Barcode in Back

D1606453

T

Praise for *How to Build Your Financial Advisory Business and Sell It at a Profit*

"For too long, financial advisors have focused on pushing product instead of building relationships, the true measure of a practice's worth. In *How to Build Your Financial Advisory Business and Sell It at a Profit*, Al Depman shows advisors how to build a practice they can be proud of, and one that they can easily sell or transfer when it's time to move on. Depman's goal of helping agents build new relationships with clients while sustaining their relationships at home is a goal we all should be focused on. His new book is destined to become 'must-reading' for all advisors who want to have a successful practice along with a fulfilling life."
—Mitch Anthony, author of *StorySelling for Financial Advisors and The New Retirementality*

"Going through the practice checkup allows you to examine where you are in the life cycle of your practice. It lets you envision where you want and need to take it—but even more important, it empowers you to get it there."
—Mike Brozzo, portfolio consultant, Charles Schwab

"For years, Al Depman has proven a valuable resource for financial advisors. His field experience combined with his practical understanding of the industry and our financial services business have led to his development of core principles that, when applied consistently, will improve results for both experienced and new financial professionals alike. Numerous advisors have benefitted from Al's one-on-one coaching and mentoring. He moves individuals from 'sales uncertainty' to 'sales success' by implementing the actions that separate the winners from the rest of the crowd. With this book, it's exciting that his proven training system can now reach even further. Get ready as Al helps you take your practice to the next level!"
—Thomas P. Burns, chief distribution officer, Allianz Life Insurance Company of North America

"This book is a clear, systemic, and practical approach for the financial advisor or insurance agent to design their business around—a road map to practice management success!"

—Susan Clements, executive director,
E-Myth Benchmark

"My work with Al Depman has taken my practice to an entirely new level. He has also inspired me to mentor others. By helping other advisors reach to the next level, it enforces my practice management and development."

—Lisa Dale, CFP, Waddell & Reed

"Al's richness of experiences, attention to detail, systems-driven approach, and ability to relate to advisors make him a resource that truly impacts advisors' practices. Many of North Star's top advisors have benefited from Al's work and guidance. North Star has benefited from Al's work and guidance, but the best part is that Al does all of this for the right reason—to bring out the best in all of those he works with."

—Edward Deutschlander, CLU, CLF, copresident,
COO, North Star Resource Group;
immediate past president of GAMA International 2008–2009

"Whether your goal is to fast track to success a new financial planning practice or breathe new life into an existing book of business, Al's book is your e-ticket to success. It's an informative, effective, and enjoyable tool in helping you to develop your practice. Al's unique (one-on-one or 'coffee shop') approach has you believing he wrote the book just for you. This is a must-read for anyone who's ultimate goal is to sell a successful practice."

—Peggy Fisher, CEA, CFP, CLTC,
registered investment advisor, Torrance, California

"I've been in the financial service business for 40 years. The material in Al's book has been a great help to my staff and me in maximizing the use of all of our combined resources. For the experienced advisor, this is a must-read. For the new advisor, it's a track to success."

—Mike Schmitz, financial advisor,
Minnetonka, Minnesota

HOW TO BUILD YOUR FINANCIAL ADVISORY BUSINESS AND SELL IT AT A PROFIT

HOW TO BUILD YOUR FINANCIAL ADVISORY BUSINESS AND SELL IT AT A PROFIT

CREATING, RUNNING, AND CASHING OUT OF YOUR PRACTICE

AL DEPMAN

New York   Chicago   San Francisco   Lisbon   London   Madrid   Mexico City
Milan   New Delhi   San Juan   Seoul   Singapore   Sydney   Toronto

The McGraw·Hill *Companies*

1 2 3 4 5 6 7 8 9 0   DOC/DOC   0 1 0 9

ISBN: 978-0-07-162157-1
MHID: 0-07-162157-1

McGraw-Hill books are available at special quantity discounts to use as premiums and sales promotions, or for use in corporate training programs. To contact a representative, please e-mail us at bulksales@mcgraw-hill.com.

This book is printed on acid-free paper.

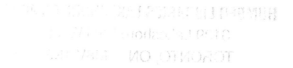

To Chris Jenkins without whose unwavering support this book would still only be a good idea. He challenged me to follow my own mission statement and gave me honest feedback. He continues to light the practice management way. Thank you, Chris.

Contents

Acknowledgments

Many people helped in the course of bringing this book to market.
Kudos to:

All the advisors who shared their stories with me over the years

Tom Burns for making the fateful decision to hire me in 1984 and believing in my potential

Heidi Wacholz for being an early collaborator and contributor in the development of practice management processes

Sainted wife Barb for keeping the faith at home

Jean Lang for helping clarify some of my fuzzier ideas

Ed Howat for providing his punny perspective

Cindy Zigmund for proofreading the work, sometimes in transit

Leah Spiro for patiently editing the manuscript and shepherding this first-time author

The Moody Blues and Herb Alpert for providing the soundtrack while I was writing

And special recognition to:

Mitch Anthony for buying into and promoting the concept and value of practice management assessment throughout his network of clients and contacts. He understood early on the need for a book, and he provided valuable resources in bringing it to fruition. Mitch, I trust it's up to your standards!

Introduction:
What Do McDonald's and Practice
Management Have in Common?

November 1986. The wind blew an icy path across Lake Mille Lacs in central Minnesota. We were insulated from the cold, nestled in a resort cabin that had been abandoned for the winter. This was the semiannual three-day retreat for the Survivors' Club.

The Survivors' Club consisted of 10 salesmen from the Prudential Greater Minnesota Agency who each had a minimum of 20 years in the business and were proud to have survived all those years "despite management." The average age of the group was 62, and careers ranged from 20 to more than 40 years with "Mother Pru."

To be sure, it was an excuse to get away and enjoy excellent food and drink—two of the guys were amateur chefs and put on quite a spread. Another was a self-styled wine expert who sponsored the required premeal wine tasting. Evenings were filled with poker games, gin rummy tournaments, and cribbage, all played with long-standing rivalries.

The three days, for tax purposes, centered around three education events, which was my reason for attending. As the wet-behind-the-ears training manager with all of two and a half years of experience, I was to lead a session on "making sense of a variable life prospectus," which at the time was a new product. The tiny print and thin sheets of the prospectus were the reasons I was brought in; I was to provide the essentials to the attendees to save them from having to read the fine print. As Jim, one of the more curmudgeonly agents put it: "You young punks know all about this stuff. Tell us what we need to know."

So, after the postlunch naps, I addressed the group on my topic. The discussion eventually turned from prospectuses to why variable life is a viable product and then ended up with guys describing their client relationships. What struck me about the conversation was how strong many of these client relationships were. After all those years, most of the agents' best clients were also their best friends.

As we were wrapping up the session, I made an observation about that friendship factor:

"That's very interesting," I said. "You have these personal relationships with your top clients."

"Sure," they answered, and they proceeded to cite more examples of how they played golf, attended sports events, and socialized with their top clients.

A thought struck me and I asked:

"So what would happen to your best friends/best clients if you were to have a stroke or be unable to work, or worst of all, you die?"

Silence. The 10 senior agents variously looked down at the prospectus or out the window at the whitecaps on the lake, or they just blankly stared ahead.

"You can't be serious," I stated. "If something happens to you, your top clients—your best friends—are just going to be sent to the orphan pool? You know what happens then: some new agent will call on them and try to sell them something. Is that really what you want to have happen?"

More silence.

"Um, well, I think we can get them reassigned to someone of our choice," offered Bob, "but there's really no formal plan in place."

This was the reality in the old agency world. Companies encouraged agents to never really retire, and when they did retire or pass away, the companies put the agents' clients into the vast orphan pool. This orphan pool was continuously worked by newer agents, most of whom didn't make it in the business.

There was little incentive for a senior agent to build a true practice, one that had systems and a succession plan. There was usually no apparent buyer, and even when there was, most of the book value had already been spent through the life insurance upfront commission compensation structure.

So it was that these gentlemen were faced with eventually letting down their best clients/best friends. It was evident in the room that this realization was a painful one.

Subsequently, over the next two years, three members of the Survivors' Club each adopted a younger agent to work with and inherit his clients through reassignment. The others never did.

Thus it was that my life's work was defined. It was unconscionable that these deep client relationships were to be squandered in the orphan pool. These men had spent decades building their practices, and in the end, they had no continuity, no legacy, and no way to profit from the value they brought to their clients.

I reasoned that there must be a way to help younger agents and advisors build their practices with integrity and solid, transferable systems. This transferability would enable the value of the practice to be passed on to a successor later in their careers for a fair price. To the clients, who are after all the real value of the practice, this transfer should be seamless.

That's when I had my Big Mac Attack.

The McDonald's Experience

Fresh out of the University of Notre Dame with a liberal arts degree in 1973, I stayed in Indiana to find out what the real world was like. I spent a year enduring a few false starts in finding meaningful work. Meanwhile, my post-college diet consisted of at least four meals a week in a fast food restaurant. Consequently, I found myself studying the controlled chaos going on behind the counter while munching on a Big Mac and fries. It was fascinating in the same way I enjoyed a good ice hockey game: players who seemed to skate about randomly suddenly coalesce into a polished team to shoot on goal.

How does that happen? Intrigued, I joined McDonald's corporate management training program after hearing the company recruiter's pitch at a career fair. So began my restaurant management career, doing a rotation through all of the crew positions at a company-owned McDonald's in southeast Indianapolis.

What I learned very quickly is that there was a system for every station and a protocol for all contingencies.

The fry station was a good example. The frozen, precut fries came in a 36-pound case containing six 6-pound boxes. They had to be stored in the freezer at 0 to −10 degrees and never stacked more than five cases high. Each 6-pound box would make four 1.5-pound baskets of fries.

The frozen fries were to be poured from the box into your hands, gently letting them fall into the basket. Breaking the fries was frowned upon since longer fries are more appealing, easier to eat, and give a much better yield. The yield is the number of servings derived from the raw product. To pmaximize both customer satisfaction and company profit, McDonald's wanted 420 to 445 bags of fries per 100 pounds of frozen fries.

Back then, a small order of fries was to weigh 2.50 to 2.75 ounces, and a large order, 4.00 to 4.25 ounces. Once cooked, the fries had a holding time of seven minutes before they had to be discarded.

The cooking shortening temperature was 340 degrees. The fry cooking computer had to be used because the immersion time could vary due to the rising and falling vat temperature. Once cooked, the buzzer sounded and the fries were taken out of the vat using the proper technique. This involved draining excess shortening from the basket using a slight shaking motion, being careful not to bang the basket against any part of the vat. Since this is where potential burns might occur from splattering shortening or touching the hot basket, you needed to take great care in pouring the cooked fries onto the bagging tray.

The mirrored bagging tray was kept hot with three 375-watt heat lamps. Once the fries were poured onto the tray, you applied the salt lightly from front to back while mixing them with the bagging scoop. The scoop, by the way, had to be cleaned every 30 minutes.

There was a list of characteristics to observe visually: if the fries were not light to golden brown, they were not to be served. Additionally, the fries had to be regular in form and uniform in length, crisp, not brittle, and mealy inside with no separation between the core and the outside. The final test was to ask ourselves, "Would I pay 25 cents for a bag of these fries?" (Ah, those mid-1970s' prices!)

We also had to keep in mind the characteristics of overdone fries (dark, greasy, brittle, hollow inside), undercooked fries (not brown, soggy, limp, raw inside), and old fries (cold, dry, tough).

Filling the bag with fries had its own set of rules. "Overfilling hurts our profit margin, and underfilling costs us customers." Fill bags as needed—the longer a filled bag sits under the heat lamps, the soggier the fries become.

There were procedures for all fry-related contingencies:

- Preparing fries during low-volume periods
- Filling the salt shakers
- Calibrating the shortening temperature and keeping the vat filled

- Keeping the floor shortening free
- Cleaning the vat daily
- Maintaining the quality of the shortening and monitoring it for the five enemies of good shortening: air, water, heat, salt, and carbon
- Stocking the fry station properly
- Working with thawed fries
- Taking care of shortening burns properly
- Testing the fry computer

And if you had free time at the fry station, you were expected to help refill stock (straws, cups, napkins), fill the ice bins, help over in the shake area, or draw drinks for a counter person.

Hungry yet? There's more but I think you get the idea. Each aspect of the McDonald's experience is rooted in a clear, minutely defined system. The systems evolve as technology gets more sophisticated and customer tastes change. The McDonald's operations manual is not negotiable when someone wants to buy a franchise. The fries will be by the book, and the result will be international consistency.

These detailed systems are the best practices for a McDonald's restaurant.

In 1977, I had the pleasure of attending and graduating from Hamburger University. It was there that I began to fully appreciate the value of systems. We applied systems thinking to not only the products' *quality* but also to *service* and *cleanliness*, creating the QSC upon which Ray Kroc founded his empire.

We studied systems for positioning crew members on the floor; crew scheduling, hiring, training, and supervising; purchasing and repairing equipment; time management; preventative maintenance; energy conservation; and goal setting. We were drilled in the expected profitability results in terms of labor costs, ratios, product yields, calibrations, and proper ordering of food and paper goods. We learned cleaning processes, the language to be used in greeting and serving a customer, and how to be a good community corporate citizen. Systems, systems, systems!

I earned my BH degree (bachelor of hamburgerology), and I use it proudly today as a constant reminder of where my systems orientation took flower.

I stayed with McDonald's, eventually joining a franchise operator and helping run his three restaurants. But the long hours, high crew turnover, and having to work holidays and weekends took their toll. It was a classic case of burnout. In 1984 I sought a fresh beginning.

Adventures in Financial Services

The ad in the paper read: "Seeking highly motivated individuals interested in a career as a sales manager. The Prudential Management Development Center is looking nationally for a select group of men and women to enter a rigorous program to build our future leaders. Management experience and college degree required."

Well, I did have management experience. If I could run a restaurant and manage teenagers, being a sales manager ought to be a snap! I survived Prudential's rigorous assessment and interview process, I was accepted into the program, and I relocated to the Newark, New Jersey, home of Prudential.

In 1984 the first year and a half of sales management training was dedicated to our understanding the salesperson's life. Our class of 10 was to sell insurance and investment products for 18 months in northern New Jersey. For most of us, this was a cold market, warmed up with a few orphans tossed our way. We learned a packaged sales process (Tom Wolfe's "Financial Needs Analysis"), product information, closing lines, techniques to overcome objections, telephone tracks, and ways to combat caller resistance.

Prospecting and marketing consisted of purchasing lists or retrieving old, discarded lists from those who graduated before us. Oh, yes, and cold calling. So we were off and running, with our agency manager diligently tracking the activity and production numbers. As sales manager wannabes, this was our boot camp. We were learning firsthand what a new sales rep needs to survive and why the agent retention rate was so low. Prudential's retention of new agents was reflective of the insurance and investment business: only one in five new hires survived to complete his or her third year. It isn't much better today, 25 years later.

My work ethic, honed at McDonald's, came in handy as our class of 10 shrunk to a class of 4 over the course of the year and a half. I made prospecting calls all day during the workweek, Monday nights, and Saturday mornings, and I went anywhere in North Jersey from Monday through Saturday for an appointment.

The good news is that I set sales records in that 18-month period. I qualified for the Prudential Business Conference and the Million Dollar Round Table (MDRT), the first in the program's history to do so, and I set a new standard for ensuing classes to chase. During that period I sold more than 250 products, mostly a mix of proprietary life, annuities, and mutual funds.

The bad news is that my marriage fell apart pretty quickly. The hours away at the office, on the road with appointments, and studying to achieve the Chartered Life Underwriter (CLU) designation all combined to create an atmosphere of intense pressure. My wife never knew what hit her: there had been little warning about this lifestyle change, and no communication from the office or from me that I'd need to be an absentee husband to "make it." A typical weekday evening ended at 11:00 p.m. with a sale and a tired husband who had no desire for small talk. She found others to fill the communication void, and the marriage ended in divorce. Thankfully, there were no children.

We married under one set of expectations, those of a fast food restaurant manager. The expectations changed as I embraced a sales management career. I found that I enjoyed sales with all its attendant challenges and rewards. She did not want to be a salesman's wife, and she took off in her own direction.

Once the emotional wounds began to heal, I wondered how many other reps were encountering a similar marital strain as a price for "success." This was a painful but valuable lesson that permeates many chapters in this book. I want to be sure you learn from my experiences.

After graduating from the program, I was placed in what was at the time the top Prudential shop in the country: the Twin Cities (Minnesota) Agency. My job was to build a sales unit from scratch. My confidence coming in—tops in the class—slowly eroded. It turned out that as a sales *manager*, I was awful.

I hired 10 reps and 1 survived to his fourth year. My big retention rate: 10 percent. My income shrunk as the initial startup subsidy vanished. My sales unit wasn't producing enough to sustain me. When I recognized that all I was doing was trying to get my agents to replicate my sales success rather than bringing out their own sales potential, I resigned from sales management.

As I would later see over and over again, good salespeople usually don't make good second-line sales managers. Prudential had made the classic sales organization error: a sales rep is successful so the company "promotes" him or her into management, expecting that success to rub off on new hires. The retention rate of sales reps going on to sales management success is dismal. Yet companies continue to ignore this reality and continue to bet on this false hope in building their field forces.

The Minnesota agency manager, Tom Burns, fortunately saw something he liked in me even as I felt like a failure, so he appointed me training and development manager. Grateful for the chance, I jumped into the classroom work. I inherited a curriculum based primarily in product knowledge, canned sales presentations, and techniques for overcoming objections.

This material felt wrong—it was all about pushing product and then fighting to keep it on the books. It dawned on me that we were teaching a transactional approach and ignoring building relationships with the clients. This emphasis was exemplified by the one-interview sale: that's where the agent meets with the clients and builds a case for selling them something, usually life insurance. Success was walking away with a check and an app.

With a broken marriage and an ugly sales management stint under my belt, I needed to make this training and development gig work. But how was I to make a significant contribution to the agency and fulfill the promise that Tom saw in me?

The answer to this question was to define the rest of my life. My quest became creating a training curriculum that was *relationship based*. This was a battle to be engaged on two fronts—helping agents build new relationships with clients while sustaining their relationships at home. To accomplish this, I would need to build new materials.

Rather than reinvent the wheel, I began to interview all the sales agents in Prudential's Minnesota field force (100 or so), from brand-new reps to 40-year veterans. My objective was simple: identify the best practices that made the successful reps successful. Conversely, I wanted to know the common "worst practices" that cropped up with those who all too often turned over.

This is about the time I was asked to help the members of the Survivors' Club understand the fine points of a prospectus at their lakeside resort in central Minnesota. Building a training system to help new reps avoid the fate of those elder salesmen became my mission. So I dragged out my old McDonald's manuals for reference, and I began the work of creating a Twin Cities Agency best practices manual filled with systems for success.

However, I was operating in a silo. I was seeing only the insurance agency system version of the financial services sales world. All I knew were Prudential materials and resources, so my early thinking was influenced by those proprietary tools. Two years later, after successfully revamping the training program, an opportunity arose to roll out a proprietary database nationwide and I jumped at it. As our little band of trainers traveled around the country introducing this client management software, I was able to continue interviewing agents all over the United States. The more data I collected, the stronger the evidence grew for identifying success and failure patterns in salespeople.

Subsequent career moves into private consulting allowed access to an even broader world of independent advisors (fee based, commission based, and some combination of the two). The success and failure patterns continued to morph, and, eventually, they solidified.

As my number of interviews continued to grow into the thousands, a consolidated list of best practices emerged.

So what are these best practices?

The Characteristics of a Prime Performer

1. A team of advocates in both marketing and administrative areas has been created, developed, and empowered. All team members have a stake in the success of the practice. While they are positioned in their areas of expertise, team members are cross trained in critical practice functions to minimize disruptions in the event of a health or relationship emergency.
2. The practice has a unique value proposition that creates a compelling reason to be sought out or recommended by others.
3. Practice leadership has established strong accountability resources, such as a board of directors or a client advisory board.
4. The practice has a deep referral and marketing process that filters throughout the organization. There is continuous growth by sifting and winnowing prospects to identify those within the practice's target profile.
5. Thorough sales and case development systems have been developed that don't leave money on the table. These systems also set up ongoing asset-gathering opportunities.
6. There is a best practices operations manual that covers the routine back-office functions (the science) as well as the higher-level processes (the art).
7. The practice has deep, legacy relationships with top-tier clients capturing multiple generations.
8. Team members provide superior, proactive service to all client tiers. Client segmentation has been done, and those that survive the cut have been promised a clear, ongoing level of service appropriate to their tier.
9. The practice has achieved a superior professional recognition standard and aspires to continuously improve.

10. The practice has embraced new technology, especially in the following areas:
    - Client relationship management (CRM) software that integrates real-time calendaring, to-do lists, and client records and notes
    - Client account data, status, and service
    - New business processing and tracking
    - Case preparation as well as product and presentation resources
11. The practice's team members give back to the community and to the profession through sponsorships, charitable concerns, board memberships, and the like.
12. There is a succession plan in place for the principals to benefit from maximizing the practice's financial value. This succession plan also assures top clients that there will be continuity in how the practice operates and that the next generation will be working under a similar philosophy.

These characteristics form the end game for practice management in the financial services world.

In order to achieve this goal and develop a practice that has value and is transferable, you need to develop tangible, incremental action steps. You also need to surround yourself with people who will hold you accountable for taking these actions.

This is *my* passion. My goal is to marry this passion with diagnostic data and the collective experience of many practitioners. Add to the mix the McDonald's dedication to detail and transferability. The result? A road map and a best practices operations manual, both designed to help you maximize your chances for success.

The book is divided into two parts:

Part I, "Why Practice Management Matters," summarizes all the elements that, when woven together, form the fabric of a valuable practice.

Part II takes the "Eight Business Systems" of your practice and digs deeper into each one.

Let's start by looking in the mirror and recognizing your own genius!

PART I

WHY PRACTICE MANAGEMENT MATTERS

1

Bottling and Selling Your Genius: How to Increase the Value of Your Practice

Whether a wealth manager, financial planner, financial advisor, insurance agent, or any permutation thereof, you are dedicated to helping clients to achieve dreams and wishes for themselves, their families, and their businesses. Your role is to ensure that clients have a sound fiscal plan that will provide them with the resources to "live long and prosper," as a certain Vulcan would say.

That's one side of the coin. On the other is doing the same for yourself, your family, and your practice. This book will work on the assumption that you want to achieve your own dreams and wishes too. In fact, my proposition is this: through strong practice management, you will be able to transcend the money issues and enhance the quality of life for your clients, your loved ones, and yourself.

Money is a fascinating topic and is at the core of the advisor's day-to-day work. Let's put some perspective on money's role in your practice.

How Is Money Positioned *with Your Clients?*

On one end of the continuum are the Scrooge-like clients who strive to accumulate the most money possible. Money alone is their objective, unattached to any other purpose. You, the advisor, exist solely to squeeze every possible profit from their portfolios. If you don't do it well enough, these clients move on and try another advisor or broker. This is a purely transactional process, and it results in a transaction-based practice.

On the other end of the continuum are the clients who have specific life goals they aspire to, and you are a primary resource in the accomplishment of those goals. The role that money plays for these clients is to facilitate their dreams, and the role that you play is to position that money accordingly as part of a holistic plan. This is a highly relationship-oriented approach, and it results in a relationship-based practice.

Our practice management model favors the latter *client* philosophy.

How Do You Position Money *with Yourself?*

On one end of the advisor continuum, money is an annually renewable, always-increasing burden. Your practice exists to constantly set new sales records and to collect more and more assets, and these are the sole measures of success. Failure is always lurking around the corner in the form of decreased production. The pursuit of money keeps you awake at night, and it has become the primary focus of your life.

On the other end of the advisor continuum, money serves your life and does not rule it. It is the means to an end, not the end itself. You have clear life goals you want to achieve. Your clients are an integral part of your journey in capturing those dreams—financially, socially, emotionally, and spiritually. Your best clients may well accompany you on this journey. Our practice management model favors the latter *advisor* philosophy.

Combining the relationship orientations of both the client and the advisor philosophies above, we emerge with a *relationship-based practice.* Given these two holistic, correlating approaches to money, it becomes apparent that in your role as a financial advisor, you bring four gifts to your clientele.

These gifts, or what I call "geniuses," are the following:

1. Relationship Building
2. Relationship Maintenance and Growth
3. Inspiring People to Action
4. Solving Problems Creatively and Interpreting Information

Let's take a look at each one.

Advisor's Genius 1: Relationship Building

We've all heard people say "He's a natural salesperson" in response to their encounter with a particularly persuasive person. It's the recognition of an intangible talent possessed by certain individuals. They seem to be able to say the right thing, to lure you into a conversation, and to have you give them information that even your spouse and best friends don't know. These persuasive people find it easy to engender trust from others while not raising any red flags.

This is the skill of Relationship Building. It is shared by honorable advisors, scam artists, politicians, and my barber, Duane. It's the *likability factor*—a positive air about some people that attracts attention and predisposes us to believe what they say.

What separates the real relationship builders from those who use their relationships only to gain short-term profits is the willingness to engage prospects in deeper conversations. The short-term profiteers maintain a relationship for only a brief period of time before they churn on to another relationship.

Duane is a real relationship builder, and he understands that I'll continue as a client of his 12 times a year (or as long as I keep producing hair on my head) because of the relationship that we've developed and that he has fostered over time through conversations in his barber's chair. I tried a number of other hair stylists, artists, and barbers before I clicked with Duane, and I heartily recommend him to others.

Similarly, my wife and I have had many financial transactions with stockbrokers, life and property/casualty insurance agents, bankers, and wannabe financial "planners." All these false starts were found wanting. My impression was that, for the most part, we were being sold something for their reasons, not ours. This losing streak ended when we met our planner, Mike, who put all our financial issues into a comprehensive, understandable perspective. In addition, he offered a sense of true caring about us. Mike came to us as a referral from a coworker.

Over the course of an advisor's career, there will be many relationships started in hopes of having them develop into fruitful clients and friendships. But only a small percentage of these relationship grafts will grow into long-lasting relationships by the advisor's choice, the client's choice, or their mutual choice.

In the financial services world, an advisor will typically start out her career trying to develop as many relationships as possible as quickly as possible. All prospects are A-list prospects because she is optimistic that they will all turn out to have unlimited funds and crave financial advice.

Reality sets in soon enough, and these burgeoning relationships with prospects settle into five patterns:

- People who make transactions without establishing a relationship ("I'll take a term life policy. Now will you go away?")

- People who establish relationships without making any transactions ("Well, we might need some retirement planning in a couple of years. Could you call back then?")
- People who reject all transactions and relationships ("Click!"—the sound of a phone being hung up.)
- Well-wishers without any substance ("How nice! You're a broker. Your parents must be proud. Good luck, but don't ask us for any help.")
- People who buy into what you are trying to build, purchase from you, and ask what else they can do ("Let's see what you've got, kid. We've been wanting to review all our financial stuff for quite a while. When can you come over?")

It's the fifth group you need to patiently cultivate to grow a successful practice. There are a number of best practices designed to facilitate the development and refinement of your Relationship Building genius. They will be found in the first of the Eight Business Systems, Client Acquisition.

Advisor's Genius 2: Relationship Maintenance and Growth

The advisor begins to segment all these various client relationships over time. He will actively court those who share his philosophy on the holistic role of money in their lives. These are relationships that need to be maintained and nurtured for they are long-range "keepers" that eventually form the core of the advisor's practice and life.

Keeping key client relationships healthy and growing requires the development of a series of "touches" that are both informative and caring. *Informative touches* include providing financial facts, performance reports, and market updates. *Caring touches* are more feeling oriented such as taking a client on a golf outing or a birthday lunch, or sending her a note of congratulations for receiving an award. The caring touches are less about the client's financial worth to the advisor than about how the advisor values the person and her family or business.

There is an art to knowing where the balance is between too many touches (smothering the client) and not enough (abandoning the client). Each top-tier client will have a unique contact preference. The advisor's genius is in setting up a scheduled sequence of client touches with flexibility for more intimate, proactive contacts.

Enhancing this Client Management genius is what the second of the Eight Business Systems is all about. Client Management covers the nature of the information the advisor collects about her top clients and how to use that information. In that context I'll also discuss client contact protocols and the importance of being careful to not overpromise and underdeliver in client servicing.

It is the mutual trust engendered through this Relationship Building and Maintenance that leads to the third aspect of the advisor's genius.

Advisor's Genius 3: Inspiring People to Action

At a most fundamental level, this genius has the advisor asking for the business and the client's agreeing to go through with it. This is also known as the "transaction," "getting the check," "closing the deal," "collecting the fee," "producing new business," and/or "bringing home the bacon."

Certainly, it's your income stream I'm talking about here. Early in one's financial services career, every transaction is vital to survival. But our relationship-based advisor seeks to transcend the cycle of product transactions by building a level of AAA clients who provide a steady flow of revenue from existing business, provide referrals on a regular basis, and are willing to commit additional assets to the advisor over time. These are the 20 percent who will produce 80 percent of the practice's revenue.

The advisor also provides inspiration to these AAA clients on a number of different levels over and above the financial by pointing out the consequences of their decisions. For example, let's look at a will. A transactional advisor will ask his clients, "Do you have a will?" and he will duly note their reply and simply move on. That information will go nowhere. An experienced advisor will ask her clients, "Do you have a will?" and if they don't have one, she will suggest they get one and provide the name of an attorney. If they do have a will, the advisor might note the executor's name and ask about some general aspects of the will's provisions. There is a proactive sense to this (suggesting an attorney's name), but in the end, the information is recorded but not acted upon.

The inspirational advisor will say, "Let's talk about your will." If the clients don't have one, the advisor will say, "Do you have a preferred attorney? If you do, I'll contact that person and have him or her give you a call about setting up a time to discuss getting a will. Otherwise, I work with attorney Sue Smart, and I'll have Sue's office give you a call." If the clients have a will, the inspirational advisor will ask probing questions about the last review date, whether the executor is aware of what needs to be done, and whether the provisions of the will are still valid. If not, the advisor will initiate a discussion of what changes should be made and how those people affected by the changes might react, and will also offer to interact with the attorney in making those changes.

The inspirational advisor knows that "the money will come" if she takes a proactive approach with her top clients.

The systematic approach to Inspiring People to Action will be examined in detail in the chapter on Core Business System 3: the Sales Process. I'll start with the initial contact with the prospective client and proceed through a sequence of discovery meetings. I'll cover the presentation and the point in the process when inspiration becomes action, traditionally known as the "close." Finally, I'll focus on the transition of the new client into the ongoing service cycle.

The inspiration to action relies to a great degree on how the advisor has developed the plan, structured the presentation, and selected the right product or service for the client. That takes us to the fourth genius.

Advisor's Genius 4: Solving Problems Creatively and Interpreting Information

The fourth area of advisor genius is that of solving problems creatively and interpreting information. There are a number of best practices underlying this gift. Primary among them is the advisor's ability to listen effectively. To solve a problem is to truly understand the problem. Stephen Covey's principle "Seek first to understand, then to be understood," captures the essence of this "listening" best practice.

The advisor understands the client's real issues and restates them for clarity before offering solutions. The solutions will be derived from the advisor's education, training, life experience, background, and wisdom. The fourth core business system, Case Development, expands on this genius area.

Many times in response to my question "Why are you in this business?" the first words out of the advisor's mouth are "I love to help people." My belief is that the creative problem-solving genius reflects the "help" part of that statement and the two genius areas of Relationship Building and Relationship Maintenance and Growth reflect the "love" and "people" parts. "I love to help people" may sound like a cliché, but it is, at its deepest levels, a necessary belief for an advisor to hold in order to develop a Prime practice (as defined in the Introduction).

Other best practices feeding into creative problem solving include the advisor's taking all the raw data and information from a client, coordinating them, analyzing them, and creating a unique set of steps to put them in order. Once in order, the advisor selects strategies to protect and grow the client's assets in line with the client's life goals. This wedding of protection and growth strategies for the achievement of client goals is one of the most powerful payoffs of the advisor's work.

"Interpreting information" can be defined as doing due diligence for the client. There is a vast universe of financial products and services out there. It is a daunting universe, to say the least, for average individuals who are trying to keep their own affairs together. There is little time to investigate the array of insurance and investment products to determine which particular products or companies are the right ones for them.

By educating, training, and collaborating with other professionals, advisors can narrow the field for their clients and identify a discrete number of products, companies, services, and strategies that will fit each situation. After all the facts have been gathered and the solutions formulated, advisors must then present choices to their clients in a clear, simple manner.

This presentation is an art. Too much information and the client's confusion will impair the advisor's ability to inspire action. Too little information and the client may become suspicious that the solution is only in the advisor's best interests. The advisor's genius is in the ability to gauge how much is just enough information to give to a particular client.

Many experienced advisors that I've worked with tell me, "Oh, I just tell them [the clients] what they need and they buy it." While this practice indicates a high trust level on the clients' part and good relationship maintenance on the advisors' part, I hope there is an element of due diligence as part of the "telling them what they need" that will withstand a lawsuit or two.

Relational Genius, Analytic Genius, and Practicide

The four areas of an advisor's genius represent the core activities that advisors can ultimately aspire to through the practice management process. In other words, the end result of Prime practice management is that the advisor can devote 100 percent of her time to being in the four genius areas and have everything else outsourced to a marketing and administrative team.

This brings up another way to look at the four advisor geniuses. The first three are *relational*—that is, they involve being face to face with clients and other key people in the practice. Building and growing relationships and inspiring action are all relational gifts. The *analytic* genius is found in solving problems creatively and interpreting information.

Frequently, an advisor will begin to lean toward either the relational genius or the analytic genius over the course of developing a practice. Advisors whose strengths are in the relational genius areas are the "rainmakers." Those with the analytic genius are the "back room" folks.

Practice management wisdom tells us that identifying which types of genius are predominant in an advisor gives some insight on how the practice should be built. This is also a lesson in what I call "practicide":

practicide: prac·ti·cide (prăk'tĭ-sīd') n.

1. The act or an instance of intentionally killing one's own business.
2. The destruction or ruin of one's own interests: *It is practicide — professional suicide — to involve oneself in illegal practices.*
3. One who commits practicide.
   [from Medieval Latin prāctica + -cide]

practicidal: prac'ti·cid'al (prăct'ĭ-sīd'l) adj.

Let's say you are a rainmaker — good at networking and meeting new people, keeping the current clients happy, and inspiring action when necessary. Case prep and product selection, however, are not as thrilling, and they tend to bog you down. What are the systems and who are the people you need to bring into your practice to enable you to maximize your relational strengths and support your less interesting back-room needs?

Obviously, an analytic person would be your first choice, like a paraplanner or administrative assistant. You could bring in a marketing assistant to help you with your relational work, setting appointments, and keeping track of all your relationships using a client relationship management (CRM) software program.

On the other hand, if you gravitate toward the analytic areas of genius and have a tough time generating leads and developing centers of influence (COIs), your first hire ought to be a marketing assistant who can create face-to-face opportunities, or you could partner with an advisor who tends toward rainmaking.

There are far too many recurring instances in our profession in which an analytical advisor hires an analytical assistant or teams up with another analytical advisor. While the work they produce is stellar, they soon run out of people to see and their practice fails.

The same issue occurs when two relational advisors team up or an advisor brings on an assistant who is also primarily relational. Lots of names are being generated, but there are not a lot of follow-up or case development actions being taken. Consequently, many good prospects fall through the cracks, and the practice suffers and often dies.

These are all examples of practicide. If caught early, these advisors would likely still be with us. Seeking out complementary people and systems is what we will be covering in the ensuing chapters of this book.

Why Practice Management Matters

- It will allow your genius to flourish by systematizing your practice and outsourcing all that prevents you from fully employing your four gifts: Relationship Building, Relationship Maintenance and Growth, Inspiring People to Action, and Solving Problems Creatively and Interpreting Information.
- This systemization will create a team approach in building your practice by clarifying roles, responsibilities, expectations, and accountabilities.
- It will allow you to maximize top client relationships for greater personal and professional satisfaction.
- It will permit you to put money in its proper place: in service to your goals.
- It will prevent a bad case of practicide by addressing both the relational and the analytical needs of your practice.
- And as we'll see in the next chapter, it will help create maximum value for your practice when you're ready to do some serious succession planning.

2

Enhancing Your Practice's Book Value

In the Old West, a cowboy died one of two ways. If he was sick or old, he'd die in bed with his boots off. If death came in a gunfight or a brawl, he died with his boots on. Consequently, he'd be buried on Boot Hill, the frontier cemetery for those who went out with guns blazing.

Over the years, that harsh reality of the cowboy era has mellowed into a romantic ideal for the hard-nosed entrepreneur. We've all encountered those aging businesspeople (mostly men) who vow to die with their boots on!

It's not coincidental that the financial services profession seeks out, nurtures, and rewards modern-day cowboys. Look at much of the recruiting material over the years and you'll read phrases like these:

- "Be your own boss! After our initial training program, you'll be in business for yourself . . . but not by yourself!"
- "You're in control of your own destiny!"
- "*You* decide what hours you work and how much you make!"
- "We offer a real entrepreneurial opportunity!"

Insurance companies from the dawn of the Industrial Age through the 1980s had a relatively simple strategy: hire huge numbers of sales agents, have them sell fast and furiously, lose 90 percent of them within four years, and then bulk up on the ongoing premium payments of the orphaned customers' whole life policies.

In effect, with only 10 percent of the agents surviving past their fourth year, there was little need for exit strategies. The compensation structure ensured that the majority of the commission was paid up front and the payments on the remainder of it dribbled off to near nothing in later years. These agents couldn't build much equity in their practices. The older agents, like my Survivors' Club guys at Prudential, did have a pension plan of sorts, based on their longevity and the persistency of their life insurance accounts (a measure of how many clients stayed on the books). But the pension was usually contingent on continued new business production. The less production in their "retirement," the lower their pension income was. The reality was that they were *expected* to die with their boots on.

This status quo was given a mighty one-two punch in the early 1980s. High interest rates prevailed, and the A.L. Williams Company was executing a brilliant strategy to take advantage of them. In what we would call "viral" marketing today, Williams employed an Avon-like approach, making almost anyone capable of passing the state life and health insurance licensing test to become a part-time agent. These agents pushed a single idea door to door: cash in your old, boring, low-yielding, company-cash-cow, whole life insurance policy. With these proceeds, you were to buy an inexpensive A.L. Williams term policy to replace the death benefit and "invest the difference" between the term premium and the whole life premium you were paying. This investment was put into the "Common Sense Trust" mutual fund, also conveniently provided by the A.L. Williams company. Money market fund returns were in double digits from 1979 through 1984, peaking at over 15 percent in 1981. Who could resist?

The A.L. Williams philosophy was quickly copied by hungry agents and brokers, and soon the dominant insurers were hemorrhaging cash from their massive general accounts that had been built on whole life policies and fixed annuities. Agents were pushing their companies to enter the investment world and provide cheap term insurance rates. As the big traditional brontosaurian insurance companies failed to respond, agents defected in droves to smaller, nimbler velociraptor-like mutual fund companies for the investment opportunities, and they found cheap term providers to provide the life coverage for their customers.

The playing field was forever changed. From the mid-1980s through today, the nature of the financial services salesperson's work has continued to evolve. Insurance agents and investment brokers used to be in different worlds, but now they work together in many combinations and permutations of financial services, often within the same company. The advent of these hybrid advisors has required higher levels of education, testing, and oversight, and it is more difficult to attract, train, and license this new breed of prospective financial advisor.

The advisor today is also savvier as to how she is compensated. Whole life insurance has given way to variable life policies, but the payout on the agent's commission on these products remains front loaded—that is, most of the commission is paid at the point of sale. For that reason, many advisors continue to espouse the buy-term-and-invest-the-rest philosophy. The reason is simple enough: you can't build your practice's value with life insurance as it's currently priced.

A practice's value is built upon assets under management and advisory fees, both of which produce ongoing revenue streams. Today's advisors are well aware of this, and assuming they are successful in building a solid asset base, they would like to see some payoff for their efforts—a light at the end of the tunnel.

Today's advisors are not willing to die with their boots on. Rather, their preference is to die with their feet up, enjoying the fruits of their labor. The expectation is that they will be able to sell their practice to a willing buyer.

Who Will Buy Your Practice?

Some forward-looking companies provide a transition plan to their advisors. These companies, acting as intermediaries, will work with a willing advisor within the same company to help him or her buy a selling advisor's book of business. The company agrees to pay the seller a stream of income from the anticipated revenue generated by the client base. The buying advisor could potentially be a seller's family member. I've assessed many multigenerational practices, and I have dealt with a variety of succession issues. For the most part, I find that clients are predisposed to trust the successor advisor who's "in the family."

Independent advisors, of course, can put their practice on the open market to find a willing buyer. They can also merge their practice with another in anticipation of eventually exiting. There are outside firms willing to broker these mergers.

Our purpose here is not to provide a calculation of a practice's value. There are far too many financial issues to address that are beyond the scope of this book. Resources for the nitty-gritty number crunching include *How to Value, Buy, or Sell a Financial Advisory Practice: A Manual on Mergers, Acquisitions, and Transition Planning* by Mark Tibergien and Owen Dahl, FP Transitions at www.fptransitions.com, and the collective work of David K. Goad of Succession Planning Consultants.

In any discussion of succession planning, what all these resources agree on is that the primary risk is retaining the selling advisor's clientele. Through our practice management process, the advisor will learn to build a practice that is highly transferable to a buyer, almost creating a McDonald's-like franchise that the purchasing advisor can step into seamlessly.

What's in It for the Client, the Company, and the Selling Advisor?

The value to the clients is a continuation of business as usual, with systems and people in place that are familiar. These clients are most likely to stay with the new advisor if that advisor has been working side by side with the retiring advisor for a period of time.

The value to the company the advisor is working for (or with, depending on the contract) is that the assets will stay with the carrier. Retention of assets is a huge financial services industry issue. According to one internal study conducted by a major broker/dealer, over 75 percent of the assets flowing into new annuity sales in 2007 were actually being rolled over from other companies. One of the dirty little secrets of the financial services world is that the majority of the revenue being generated is the result of simply moving money from one company to another. "New business" is a misnomer. It's usually "recycled business."

The value to the selling advisor is that the more likely it is that the clients will stay with the practice and the company, the higher the asking price can be.

Let's break this down.

Book Value

A practice's *book value* (BV) as defined for the purposes of this book begins with examining two elements:

- Percentage of top-tier clients
- Recurring revenue

Percentage of Top-Tier Clients

A "solid book of business" is defined as a practice in which the clientele is clearly segmented and at least 20 percent meet the advisor's definition of a "top-tier client." Top-tier clients have any or all of these three characteristics:

1. Top-tier clients contribute significantly to the practice's annual revenue stream. "Significant" varies by advisor, but a rule of thumb is Pareto's principle, which states that 20 percent of one's clients will produce 80 percent of one's revenue. This range can be as tight as 10 percent of the clients producing 90 percent of the revenue.
2. Top-tier clients have additional assets not yet under the advisor's management. These potential additional assets can include other services or products—such as long-term-care insurance—that the advisor might be able to provide and/or additional assets the clients control through their roles as trustee, beneficiary, or other fiduciary position.
3. Top-tier clients provide a stream of quality referrals (a minimum of three per year).

Recurring Revenue

A practice has a defined revenue stream each year. In other words, the advisor wakes up on January 1 and knows what his income will be from assets under management, trails, renewal commissions, and fees from his current client base (as long as those clients stay on the practice's books). Consequently, the practice's monetary value is based on the present value of this income stream for a set number of years in the future. The formula agreed upon by the seller and the buyer as "fair market value" for the practice essentially assumes the purchased client base will remain with the buyer for a set number of years into the future (commonly two or three years), and after that all bets are off. The more attrition that occurs during that set number of years, the less valuable the income stream becomes.

During the research we conducted as we developed and implemented the Business Practice Checkup, we discovered that book value is directly affected by whether or not an advisor has successfully segmented her book of business, identified top-tier clients, and cultivated strong relationships with those clients to protect the revenue stream.

BV Multiples

With this in mind, it was possible to assign multiples of an agreed-upon practice's fair market value, which we designated as BV.

The BV Practice

With a typical BV practice, the advisor will sell his book of business and then retire, and his staff will disband. The purchaser will implement her own systems and bring in her own staff to run the practice. How much of the selling advisor's business stays on the books is an unknown, but it is assumed to stay intact for two or three years. The goodwill value of the practice is probably not retained. Some studies estimate that up to 50 percent of top-tier clients will move their money within two years of the sale of a practice because they were loyal to the advisor, not to the practice or the company. My own experience in helping advisors in transition supports this finding.

The BV × 1.5 Practice

This practice has a solid book of business with defined, running systems that are documented with a best practices manual, and it is easily transferred to the purchasing advisor. There will also be at least one staff person who will continue with the practice for a transition period. The impact of having these systems and transition person in place is to increase the value of the practice by 50 percent (BV × 1.5). Maintaining systems that are proven and familiar to a practice's clients and having a familiar voice answering the phone will slow any attrition and extend the revenue stream for the purchaser. There is an increased chance of sustaining client goodwill for the new advisor.

The BV × 2.0 Practice

This practice also has a solid book of business with defined, documented, running systems, and it has a transition staff person. In addition, to provide continuity, there is an associate advisor with at least five years' experience. The presence of this associate advisor would double the value of the practice (BV × 2.0). The associate advisor might be part of the sale or perhaps even be the purchaser. The prospect of sustaining goodwill in this scenario is extremely good.

The BV × 2.5 Practice

This practice is a growth engine. It boasts a solid book of business with defined, documented, and running systems. There is an associate advisor (or more) with dedicated, licensed, productive marketing and administrative teams who will continue on with the practice. Having all this will increase the value of the practice by 150 percent (BV × 2.5). The prospects for sustaining goodwill are excellent.

After doing more than 1,000 Business Practice Checkup assessments (go to www.practicetools.net for more information) over the past five years from a variety of financial services channels, we were able to build a numerical advisor practice transferability scale based on the above BV definitions.

In developing this grid, we cross-referenced the advisor developmental (life cycle) stages with the strength of each of the Eight Business Systems that constitute Part II of this book. The grid is blind to advisor income levels, years in the business, and age. It simply represents a snapshot of where the advisor's practice systems are as compared to the best practices in the financial services profession.

To be clear, this model addresses those advisors who grow through *relationship-based practices* as opposed to highly transactional practices.

To encompass all the variations and permutations of relationship-based financial services practices, we constructed a 1,000-point scale as a common measuring stick. Each of the Eight Business Systems had a series of best-practice questions. The questions were assigned varying weights as each business system was scored. The overall average of the Eight Business Systems scores provided each practice's final score. With all this information, we were able to identify where each practice was in relation to the five basic life cycle stages: Prime (discussed in the Introduction), Mature (Early and Late), Emerging (Early and Late), Developing, and Formative.

Aligning book values (BVs) with practice scores allows financial advisors to review and consider the very practical, tangible, and tactical aspects of a practice and ultimately its salability. There are also intangible, hard-to-measure factors that play into a sale. These include family situations, business relationships, debt loads, contractual obligations, and advisor health and preexisting conditions. The scores and BV multiples on the next page provide an excellent starting place for negotiations.

Here, then, are the BV benchmarks as lined up with the life cycle stages of an advisor's practice:

An advisor whose practice scores 700, for example, is in the Early Mature stage, and she can make a strong case that she has built a transferable business that would be beneficial to the buyer. Why? Business systems are in place and can be easily transferred to new or existing staff members on the purchaser's team. This will be facilitated by a staff person who is willing to stay for a transitional period. A best practices manual is in place detailing the core business systems as well as defining who is accountable for what tasks.

Consequently, the purchasing advisor would be buying a clientele that looks like this:

Life Cycle Stage	Characteristics for Sale of Practice	Practice Tools Assessment Scores	Book Value (BV) Multiple
Prime	Multiple advisors, marketing and administrative teams, and sophisticated systems are all in place and turnkey in nature. The result is a seamless transition, and the practice keeps growing.	900–1,000	BV × 2.5
Late Mature	Transferable systems and marketing and administrative staff are in place. An experienced associate advisor provides smooth transition.	750–899	BV × 2.0
Early Mature	Transferable systems have been implemented, and a staff person is in place and is willing to help in a transition.	650–749	BV × 1.5
Late Emerging	Transferable systems are beginning to be implemented, and the practice is experimenting with assistants. No transferable processes are yet in place.	500–649	BV
Early Emerging, Developing, and Formative	Practice is in solo survival mode, and it is searching for systems to implement.	Under 500	BV × 0.5

- These clients are highly likely to stay with the new advisor because they are familiar with the buying advisor's staff and the systems.
- The opportunities for future sales to these clients have been clearly identified.
- The referrals these clients are capable of making have been clearly identified.
- Those monies that these clients control in their roles as trustees or beneficiaries—that is, their legacy dollars—have been clearly identified.

In short, the practice's top-tier clients have been well prepared for the purchase, and the key revenue streams are secured from attrition. This practice could be sold for 1.5 BV.

Keeping it simple, let's take Joe as an example.

Joe is a 20-year-veteran who has established a primarily fee-based practice, managing assets and doing financial plans. He does some insurance business, mostly term life and long term care. Jill is thinking of buying Joe's practice. They agree to take a look at his recurring income stream projected for three years.

His annual recurring income breaks down as follows:

Assets under management (wrap accounts, mutual funds)	$180,000*
Planning clients' annual retainer fees	$30,000
Annuity trails (expected annually for the next three years)	$25,000
Insurance product renewals (expected annually each of the next three years)	$15,000
Total annual revenue	$250,000

*From ongoing fees to manage this money.

Projecting three years out, the total is $750,000. The present value (PV) factor (from the PV tables) of this lump sum, assuming a 3.5 percent inflation rate, is 0.901943. Multiplied by the $750,000, we arrive at present value of $676,457. At its most fundamental, this is the BV—$676,457—that Jill would agree to pay.

Joe, however, has assessed his practice, and it scored a 700 as an Early Mature practice. This score permits him to increase the sale price to BV × 1.5, or $1,014,686. He can confidently do this by demonstrating to Jill that she will likely be able to sustain the income stream by keeping his existing top-tier clients beyond the average advisor's three-year point and perhaps indefinitely. Joe will be passing on to Jill his functioning practice management business systems (including a best practices operations manual) and providing his experienced full-time assistant for a two-year transition period until Jill gets her own staff up and running and acclimated to Joe's clientele.

Joe's reward for building, maintaining, and growing strong systems and people? A million-dollar nest egg.

Keep Joe's story in mind as we embark on a voyage of exploration in the Eight Business Systems of a financial services practice.

PART II

EIGHT BUSINESS SYSTEMS

3

Transferability: An Overview of the Eight Business Systems

Transferability. That's the word at the heart of building a successful and valuable financial services practice.

During the lifetime of a practice, the advisor strives to build systems that work, the result of trial and error, targeted markets, and product mix. Once constructed, the advisor then transfers these systems to others until he has delegated all but the activities he finds most rewarding. In most practices, a staff person or two exists to support these day-to-day business systems. Sometimes it can be cost effective to outsource some of the more routine work to third parties.

When an advisor decides to wind down and exit the business, she steps back and takes a look at the entire practice. What has she built? How much is the practice worth? Is there a willing buyer?

When selling a home, the owner can clean up the yard, paint some rooms, fix the dripping faucet, and bake bread during showings to enhance the perceived value. Serious buyers look past the amenities and require an inspection that will reveal the strength of the house's core systems and infrastructure. Is the electrical system up to code? Is the roof secure? Are the pipes rusty? Is there water in the basement? Are there cracks in the foundation?

Similarly, the prospective buyer of a financial services practice will want to know if its systems are in place and working. If the selling advisor has been haphazard in building systems during his growth years, it's too late to retrofit them before a sale. Consequently, the value of the practice suffers.

It is during the Developing and Emerging practice years that an advisor has the opportunity to build and delegate systems. The integrity and transferability of these systems will pay large dividends in an exit strategy, especially if they are developed in accordance with proven best practices. Getting the maximum value from a practice is at the heart of a mature business plan. And at the heart of a mature business plan is an effective best practices operations manual.

Every revenue-producing activity in an advisor's practice has a process attached to it. This not only includes the administrative work but also the Client Acquisition, Case Development, and Client Management systems. Each process can be broken into specific steps, and each step can be assigned to a particular individual.

The deeper and more complete these processes are described and recorded, the more transferable they are when bringing on new associates, cross training existing team members, and being scrutinized by potential buyers. These detailed processes are recorded in a best practices operations manual.

The best practices operations manual is not a routine operations manual that spells out office policies, vacations, HR rules, and whose turn it is to make the coffee. The best practices operations manual exists separately as a companion to the traditional operations manual. It is a detailed breakdown of each of the practice's business systems that are germane to the generation and preservation of revenue.

There are Eight Business Systems common to all financial service practices: the *Core Four* and the *Infrastructure Four*.

The Core Four business systems line up directly with the advisor's four areas of genius discussed earlier. Recall that they are Relationship Building, Relationship Maintenance and Growth, Inspiring People to Action, and Solving Problems Creatively and Interpreting Information.

You might think of these first four business systems as ways to capture and bottle the advisor's genius, making it as transferable as possible to the other members of the practice.

The Core Four business systems are the following:

> *Client Acquisition.* The Client Acquisition system reflects the advisor's
> Relationship Building genius. It includes primarily the practice's
> methods for attracting quality prospects. It involves identifying
> referral processes, seminar procedures, product- or service-driven
> marketing campaigns, and other name-generating sources. These
> processes are spelled out in detail and coordinated with available
> staff, database capabilities, and tracking accountabilities. The case
> study that follows in the next chapter will delineate the best-practice
> elements of a Client Acquisition system.

Client Management. The Client Management system reflects the advisor's Relationship Maintenance and Growth genius. It includes the practice's techniques for maximizing client satisfaction through segmentation and service protocols delivered to each identified tier of clientele. Additionally, the advisor looks at the processes in place to attract additional assets from current clients and encourage quality referrals on a regular basis. Staffing, database coordination, and accountabilities are all recorded as part of the Client Management system.

Sales Process. The Sales Process system reflects the advisor's genius for Inspiring People to Action. This system embodies how the advisor orchestrates the experience a prospect goes through in becoming a client. Best-practice steps include initial contact, first appointment, discovery interview (facts and feelings), postdiscovery communication, presentation, close, issue, delivery, and segue into becoming part of the Client Management system. Each practice documents its unique implementation of these steps and the assigned roles for advisor and staff.

Case Development. The Case Development system reflects the advisor's genius for Solving Problems Creatively and Interpreting Information. Here we find the advisor's processes for taking the discovery materials, analyzing them, and then preparing solutions, recommendations, and a presentation. This sequence is documented, the software and formats are identified, and roles assigned to advisor and staff are noted.

The Core Four systems all directly generate income, and they are implemented usually in face-to-face meetings with prospects and clients. They need to be developed quickly for survival, and they must be continually refined to meet the advisor's increasing cash flow obligations.

The Infrastructure Four systems, on the other hand, are implemented behind the scenes. They exist to build efficiencies in the practice, which enables the advisor to spend the majority of her time in revenue producing endeavors. While the Core Four systems *reflect* the advisor's genius, the Infrastructure Four systems *serve* her genius by allowing that genius to flourish and grow.

The Infrastructure Four systems are the following:

Time Management. This practice system focuses on two core concerns: (1) keeping the advisor and his staff in control of the advisor's time as opposed to allowing it to be dictated by clients and environmental factors; and (2) maximizing the advisor's time as a rainmaker in meeting face-to-face (or ear-to-ear) with top clients, prospects, and centers of influence, as well as engaging in other networking and business building activities. Responsibilities are delegated to both the advisor and his team in the areas of telephone coverage, call prioritization, calendar coordination, and overall team integration with the database and portable devices. The execution of a "model week" that addresses the personal and professional aspects of the advisor's life is addressed.

Communication. This system spells out the advisor's methods for interacting with staff, centers of influence, networks, community contacts, and company contacts. The tools that facilitate these communications are identified. Processes are examined and roles assigned in the hiring, supervision, and review of staff members. Methods for contact with business associates other than clients are examined. Mail and e-mail screening is covered as well as some of the ways the staff can use the Internet effectively for prospecting and deepening client relationships.

Education. This system includes acquiring and encouraging designations, staying current on financial events, using the Internet proactively, growing and developing staff, and educating clients. Responsibilities are delegated to both the advisor and her team in the areas of continuing education, study groups, sharing of motivational goals, exploring and developing new markets, joint work with other professionals, and staff cross training.

Financial Management. This system includes the practice's processes for creating a business entity that makes money and can stand up to the due diligence requirements of a potential purchaser. Elements of this system include auditing income, creating budget and cash flow statements, managing death and disability plans, using credit, and tracking advisor and staff bonus points and achievement levels.

Infrastructure Four systems do not directly generate revenue but instead build efficiencies into the practice, permitting the advisor to concentrate on the Core Four systems. With each system, the advisor needs to pinpoint best practices, identify duties and assign them to junior-level advisors, staff members, or other support services.

As stated earlier, the entire purpose of a best practices operations manual is to increase the value of your business. The following chapters are devoted to examining each business system in detail and will provide you with templates to construct your own best practices manual.

4

Core Business System 1: Client Acquisition

The ultimate objective of practice management is to have a completely transferable practice. The difficult part of attaining that transferability is systematizing, or "bottling," your genius.

The first of the advisor's geniuses is Relationship Building. The Client Acquisition system is the embodiment ("embottlement?") of this genius. The objective will be to identify the more routine functions of the advisor's Client Acquisition system and outsource them. Doing this will free the advisor to concentrate on high-impact interactions with people critical to the growth of the practice. The more turnkey the Client Acquisition system becomes, the more value your practice generates. The second core business system, Client Management, will then build on these new relationships, developing and deepening them.

The Client Acquisition system covers all the processes the advisor uses to find prospects and try to build relationships with them.

The three basic reasons for prospecting are to grow the number of clients in your practice, to offset attrition of current clients who pass away or move their business elsewhere, and/or to replace C- and D-level clients with A-level prospects, thereby upgrading the aggregate client profile.

In all practices at least one of these reasons to prospect is in play. The first five years of the advisor's career is all about building up a volume of clients. The senior advisor who has all the clients she can handle will still be looking for that ideal prospect to spend time with and will happily have a C client reassigned to a less experienced advisor in return.

The common denominator is that in every type of practice, there is a need to have a flow of names passing through at all times so that the advisor can be selective about whom to take on as a prospect. This flow can be large or small, passive or proactive, but it must be constant.

Steps in Creating a Client Acquisition System: VALUE-TO-ME

Value. Determine what you have to offer in a potential relationship. Design a brief, iconic presentation to describe this value and convey why someone should talk to you.

Approach. Identify the types of markets and prospects you would like to approach.

Link. Connect with people who can help introduce you to those prospects and enter those markets.

Understand. Know who you would like to approach by interviewing your link contacts. In doing so, you get a profile of those people you would like to pursue: their communication methods, benefits packages, occupations, and other opportunities where your products and services would fit.

Engineer. Develop your approach strategies: coordinate your initial contact with your initial presentation and materials—then rehearse!

Tactics. Determine how you will spread your message: referrals, seminars, mail, e-mail, phone calls, and other tactics.

Ongoing. Position yourself as the go-to person in that market for financial services.

Maintenance. Outsource as much of the day-to-day prospecting and marketing details as possible to a staff person.

Evaluate. Review what worked and what didn't in preparation for entry into another market. This entails studying the statistics you have been collecting over time.

Value: The Iconic Self-Introduction

Before setting off down the road of name accumulation, you should have a consistent message that will resonate with those who are willing to listen to you. This best practice will accomplish the following:

1. Provide you with a simple, *iconic method* of articulating the value you can bring to a relationship and intrigue a prospect to hear more about you
2. Be transferable to other advocates of your practice to use in explaining what you do when you aren't present
3. Provide you with a touchstone for ongoing client interaction and growth

Icons are used on computer desktops to serve as gateways to entire programs. They are graphic symbols of what lies behind the double click. Similarly, your icon should be a simple representation of the processes and passions you bring to a client relationship.

The iconic image is *not* the equivalent of the so-called elevator speech. The "elevator speech" idea evolved as a way of responding to the question "What do you do?" in a quick, efficient, and brief manner.

While there is a place for having this type of handy phrase, I've always found it curious that waiting for an elevator is used as a prototypical situation in which to utilize this phrase. It's taught to new advisors in many classrooms as a snappy dialogue starter, the setup being that you are to imagine you are waiting for an elevator and want to strike up a conversation with a likely looking prospect also waiting for the same elevator. The idea is to have both of you enter the elevator talking and then end up walking out in agreement to get in touch about your products and services. You get about 15 seconds to snare the prospect's attention (unless it's a really slow elevator).

My preference is to call these "power phrases" instead of "elevator speeches." If you can pull off a power phrase one-liner, more power to you. In the course of my consulting, I've heard plenty of catchy come-ons designed to have the prospect say "What's that again?" in order to engender a conversation. A few samples:

- "I'm in the business of saving lives." [Huh?] "Financial lives." [Oh.]
- "I help people get off of their assets." [Huh?] "Investing wisely for retirement." [Oh.]
- "I tame bulls and bears." [Huh?] "Investment counseling." [Oh.]
- "I'm a planner for all seasons." [Huh?] "Financial planning from birth to senior years." [Oh.]
- "I'm a money counselor." [Huh?] "Investments and insurance." [Oh.]

If the result is getting into a dialogue with a prospect that results in an appointment to explore what the advisor does, then the power phrase is successful.

The biggest issue is that a power phrase, clever as it might be, usually triggers a suspicion in the recipients that they are going to be confronted with someone trying to sell them insurance or a hot stock. In other words, the downside of using a power phrase is that it could unnecessarily stereotype the advisor.

It's true that advisors need to be able to bring prospects into a conversation and provide them with the opportunity to express an interest in what they do. A simple "I'm in financial services, planning, and/or investments" should suffice. By all means, try out some power phrases that you feel comfortable with.

However, the actual presentation of the what, how, and why of your practice should be a separate meeting and not part of a repartee at a social function. This is the gist of the *iconic presentation*.

In researching iconic presentations, I've come across many that work well in a variety of situations. Some advisors use a pyramid to demonstrate their ground-up building block program to financial well-being. Others use interlocking circles or boxes to explain how they approach tax planning. I work with one advisor who is an avid college football fan and describes himself as a "financial quarterback" and hands out minifootballs with his logo. In the Case Development system we'll look at a "Building a Financial House" iconic presentation. The unifying characteristic of all of these icons is that they involve establishing and using memorable images. Memorable images can be taught to others and used by those folks to convey your values and the depth and breadth of what you bring to the table.

Research indicates that we retain only 10 percent of what we hear, 20 percent of what we see, 65 percent of what we hear and see, but 90 percent of what we hear, see, *and* do.

With that in mind, an iconic presentation should seek to be visual and verbal, and it should involve the person you are sharing it with. It can be used in one-on-one situations as well as in group seminars to demonstrate what it is that you do.

As an example, here is the "Line Presentation" developed by an advisor and adapted for general use.

You draw a line on any available surface:

B _____ D_ _ _ _?

Here's where you were born (B), and here's where statistically you will die (D). However, with medical and scientific advances, chances are you'll outlive that age so I'll put a question mark at the end [dotted line and ?].

This line and the dotted line represent your income stream during your lifetime. Hopefully, it's an ever-increasing income stream. My life's work is to protect that income stream from all possible disruptions. Now what would you think could possibly interrupt your income stream?

Allow prospect to answer: "Dying, illness, a lawsuit, job loss, sending the kids to college, starting up a business."

That's great! And there are many others. Generally, though, they fall into two categories: Things we can insure against and things we can't [write "INS" under the solid line].

B _____ D_ _ _ _?

INS

Of the situations you suggested, we can buy insurance against dying too soon, illnesses, disabilities, accidents, lawsuits, and infirmity in old age. But there are other things that can interrupt your income stream that we can't buy insurance against. As you mentioned, some of those things are losing a job, needing college funds, living too long, getting divorced, or starting a business. We need to build pools of money to provide us with income during these often unexpected and stressful situations. For this, we invest for such contingencies [write "INV" above the solid line] to build that pool of money to supplement your income as necessary.

INV

B _____ D_ _ _ _?

INS

That's a picture of what I do: I help you protect your income from being disrupted from those things we can insure against and from those things we can't. I feel very strongly that everyone should have both sides of this line assessed and secured. Is anyone taking care of these issues for you?

If not, because this is my life's work, I would be happy to be that person.

Results:

- It's a simple and transferable visual icon: a line. Top clients and centers of influence can replicate the presentation to explain what you do when you are absent.
- It provides a forum that allows your passion to come through.
- When prospects respond to your request for "income interruption" items, they are participating, thereby increasing the buy-in to your message.
- As they suggest income disruptors, you may be hearing top-of-mind concerns (hot buttons).
- It describes the depth and breadth of your products and services.
- It gives you a piece to use with clients during reviews to summarize their particular situation.
- Repeated use of the line icon will strengthen and reaffirm your role in advising the client on both the insurance and investment sides of the line.

Approach and Link: Determining Your Markets, Prospects, and Who Can Help You Connect with Them

The iconic presentation reflects and communicates your areas of genius. It defines the value you bring to a client relationship. In the line presentation above, the advisor using it might be considered a *generalist*—that is, a financial planner who provides both investment and insurance products and services. Advisors who work closer to either the investment or insurance side of the equation should create an appropriate iconic image that shares this preference.

The next step is to find people who need what you have to offer and decide how to approach them. Taking a systematic approach, we look for links that you might already have in place to access these potential prospects. We can look ahead for links that can be developed over time.

Before we get started, let's take some time out for a couple of definitions:

Market. A group of people who have common interests, needs, and communication links

Prospect group. A group consisting of both people in a specific market and people in the general population

Many times *market* and *prospect group* are used interchangeably. This is due to fuzzy definitions of markets like "business owners" that are far too broad. Business owners as a group don't have common interests, needs, or communication links. They come in a rich variety of shapes and sizes. They are a great example of a prospect group—one that an advisor might send a mass mailing to, create a telephone campaign for, or canvass and invite to a seminar. However, until it's narrowed down to specific types of business owners, it remains a prospect group.

For example, architects make up a market in the business owners group. Independent architects who don't work for large architectural firms make up a narrower market group. Finally, independent architects who have fewer than 10 employees and have been in business for at least five years make up an even narrower market group. The narrower the targeting, the more intimately an advisor can get to know the common interests, needs, and communication links its members share.

There are many ways to prospect in these markets, which we will examine later in this chapter. Right now, let's take a look at a best-practice method of finding potential markets in which to prospect.

The successful advisor is positioned to utilize his or her influence and the influence of other key people to gather qualified prospects. There are three tools to determine the extent of one's current and potential centers of influence: (1) Project Brain-Dump, (2) Mapping Exercise, and (3) Market Focus List.

Project Brain-Dump

Project Brain-Dump is used to gauge the depth and breadth of the advisor's network of currently active contacts. It's created by having the advisor list—brain-dump—all the people whom they have been in contact with during the past year. This list can be made on a simple spreadsheet. Names can be gathered from PDAs, cell phones, address books, party and social event lists, phone directories, e-mail lists, and holiday card lists.

Analysis of Project Brain-Dump reveals the advisor's possible range of influence. How many names is the advisor able to generate through this exercise? While 300 is a good sign, 50 is not. What does the range of names look like? There ought to be a reasonable variety in the areas of occupations, income, geographic locations, and nature of relationships (business, personal, avocation, relative).

The more variety the better. For new advisors in their Developing life cycle stage, this exercise should produce a volume of names large enough that the *law of large numbers* can be applied as it is with batting averages in baseball. The law of large numbers says simply that a new advisor needs to have plenty of opportunities at bat. Calculating success in converting these times at bat—contacts with people in the Project Brain-Dump—will be similar to calculating batting averages: a player who hits .300 is doing extremely well.

With only 50 names to work with, an advisor batting .300 will get in contact with 15 people. Even in the unlikely scenario that all 15 become clients, the pool of names has been exhausted for the time being. To generate prospecting activity, the advisor may well have to turn to cold calling or another mass prospecting endeavor in which a response rate of 2 percent is considered stellar. With 500 names from the Brain-Dump at the same .300 average, the advisor will get 150 contacts, which is a healthier number from which to work, network, and gather referrals.

The resulting names from Project Brain-Dump should be taken from the spreadsheet and entered into the client relationship management (CRM) software to put into a contact cycle. Only basic information about the people should be entered at this point since their future potential is still unknown. At minimum, record their name, contact data, and occupation and the nature of the person's relationship to the advisor.

Determining the potential influence an advisor has with these people is the key element to the effective hiring and retention of advisors. In my consulting work, I encounter many seasoned veteran advisors who are looking to bring on and mentor new advisors. In the past, much of this recruiting work was done by large agencies or firms. Nowadays, more and more of it is falling on the shoulders of the senior advisors, who are forced to make advisor hiring decisions. This is normally not their strong suit and can be very costly—financially and emotionally—if the new advisors don't work out. Being able to determine the candidates' chances for success is imperative. Too often a new advisor is brought on with a Project Brain-Dump that looks good on paper but turns out to be unresponsive and unhelpful. To dig in and determine an advisor's influence range, we use the Mapping Exercise.

The Mapping Exercise

Mapping is used to plot out all the roles the advisor has played in life with their respective relationships to other people: family and friends, education, occupation or profession, community, and avocations. These maps can unlock relationships that have gone dormant or have been forgotten or that are part of someone else's network. These roles and relationships make up potential prospecting groups that can be approached on a warm basis.

In mapping the networks of those key people in the advisor's life— spouse, children, friends, former coworkers, or parents—the real power of this exercise is unlocked. The advisor can look at this mapping exercise as the uncovering of potential influence in others close to the advisor.

What the Mapping Exercise Looks Like

As shown in Figure 4.1, a free-form drawing is used to complete this exercise to allow for the fact that each advisor's map will be unique. The map begins with putting the advisor into a circle at the center of the page, as we have done with Paul, an advisor in business for five years. We then created adjoining circles for his wife, Beth, their children, Courtney and Sam, and his parents, Al and Cora.

From each circle extends an area of the advisor's life (a spoke) that intersects with other people and might result in possible markets and prospects. In Figure 4.1, you can see that spokes were used to radiate from Paul and key people in his life. These spokes connected them with more people and organizations where possible centers of influence might reside.

We then asked Paul about every close relationship these key people might have in each of the following categories:

- *Family.* Parents, siblings, and children
- *Relatives.* In-laws, cousins, and aunts and uncles
- *Friends.* Hometown, high school, and college

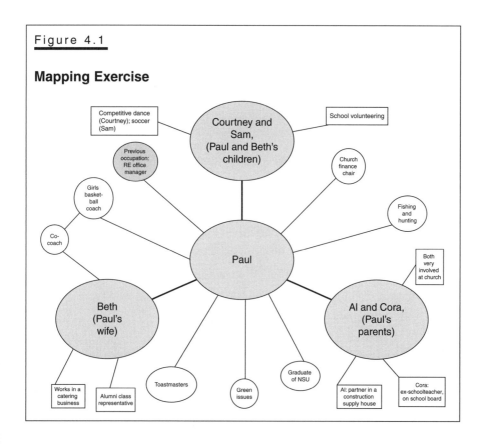

Figure 4.1

Mapping Exercise

- *Professionals.* Close working relationships
- *Previous work experiences and organizational structures*
- *Community.* Neighbors, community leaders, and business owners
- *Worship*
- *Nonprofits or volunteer organizations*
- *Sports.* The advisor's activities, health club memberships, and children's sporting groups
- *Hobbies*
- *Networking organizations*

Next we asked the following questions about Beth, Paul and Beth's children, and Paul's parents:

- What sports, hobbies, or interests do they pursue? Whom do they know through these activities?
- Do they belong to any organizations or networking groups? Who are the other members?
- Are they involved in their church or community in any ways?
- What did they do previously [work experience, position]? Whom do they maintain contact with, from the previous position?
- What other professionals or people do [or did] they work with?
- What other contacts can these people provide?

Repeat the questions for any new names that arise during the process. Work through each name until there are no new names generated.

In our example, Paul has noted the following about himself as possible sources:

- Previous occupation as a real estate office manager
- Church activities
- Avocations of hunting and fishing
- Interest in environmental issues
- Coaching of local girls basketball (which he does with Beth)
- Long-standing involvement with Toastmasters
- College alumni club activities

Once these lines (spokes) have been mapped, each resulting circle or box can then be analyzed in more depth.

To illustrate the power of the Mapping Exercise in determining the level of influence at the various points in Paul's network, let's take a look at one of his spokes. I've chosen the spoke that leads to his previous employer—previous occupation: real estate office manager—to demonstrate how this would work.

When we drilled down into Paul's experience as an office manager, we discovered that he regularly dealt with six different groups of people. These six groups could be considered nests of possible influence. As shown in Figure 4.2, we further mapped these groups into (1) real estate sales representatives; (2) attorneys and real estate consultants; (3) architects and construction contractors and subcontractors; (4) mortgage bankers, brokers, and lenders; (5) commercial developers and property managers; and (6) title companies and appraisers.

The Mapping Exercise leads to the creation of an Influence Worksheet. In Paul's case, we referenced each group from the spokes in the Mapping Exercise to an accompanying contact sheet, as shown in Figure 4.3, "Influence Worksheet." Paul listed on his contact sheet all the people he knew in each category by their position, job, and duties. He then indicated how much influence he felt he had with each person:

1. Paul's ability to get an appointment with that person for the purpose of reintroducing himself and what he's now doing

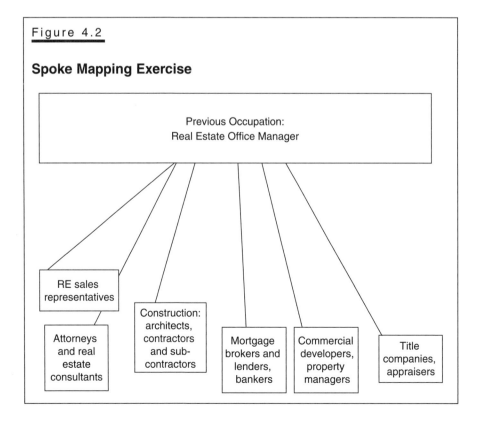

Figure 4.2

Spoke Mapping Exercise

Previous Occupation:
Real Estate Office Manager

RE sales representatives

Attorneys and real estate consultants

Construction: architects, contractors and sub-contractors

Mortgage brokers and lenders, bankers

Commercial developers, property managers

Title companies, appraisers

Figure 4.3

Influence Worksheet

	RE Sales Reps: Contact name	Position/ occupation/duties	Influence level		
			High	Med	Low
1					
2					
3					
4					
5					

	Att./RE Consultants: Contact name	Position/ occupation/duties	Influence level		
			High	Med	Low
1					
2					
3					
4					
5					

	Construction/Architect: Contact name	Position/ occupation/duties	Influence level		
			High	Med	Low
1					
2					
3					
4					
5					

(continued)

Figure 4.3

(Continued)

	Mortgage/lenders: Contact name	Position/ occupation/duties	Influence level		
			High	Med	Low
1					
2					
3					
4					
5					
	Commercial/Property: **Contact name**	**Position/** **occupation/duties**	**High**	**Med**	**Low**
1					
2					
3					
4					
5					
	Title/appraisers: **Contact name**	**Position/** **occupation/duties**	**High**	**Med**	**Low**
1					
2					
3					
4					
5					

2. The person's predisposition to give Paul credibility in his new financial services role versus his old real estate office manager role
3. The likelihood that the person will introduce Paul to others

A contact having all three factors indicated that Paul had *high influence* with that person. Two of the three indicated *medium influence*. One or none of the three indicated *low influence*.

The resulting worksheet revealed the links—or relationships—for Paul to foster in reaching out to spread his message.

In general, many of the people who are on an advisor's high end of the influence scale should be asked to be centers of influence (COIs). A *COI* is defined as someone inside a network who is willing to help the advisor penetrate that network. In addition, all of the names with high or medium influence should be entered into the CRM for contacting.

Understand: Understanding the Markets and Prospects

Once Project Brain-Dump and the Mapping Exercise have been completed, Paul will have a strong picture of which markets he would be able to enter effectively. Additionally, he has identified people who could be considered potential centers of influence in each of these markets.

Paul can now dig deeper to uncover characteristics common to those prospects who make up each market. With this information he can tailor a selection of his products and services to the market's membership, find effective ways to prospect and communicate his message, and learn what pitfalls to avoid.

This insider information is best collected using a Marketing Research Questionnaire (Figure 4.4). After completing the interview, study the results to determine strategies and tactics.

Engineering and Tactics: Approach Strategies and Methods of Gathering Names

To summarize the Client Acquisition system thus far: we have a succinct, iconic story to tell, one that demonstrates the *value* you bring to a client relationship. We've identified the types of people we are interested in *approaching*. We uncovered our networks of potential contacts to *link* us to these prospects, gauged our influence with them, and sought to *understand* the markets by surveying key members.

Now it's time to go and actually do it: by *engineering* the flow of names into the practice's pipeline. Sources that can provide this flow of names include referrals, natural markets, lists (both personal and purchased), public forums (seminars, work site visits, speaking, writing, shows), and observation and face-to-face calls.

Figure 4.4

Marketing Research Questionnaire

Market: _____

Person interviewed: _____

Date: _____

Common Characteristics

What observations can you offer about the following demographics of this market?

- Age range

- Male/female ratio

- Ethnic mix

- Marital status

- Percentage with children

- Educational level achieved

- Work schedules

- Best time to catch them

- Recreational activities and/or hobbies

- Religious preferences

- Social activities

- Volunteer activities

- Legal or political concerns

- Other outside interests

Common Needs

What observations can you offer about the following financial and business aspects of this market?

(*continued*)

Figure 4.4

(Continued)

- Office location

- Typical organizational chart; number of staff

- Who are the key people, and are they hard to keep?

- Top 5 day-to-day problems that are always being wrestled with

- Benefits package offered

- Who usually coordinates the benefits?

- Retirement plans offered

- Business entity for taxes

- Financial concerns

- Cash flow problems

- Retirement

- Business plan: Short range

- Business plan: Long range

- Other professionals retained, like CPA, attorney, P&C agent

- Financial go-to counselor

- General understanding of how a profit is made

- Average earnings per year: New, growing, established

- Biggest financial issues faced

Communication Links

What are the common communication methods that the members of this market share?

- Newsletters, paper and online

- Magazines and journals, paper and online

- Associations

(continued)

Figure 4.4

(Continued)

- Clubs

- Regular meeting places, formal and informal

- Internet sites

- Continuing education

- Type of customer relationship management software

- Special services or contacts for top clients

- Special incentives for staff members

- What is the wrong way to approach the members of this market [bad experiences]?

- What is the right way?

Concluding Items

I have a list of some members of this market that I'll be contacting. Is there anyone on this list that you might know about or can provide me an introduction to?

- Thank the interviewee.

- Be sure to send a thank-you note.

Schedule a follow-up meeting in a month or so to keep the interviewee apprised on the progress of your market penetration, especially if he or she has provided an introduction.

Of these, a strong referral process is the most effective in finding the quality of prospect the advisor seeks.

Referrals

There are many good-quality referral systems used traditionally throughout the financial services profession. However, many advisors are uncomfortable with these traditional methods of referral gathering, which I describe as "tacky" because advisors have been taught to tack a referral spiel onto any and all appointments.

I see this tactic as a form of bait and switch. The advisor is with the clients or prospects ostensibly for one reason—to fact find, present a case, or to do a review, for example. The advisor then attempts to gather names of referrals as an afterthought, an "oh, by the way." This approach catches the clients off guard or, worse, confirms what they had been fearing all along: the dreaded "who do you know?" question. Whether or not the tacky referral approach comes as a surprise to the clients on the other side of the table, it's never a way to get good-quality referrals.

My research has confirmed that referral gathering should be a planned event, an expectation, and not a surprise. It can be part of an interview with a client, but it needs to be a *planned* part. The language might be the following used in confirming an annual review appointment:

We'll be reviewing your portfolio, looking at adjusting strategies if necessary and ensuring that all of your profile information is current. Also, I'd like to carve out a few minutes to ask for your help with my marketing plan. I'm opening up a couple of new sources and would like to run them by you if I could. Would that be all right?

Note that permission is obtained to broach the marketing process. The new sources are reflected in the Market Focus List we will be discussing shortly.

The best practice in referral gathering is to hold an interview with a center of influence for the sole purpose of gathering names. It's an honest, straightforward approach that leverages both the influence of the advisor and that of the COI.

Paul, our advisor from the Mapping Exercise, has a very deliberate referral process. He has identified 20 COIs who can provide quality names in his client and market profiles. He has a regularly scheduled meeting with each one on a semiannual basis, which is roughly one a week over the course of the working year (net vacations, conferences, holidays, and other schedule disruptions). The sole purpose of these meetings is to brainstorm for prospects.

His COIs understand this and are familiar with the routine. Before we take a look at his COI meeting agenda, how might you invite a person to become a COI? Paul's script is straightforward. He's coming from a position of strength—being already successful—and asking for help in expanding into specific markets he has identified.

Asking someone to be a center of influence might sound like this:

Hi, Jim. This is Paul. Do you have a minute? Thanks. As you know, I've been in the financial services business for a number of years now, and I have reached a level of success. This is truly what I was meant to do in life, and I've been blessed with great clients and associates.

I've been working on identifying what I'd like my practice to look like in the upcoming years. It's a bit ambitious and will probably keep me and my team very busy. I've also identified the profiles of the types of people I'd like to work with—and the markets I'd like to work in.

I'm hoping you'd be able to help me in this marketing effort.

I respect you and what you have accomplished in your life, and I would be honored if you could share some of your experience and wisdom with me as I strive to get to my own next level of success.

We'd meet twice a year for 30 minutes or less. During those meetings, we'd discuss my markets in some depth and see if you could help identify resources, people, and tactics for entering these markets. My expectation is simply that you challenge me to keep on track with what I say I want to do.

If it's affirmative, he sets up the initial appointment. Paul then sends an e-mail or handwritten note of appreciation and confirms the appointment date.

If the person declines, Paul acknowledges the reason why the person won't—"You've had a bad experience in the past, and I appreciate that"— and thanks the person for his or her time.

The COI Meeting

When Paul meets with those who say yes to helping him as a COI, the meeting has three agenda items:

1. Paul updates the COI on his practice. This might include new products or services, investment strategies, and marketing pieces being offered by his company. He always ensures that the COI knows how to promote him to potential prospects. He reinforces his use of an iconic presentation—a financial pyramid—by pointing out where the new products or services impact the pyramid.

2. Paul utilizes a Market Focus List for the COI to react to: "These are the types of people I am actively seeking to work with. I know something about their occupation, avocation, or situation, and I would like to work with them from a financial perspective. Who are some people you know who are in or are associated with

these profiles?" The list includes a number of bullets for specific demographics, occupations, community involvements, and other key traits that Paul is looking for.

3. Paul and his marketing assistant put together lists of people they would like to approach who are not warm. This could be a list of architects (one of Paul's focus markets) in the community or in a particular zip code. Paul would then test the names on the list to see if his COI could provide some insight or contact information for anyone on it. Paul has also identified people from other sources whom he would like to have as prospective clients. This could include people who have appeared in the media after having accomplished something of significance or experienced a life-altering event. The COI can review these lists of names with an eye toward helping Paul create a warmer introduction.

Paul doesn't have to continually ask clients for referrals at every opportunity because he has set up a constant source of prospects. The centerpiece of this best-practice referral approach is the Market Focus List.

Market Focus List

The Market Focus List builds on and is used to direct the referral process. The bullet points on this list are specific types of people you would like to work with based on experience, involvement, and/or interests. Reviewing the advisor's brain-dump and mapping exercises will also point to some possible markets to target.

Figure 4.5 shows what Paul's Market Focus List looks like. Each of the categories on the list should have a story behind it. The story should connect the category (market) to the reason the advisor has an interest in it. Let's look at an example of how this story connection might work in an interview with a center of influence (COI) and architects as a market focus.

> *I appreciate your time in helping me with my marketing.*
>
> *Let me explain how I'm going about my marketing. It's essentially a word-of-mouth system. I've identified a number of markets and networks I'd like to pursue going forward. [At this point, the advisor presents the one-page Market Focus List, facing the COI.] We won't cover all of these bulleted points today, but I'd like to review a few of the categories. Is that fair?*
>
> *Thanks. Now about architects . . . : I worked as an intern in an architecture firm for a couple of summers during college. Watching them take a concept of a structure, mentally visualize it, put it into*

Figure 4.5

Sample Market Focus List

- Architects
- Soccer coaches
- Involved parents
- Middle school sports fans, especially girls basketball
- Toastmasters members, past and present
- NSU grads
- Real estate developers
- Construction business owners
- People involved in their place of worship
- Fishing and hunting enthusiasts
- People interested in environmental issues
- Competitive dance participants and sponsors
- School board members or interested parents
- Catering-related business owners

---

a blueprint, and shepherd it into a real building was amazing. They are true geniuses.

I learned to appreciate the art and science of what an architect does. In my previous position as a real estate office manager, I occasionally came in contact with architects, but I still don't know enough about how they think about money and benefits, so I'm going to reapproach them from a financial services viewpoint. Does that make sense as a marketing strategy?

When you think of architects, who are the successful people that come to mind?

How about successful people in related areas, like construction, building contractors, and real estate developers?

As you were thinking about [name], who else came to mind?

Paul repeats this process with three or four other categories in which the COI might have contacts. He writes down the names as they come up, but he doesn't stop the flow by trying to get additional information. After all the names have been written down, he sums up the conversation and closes:

Thank you for your help. Now reviewing this list of people, I'll be contacting them by letter first, then by phone. My purpose in doing so is to briefly meet with them, tell them what I do, hand them my business card, and stay in touch with them until they might have need of an additional financial service or product. Does that sound like a fair way to do business?

Great. I'd like to use your name in my approach to these folks. Is there anyone on this list with whom you would prefer I not use your name in my initial contact?

At this point, if the COI objects, the advisor can acknowledge the objection and steer the conversation to address it:

I understand. Assuming they are successful people, I'm thinking that in the next two years or so, they will probably be making some major financial decisions, right?

I'm simply going to contact them, tell them what I do, hand them a business card, and stay in touch until that financial decision time arrives. It's at that point I'd like to be available to them as a choice to turn to for advice. Does that make sense?

With that in mind, your name is my best calling card. How are you feeling about that now?

Could you give me a little background on each of these people such as contact information, where they work, family, or how you know them?

Thanks! I'll be keeping you in the loop on all my contacts with these folks so you will know exactly how I sit with them at any given time.

After the meeting, Paul sends the COI a thank-you note, a copy of the initial contact letter and who received it, the status of previous contacts and meetings with the COI's referrals up to the point where confidentiality takes over, and a suggested time to get together again to review a few more of the listed Market Focus List categories.

As a result of the interview, Paul has positioned himself as a businessperson, directed the referral discussion by leveraging the COI's areas of influence, secured warmer names to call, and "trained" his COIs to help with his marketing.

The Market Focus List should be a tool that is with you constantly. It can be used as part of any interview in which you have gotten permission to discuss your marketing plan. It is also a list that's under constant reconstruction. You may be adding and subtracting categories as your practice evolves. It's this constant rebuilding that keeps it fresh and interesting to your COIs who are viewing it twice a year.

While referrals are the primary source of names in our relationship-driven financial services profession, there are a number of other ways to gather prospects.

Natural Markets

The term *natural market* is really the result of Project Brain-Dump and the Mapping Exercise. Your natural market is composed of those people who are part of your day-to-day and month-to-month activities. These are folks whom you encounter on a regular basis and have formed a relationship with. The relationships may be tenuous, but you have the ability to approach these people on a warm basis. Normally, a natural market encompasses friends, family, relatives, coworkers, those in organizations you belong to, service providers, business contacts, and the like.

Revisiting the Project Brain-Dump and the Mapping Exercise every couple of years would be advantageous in ensuring this source of names is alive and well. Why? In many cases, a member of your natural market may sit back and wait until you've "made it in the business" before meeting with you. Or, of course, situations change, and where you were once not offering anything of value to particular contacts, suddenly you may become a needed resource if a windfall, emergency, death, or disability has occurred in their life.

Lists: Personal and Purchased

The use of lists has evolved in the face of junk mail oversaturation and state and federal do-not-call legislation. There was a time when an advisor got a list and proceeded to make cold calls. A softer (but still cold) approach was to send a precall letter to members of the list before calling them. This was my favorite tactic in my first two years as an advisor. It always felt better to make a call that started out: "I'm calling to follow up on a letter that you should have received." This worked even if the caller never sent a letter in the first place. While there still may be demographic pockets where these strategies work, the sophistication of the general public and the use of call screening technology are rendering them ineffective. Certainly, if you are an advisor who is relationship focused, you wouldn't find these approaches palatable.

Used wisely, however, lists can be very productive. The best-practice use of lists is to present them as names for others to review and possibly warm up for a contact. These are known as "feeder lists."

Prior to visiting with a COI in his architect market, Paul and his assistant prepared these feeder lists. Using the Internet, subscription services, reverse directories, and the phone book, they created the following lists:

- Architects and architect firms in the surrounding geographic area
- Property developers in the same area
- Construction firms in the same area
- The COI's home neighbors
- The COI's business neighbors, if in an office environment
- Names obtained from the media whom the COI might know
- Names obtained from lists purchased from vendors such as Dun & Bradstreet

Paul could then say to his COIs: "Here is a list of people whom I would like to contact, but these would basically be cold calls. Would you mind scanning the list to see if there is anyone on this list whom you might be able to warm up for me?"

When the COI identifies someone on the list that he or she can provide some information about, or an introduction to, Paul highlights the name. Once a number of names have been highlighted, Paul then completes a prospect card on each one. His assistant will then put the names and contact information into the database noting a scheduled contact time and whether that contact would be by letter, call, visit, or e-mail.

Public Forums: Seminars, Work Sites, Speaking, Writing, and Shows

For many advisors, public forums are the primary source of new names. In the many interviews I've conducted with advisors, I am constantly amazed at how some have created prospecting machines from their efforts in this area.

Rick, based in Washington, D.C., holds six seminars a year that yield all the new prospects he needs, based on his prior year statistics. The invitees are all the result of center-of-influence and top-tier client referrals. Using a personalized variation on Paul's referral approach discussed above, Rick acquires approximately 72 prospect units (couples are one unit, as are some business partners) over the course of a year.

Each seminar presentation on his financial planning and wealth management practice is tied to a meal. Not just any meal, but a meal at a featured restaurant with unique cuisine. Rick's client base includes high-powered

Washington insiders, lobbyists, attorneys, CPAs, and all levels of government appointees so his attention to detail is very acute.

The referral is alerted by the COI to expect Rick's office to call. Rick's top assistant makes the initial call to schedule a phone meeting between Rick and the referral. Rick has an initial phone conversation with the 72 prospects to further qualify the candidates. This will usually eliminate 12 who are happy with their advisor or just not interested. The remaining 60 are invited to a dinner seminar that is crafted to their choice of cuisine, wine, and ambiance. The referring COI or top client is also invited.

For every 60 invitees, statistically an average of 8 prospect units and 4 referrers end up attending each event. Rick would like to recruit 4 new clients from each seminar and usually succeeds, which reflects his goal of adding 25 new clients each year for the next five years.

These focused seminars work well for Rick. He feels the days of "mass invitation" seminars are over or they have been relegated to the transaction-driven sales agents. He is a relationship genius in a politically drenched environment where every action can have multiple cross purposes and interpretations.

Anthony and Allan, in Phoenix, Arizona, and Portland, Oregon, cultivate all the prospects they need through the year by being the sponsored financial services provider for teaching hospitals, working primarily with resident physicians. They understand that this is a strategy for the long run since residents have minimal incomes. Both advisors have mentors who have made this strategy a turnkey process. Once the resident completes her tour, then there is a huge jump in income that can be managed with the advisor's help since the relationship has already been established during her residency.

How did they get into these teaching hospitals? "It's why I was hired on," says Allan. "I come from a family of physicians, and my dad and older brother have made many good relationships in their hospital. That hospital was added to the two already developed by Shelly, my mentor. We're negotiating with another university medical center that was referred to us by my dad."

Anthony took a different track. "My background was office management for a large physician group. I recognized a huge need for educating doctors in how to run an office efficiently, and I began holding seminars to communicate that knowledge. This caught on, and soon I wanted to do these seminars full time. But I needed a long-term 'hook' if you will. I found that hook in the financial planning area. The 'Financial Management for Growing Physician Practices' material developed by Shelly provided the backbone of my presentation. It's of particular interest to residents getting ready to jump out on their own. I presented the program to a couple of hospitals, and since they had never seen anything like it, they bought into it and permitted us to offer it throughout the year. We've had great success since. I've had to bring on two other advisors to keep from getting overwhelmed."

Richard, in Minneapolis, Minnesota, has made a career out of selling 401(k) plans to large companies and providing work site seminars to the employees. Richard has mastered the penetration of a corporation. In his early years, he obtained a foothold working individually with the rank and file members of three large companies, and then he referred his way up the chain of command. These days, he starts with the executive group and provides seminars to the various employee levels within the corporation. Richard specializes in executive compensation and 401(k) plans. His advisor team of four works through the rest of the organization. As a result, he has never met many of his clients. Rather, he spends the majority of his time rainmaking—cultivating the top-level executive relationships.

Leslie, in Sacramento, California, gathers all the prospects she needs from her radio call-in show. Succeeding with this approach was an exercise in patience. Five years ago, she had the opportunity to be a guest on a local financial talk show. This turned out well, and she returned frequently as a regular guest, but there was little tangible business that emerged. When the host of the show decided to move on, Leslie was a natural replacement. In the past two years of hosting the show, she has developed a strong following, and a steady stream of prospects and referrals has evolved from her audience. When she sponsors live seminars in the area, her reputation guarantees a high turnout. But, she cautions:

> I don't recommend this as a strategy while you are building a business. For 10 years, I was running around looking for the markets and referrals that were necessary to survive and grow. Now I can look back and say that radio was a smart strategy but not one I would have bet the house on.

Observations and Face-to-Face Calls

Two final approach strategies are time-honored methods. *Observation* is exactly what it suggests: the advisor observes someone in the course of daily events who fits the advisor's target profile and either approaches the prospect on the spot or arranges to meet with him or her for an initial interview.

Morgan, in Tulsa, Oklahoma, enjoys this interaction: "I like to catch people red-handed doing something really well. Yesterday, I was out at the mall purchasing a new pair of shoes. The salesman who assisted me was very courteous and patient, and he spent a little extra time and effort in selecting the best possible pair of shoes for my feet. I thanked him and asked to see the owner. I spent 10 minutes with the owner, both to compliment his employee and the excellent training he obviously received and to learn how he started his business. We continued the conversation over coffee the next day. As part of the give-and-take, I showed him how I help small businesses with their cash flow issues. Now we're working on an exit strategy for him. That's the sort of thing I love about what I do. It's all interrelated—business and pleasure."

Face-to-face calling is the advisor's dropping in unexpectedly to greet a potential prospect. It demands a certain outgoing personality combined with a defined geographic area. Greg, in the western Boise, Idaho, suburbs, has mastered the technique. "I'm pretty well known in our Boise area, having built my practice over the past 25 years and watching the exponential growth of our metro region. So it's no problem for me to see a name in the newspaper and simply stop by and meet them. Here's a good example:

> *In June 2006, I saw in the newspaper that a new law firm was being formed from two attorneys' practices. I had met one of them, Rob, but I had never met his new partner, Laura. Neither were clients, but they certainly fit my prospect profile. After they had been together for nine months, I stopped by their office one day with a framed copy of the article in the newspaper that announced their merger with a proclamation signed by the mayor honoring the merger date on June 1 as "Rob and Laura Day." We had a blast with that concept—I hosted the in-office open house on "Rob and Laura Day," and the mayor was there, as were the firm's top clients, the local media, and the manager of my office. And me, too, of course. Are we good referral sources for each other? You bet. As they expand, who will they turn to for advice? Our firm and its planners and specialists. Face-to-face calling can be a disappointment, naturally. A lot of people don't know what to make of it, but I'm resilient, and more often than not, I get to hear their story and end up with a solid lead.*

Ongoing: Managing Prospects

Once an approach has been engineered and the tactics for gathering names set in motion, the next piece is to have a system for tracking people through the prospecting phase and to not let the better candidates fall through the cracks over time. The tool for this system is a good CRM database with an integrated calendar.

There are multiple CRM programs in the marketplace, running the gamut from basic to complex. We will be examining the best practices concerning the selection of a CRM in the next chapter. For purposes of the Client Acquisition system, a good CRM should be able to accommodate the following data for prospects:

- Prospect name
- Age and date of birth
- Employer
- Occupation
- Client address
- Client phone numbers
- Client e-mail and Web site
- Referring party's name if the prospect is a referral
- Source of the prospect

The CRM should also be able to track, record, and schedule the following contact points in the advisor's prospecting sequence:

- Scheduling an initial introductory letter or mailing
- Recording the date of the mailing
- Scheduling an initial call to the prospect on a to-do list
- Recording the outcome of the initial contact:
  - Yes to an appointment
  - Not right now, with permission to stay in touch
  - No, but meets your criteria and you want to stay in touch
  - Flat no
- Scheduling a next contact based on one of these outcomes

The CRM should also be able to record the following in the notes section:

- Information picked up during phone conversations
- Additional information provided by the referring party
- Outside information collected from search engines
- Areas of interest in which the prospect expressed interest

The further the prospect goes into the process of becoming a client, the deeper the amount of information that will be collected. This additional depth will be examined in the next chapter, but to summarize, processing a lead in your CRM includes these four elements:

1. Populating the entry with basic information and notes
2. Scheduling and tracking the initial activity
3. Posting outcomes from the initial contact
4. Indentifying the next contact steps

Maintenance: Assistants

In an advisor's Developing years, he or she should experience, hands-on, the processing of a prospect through the CRM system. This is essential to learning the CRM's capabilities. As soon as possible, however, it is prudent to outsource these duties to an assistant. At first, this is probably a marketing/administrative hybrid assistant. As the practice approaches the Mature stage, there is the need for two distinct functions: marketing and administration. We will cover the basics of hiring, training, and supervising these resource people in Chapter 9.

What does an assistant do to facilitate the Client Acquisition system? To answer this question, we have developed a series of best practice checklists for each of the Eight Business Systems. With these checklists, the advisor can assign team members to specific tasks. While the team members might change, the tasks themselves will remain the same. To help you create a best practices operations manual that works for your own practice, we have included these detailed checklists. The first is for Client Acquisition and appears at the end of this chapter.

Evaluate: Monitoring Your Client Acquisition System Activity Statistics

To measure the effectiveness of the advisor's Client Acquisition activity, a few key statistics need to be monitored:

- Number of warm prospects obtained, tracked by markets and sources, per week
- Number of these prospects who agree to initial meetings
- Initial meetings that result in a commitment to work together
- Number of commitments to work together that result in in-depth fact/feeling finders (that is, discovery interviews)
- Number of discovery interviews that go on to become presentations

- Number of presentations that result in asset capture and/or product sales

A simple weekly activity spreadsheet might look like the one in Figure 4.6. The shaded statistics are specific to the Client Acquisition system, indicating the gathering of names and meetings with people who are not yet clients. For a fee-based advisor, the prospect may become a client at the end of the "agreement to work together" meeting when the required Form ADV is signed and a fee collected. The statistics listed are typical of an Emerging practice.

Client Acquisition System Best Practices Checklist

There are 60 specific steps in the Client Acquisition Best Practices Checklist (Figure 4.7). It's the blueprint for the first section of your best practices operations manual. Subsequent checklists for the remaining seven business systems will be in the same format.

The first column identifies the step number of the best practice, and the second identifies the specific step.

Columns 3 through 6 are possible people to hold accountable for the execution of those steps: advisor, marketing assistant, administrative assistant, and firm. A *firm* is defined as a larger entity the practice may be part of (office, agency, company, or broker/dealer), and it might pick up some of these steps in this system. There is a primary accountability person (X) and room for a shared accountability person (S).

The last column indicates what resources are being used to fulfill these steps, if any. The resource should also point to the location of other processes that are available and spelled out elsewhere.

In the example in Figure 4.7, it is assumed that the advisor is with a broker/dealer in a detached location, with a full-time administrative assistant and a full-time marketing assistant. The advisor is in a Mature life cycle stage.

Each practice is unique, of course, and the checklist can be modified for each advisor. The resources referred to on the checklist are suggestions based on various best practices observed in the field. Any resource in italic type is a piece that is reviewed or illustrated earlier in this chapter.

Figure 4.6

Weekly Activity Spreadsheet

Statistic	Weekly Expectation	Actual	Difference
Warm prospects obtained	6		
Percent who turn into a current appointment	50% (3)		
Percent say "call back"	33% (2)		
Total appointments held	14		
Number of COI appointments	1		
Number of initial meetings	3		
Number of agreements to work together	2		
Number of discovery interviews	2		
Number of presentations	2		
Product sales	2		
Assets captured	$10,000		
Number of review appointments	2		
Number of networking appointments	1		
Number of other appointments	1		
Face-to-face time with key people: Hours per week	25		

Figure 4.7

Client Acquisition System Best Practices Checklist

Client Acquisition Activities	Advisor	Marketing Assistant	Administrative Assistant	Firm	Resources
Advisor Prospect Pool					
1.1 Complete Project Brain-Dump.	X				
1.2 Record Project Brain-Dump names on a spreadsheet or in the database.		X			CRM database
1.3 Complete Mapping Exercise to determine the extent and influence of your contact universe.	X				*Mapping Exercise*
1.4 Record Mapping Exercise names on a spreadsheet or in the database.		X			CRM database
Marketing Preparation					
1.5 Define markets to approach from prospect pool analysis.	X			S	
1.6 Identify centers of influence (COIs) in these markets.	X				*COI script*
1.7 If no specific markets are being pursued, identify COIs from your network who will help you generate names of prospects.	X				*Mapping Exercise*
1.8 Interview COIs to deepen understanding of selected markets.	X				*Market Research Questionnaire*

Note: X denotes primary accountability person, and S denotes shared accountability person.

1.9	Package a presentation of your products and services for members of these markets.	X	S		S	
1.10	Complete a profile of your target prospect in each selected market.	X				Prospect criteria
1.11	Establish a list of standard information to gather about a prospect.	X	S			
1.12	Develop a method to record prospect information.		X			Prospect information card
1.13	Prepare prospect feeder lists by market to have COIs warm up if possible.		X		S	List vendors, Internet search
Referral Process						
1.14	Review referral processes available.	X			S	Referral vendors
1.15	Select a referral process and language complimentary to your style.	X				
1.16	Refine an iconic introduction of yourself and what you do.	X				*Line Presentation*
1.17	Establish a stand-alone, dedicated interview for the purpose of gathering names.	X				*COI meeting*
1.18	Integrate name gathering—with permission—into all forms of face-to-face encounters with key people in your practice (reviews, discovery interviews, service calls, deliveries).	X				

(continued)

Figure 4.7

(Continued)

Client Acquisition Activities		Advisor	Marketing Assistant	Administrative Assistant	Firm	Resources
1.19	Obtain referrals.	X				*Market Focus List*
1.20	Gather and record standard information about referrals.	X				Prospect information card
1.21	Do Internet research on referrals.		X			Google, LexisNexis
1.22	Transcribe referral information to spreadsheet or database.		X			CRM database
1.23	Commit to and sustain a referral/prospect activity level and weekly expectation.	X	S			
1.24	Establish an accountability person to monitor this activity.	X	S		S	
Preapproach (All Prospects)						
1.25	Select preapproach letters for new prospects from approved literature.	X	S			
1.26	Package introductory material to include with prospect precall letter or e-mail (business card, brochure, testimonials).	S	X			
1.27	Mail the precall communication; record date sent.		X			CRM database
1.28	Post a follow-up call date.		X			CRM database, calendar

60

1.29	Contact prospects to schedule appointment.	X			Script
1.30	Post results of prospect contact.	X		S	CRM database
1.31	If prospect says "no" or "not now" post a call-back time or drop the prosect.	X		S	CRM database, calendar
1.32	If prospect says "yes," schedule appointment (go to Sales Process).	X		S	CRM database, calendar
Mail Campaigns or Other Cold-List Approaches					
1.33	Research and purchase (or obtain) a targeted list.	X		S	List vendors, Internet
1.34	Select letter—precall or return-requested—from approved literature.	X		S	
1.35	Coordinate mail-merge and mailing sequence.		S	X	CRM database, calendar
1.36	Schedule follow-up phone date.			X	CRM database, calendar
1.37	Make the follow-up call.	X			Script
1.38	With warm responders, set initial appointment (go to Sales Process).	X			CRM database, calendar
1.39	Determine what to do with nonresponders: keep in database or eliminate.	X		S	CRM database

(continued)

Figure 4.7

(Continued)

Client Acquisition Activities	Advisor	Marketing Assistant	Administrative Assistant	Firm	Resources
1.40 Track the success of the campaign.		X	S		CRM database analysis
Seminars and Public Presentations					
1.41 Determine which seminars or public presentations to use from approved materials.	X			S	Approved vendors
1.42 Calendar: Set an annual seminar schedule.	X	S			CRM database, calendar
1.43 Find a sponsor: wholesaler, fund rep, home office department.	X			S	
1.44 Create a budget.	X	S			
1.45 Create a timeline checklist for preseminar preparation: • Invitation selection and mailing • RSVP tracking and confirmation • Phone call follow-up for nonresponders • Food and beverage, catering • Location, room rental, room setup, cleanup • Directions and parking • Speakers and presenters booked and prepped • Audio-visual equipment	X	X			CRM database, calendar Follow suggested vendor steps (e.g., Emerald) if available.

	• Promotional materials; ads • Handouts, workbooks, feedback forms • Door prizes • Photographer • Rehearse presentation		S	Videotape for rehearsing
1.46	Conduct the seminar: • Arrival procedure; check-in table • Agenda provided • Mingling, informal time, eat and drink • Presentation • Questions and answers (Q&As) • Postseminar feedback forms completed and collected	X		Follow suggested vendor steps (e.g., Emerald) if available.
1.47	Postseminar: • Send thank-you notes, with photos, from approved material. • Send "sorry we missed you" notes. • Post additional information about attendees gathered at the seminar.		X	CRM database, calendar
1.48	Schedule follow-up phone calls to attendees.		X	CRM database, calendar
1.49	Make the follow-up calls.	X	S	Script
1.50	With warm responders, set initial appointment (go to Sales Process).	X	S	CRM database, calendar
1.51	Determine what to do with nonresponders: Keep in database or eliminate.	X	S	CRM database

(continued)

Figure 4.7

(Continued)

Client Acquisition Activities		Advisor	Marketing Assistant	Administrative Assistant	Firm	Resources
1.52	Track the success of the seminar; calculate ratios for the following: • Invites to accepted invites • Accepted invites to attendees • Attendees to OK to contact • OK to contact to actual appointments • Appointments to sales	X				CRM database analysis
1.53	Add results to cumulative seminar experience.		X			CRM database
Key Client Acquisition Statistics						
1.54	Track number of prospects obtained.		X			
1.55	Track number of prospects by source (e.g., referral, seminar, COI).		X			
1.56	Track number of prospects by market.		X			
1.57	Track ratio of prospects to initial appointments.		X			
1.58	Track ratio of initial appointments to presentations.		X			
1.59	Track ratio of presentations to sales.		X			
1.60	Create monthly ratio summaries		X			

64

5

Core Business System 2:
Client Management

In September 2008, the financial markets imploded. In a complex cascading of credit derivative write-downs, whole companies went under, and it became imperative to rescue others to prevent a Depression-like catastrophe. One of those rescues involved AIG, a world insurance giant, brought down by the need to cover its default credit swap instruments. With these events swirling around him, Scott, an AIG Retirement advisor in the Philadelphia, Pennsylvania, area, took to the offense.

He and his marketing advocate, Fran, executed a methodical Client Management strategy the day after the AIG news broke. Putting everything else aside, Scott reached out to each of his top-tier clients, reassuring them that their money was safe. AIG Retirement, as a subsidiary, was well capitalized and protected by the network of state insurance commissions. Scott and Fran went to their database and quickly extracted a list of A- and B-level clients. They sent a blast e-mail to those whose addresses were available with a "don't panic" message. Simultaneously fielding incoming calls and trying to make outbound calls, Scott and Fran eventually reached all their clients who had $50,000 or more in assets. The result was phenomenal.

"Nearly everyone was worried but reassured by our call," Scott said. "Most clients could tell me that their strategy was for a longer term and while the value of their portfolios dipped, they had no plans to move the money. In fact, I received quite a few compliments for taking a proactive stance."

Having worked with Scott on systematizing his practice over the previous two years, it was obvious that his Client Management system was working in the face of a worst-case scenario. His clients, although they were justifiably nervous, knew the reasons behind the way that Scott had allocated their funds and how he was managing their portfolios. He and Fran had been strongly reinforcing these reasons during each annual review. In addition, there were a regimented number of contacts throughout the year to further solidify the client relationships.

"The clients had a relationship primarily with us," Scott said. "The company was a secondary relationship. We didn't lose much in assets because of the AIG crisis. We're continuing to keep our top clients up to date on the market's events as they are unfolding."

Client Management is the second of the Core Four business systems. It is the "bottling" of your Relationship Maintenance and Growth genius. In practice management's quest to have a completely transferable practice, we seek to create a turnkey Client Management process to further enhance the value of a financial services practice. Scott and Fran's ability to react quickly in the face of adversity is a testament to having a strong Client Management system that "leaves no client behind."

The Client Management system covers all the processes you use to create a unique client experience.

An advisor's meat and potatoes are the relationships that are developed over time through providing this experience. The advisor's team is dedicated to keeping these client relationships alive and kicking. It's through these relationships that the practice grows and prospers, often through many client generations.

The approach to building a transferable Client Management system begins with client segmentation. We'll take a look at how to segment your clients and then take a look at each tier in terms of the client relationship management (CRM) database needs, service protocols, and annual reviews.

Segmentation of Clients

Early in their careers, many advisors want to treat all their clients equally. While philosophically appealing, this is a practical nightmare the larger one's client base grows.

Generally, after you've recruited your first 100 clients, segmentation begins to take on significance. Up to that point, almost everyone's a top-tier client—they're all important in building that initial client base. Starting segmentation at the 100-client mark allows for a systematic series of proactive contacts that helps keep you, the advisor, in control of Client Management.

Without segmentation, the demands of 100 and more clients may quickly overwhelm you and your staff. It is therefore important to keep in mind the Pareto principle, or the 80/20 rule, because it is especially true in Client Management. We don't want the 20 percent of your clients who drive 80 percent of your revenue to be lost in the day-to-day transactional issues that are constantly arising from the entire client population. Ideally, the advisor should not be involved with the majority of lower-tier service work. These tasks should be delegated to others on the team or within the company.

Once the initial segmentation is completed, client segments should be reviewed on an annual basis and adjusted as needed. People change, situations change, relationships change, earning powers change, and health circumstances change. All of these factors, and more, can affect a client's ranking. The focal point for arriving at a segmentation score and then periodically reassessing it is the annual review.

The annual review is best set at six months from the birthday of the client. The reason for this is to form a basic skeleton for the Client Management system in which there is one touch that's purely nonbusiness (birthday) and one touch that is all business (annual review). The remaining contacts can flow from those two key events.

Remember that a client can be defined as an individual, a head of household, business owner, or other key person controlling the wealth of others. For example, if a family is a client, the head of the household's birthday drives the reviews for the entire family's holdings. This keeps things simple, as multiple products will generally be part of a family's portfolio, all purchased at various points over the years. Time was when a life insurance policy date drove the review process. But today the variety of products, services, and timing precludes using that old yardstick.

So what are the segments? Simplicity and flexibility are the hallmarks of our flexible best-practice segmentation process. It starts with the concept that clients are either A-level or C-level. A-level clients are very important to the vitality and profitability of your practice. A-level clients will compose 10 to 20 percent of the total client base. C-level clients are customers holding a few products and not requiring or demanding a whole lot of service. C-level clients will compose 75 to 80 percent of the total client base.

What, then, of the B-level clients? In this philosophy, a B-level client is one who has yet to be designated an A or a C. B level is a holding place until a determination can be made. Most new clients fall into this category for their first couple of years. B-level clients make up 10 to 15 percent of all clients.

Finally, there is an optional D level for those clients who really need to be discarded. More about them later.

A-level clients have all, two, or one of three characteristics and are subdivided into AAA, AA, and A.

AAA. Triple-A clients have these characteristics in common:

1. They provide a significant source of recurring revenue for your business. "Significant" needs to be defined by you, based on your practice's life cycle stage, cash flow, and budgetary needs. "Recurring" revenue is ongoing income available through money management fees, planning retainers, or product trails.
2. They have the potential to attract more business: more assets to move, additional product needs, or ancillary services to be provided. These clients can also be in the driver's seat for others' assets. Perhaps the client is a beneficiary of a large estate, controls a trust, or is the decision maker for a company's pension plan.
3. They provide quality referrals. My rule of thumb is a minimum of three solid introductions per year.

AA. Double-A clients have two of the three characteristics. Usually, these clients contribute significantly to your recurring revenue and either they give referrals but don't have further potential or they have further potential but don't give referrals.

A. Single-A clients or prospects have just one of the characteristics. Note that a single-A contact might not be a client but is a *prospect* who has a lot of purchasing power (characteristic 2) or is a *center of influence* (COI) who only gives quality referrals (characteristic 3). These nonclient A's should be given A-level treatment. The A prospects can get a taste of what it would be like to actually be clients and that may help persuade them to your cause. COIs receive the A treatment to keep them active and aware of what's going on in your practice, hopefully giving them additional reasons to refer strong prospects to you.

B. B-level clients are those who have the potential to reach the A, AA, or AAA level in the next couple of years. In other words, they need cultivating. The B tier is a stopover place for either promotion to A level or placement into C level. As stated before, any new clients are initially put into the B category for a year or two until they prove to be A or C quality.

C. C-level clients are those who don't individually make a significant contribution to your revenue stream. Perhaps they have purchased a product or two and don't require much maintenance. As a group, the C clients may provide the practice with a block of renewal commissions or trails that in aggregate is important to maintain. Consequently, C clients should receive regular touches from the advisor's team.

D. D-level clients are those clients who demand far more maintenance than they are worth to your revenue stream. These folks tie up the support team's time with petty requests, service demands, and research questions far beyond their value financially. In fact, they may be taking a psychological toll on the team. Such clients need to be divested from your database. Where can they go? Some companies have an orphan pool or 800-number centers to which unwanted clients can be assigned. These orphans will then be contacted by new advisors or a dedicated team of orphan managers. Another possibility is discussed below in our Client Management case study.

We'll look in depth at each segment through the eyes of advisor Chris and his marketing assistant, Beth. Before that, however, we should take a look at the essentials of a client relationship management (CRM) program. We discussed the CRM in the Client Acquisition system as a way of processing prospects to the point of becoming clients. Now that we have a clientele to manage, it's even more imperative that there be a strong database program to provide a focal point for the Client Management system.

Client Relationship Management (CRM)

The best-practice CRM has four basic components that are integrated and searchable:

1. *Hard data on client holdings, by product and/or investment.* This information may be downloadable from the carriers and broker/dealers, or it may require some manual entry. Ideally, the values of these holdings should be updated daily.
2. *Soft data on the clients.* This is the nonproduct information that will be used to create a unique client service experience.

3. *An interactive calendar function.* This calendar should automatically record past client contacts, stamping them with a date and time. The calendar should combine e-mail capability with a to-do list. It should synchronize with most PDA models.

4. *Client notes.* This function records notes about clients such as the notes transcribed by an advisor after a meeting, call, or review. The client's file should also be able to contain Case Development records, attachments of correspondence, and scanned legal and tax documents.

The CRM's hard data could include sections and fields in any or all of the financial categories included in Figure 5.1.

Figure 5.1

Client Information Included in the CRM Hard Data

Insurances	Investments	Financial Plans, Coordinating	Additional Hard Data Considerations
Annuities	Variable annuities	Goals and objectives	Values
Variable life insurance	Mutual funds	Family and business	Cost basis
Term life insurance	Stocks	Wills	Taxes
Permanent life insurance	Bonds	Executors	Risk tolerance, asset allocation
Disability	CDs	Trusts	Transaction records and dates
Liability	Wrap account	Trustees	Charitable intent
Property and casualty	Traditional IRAs	Budgets and cash flow	Estate planning
Long-term care Health	Roth IRAs Education funding	Benefit packages Business agreements	Beneficiaries Ownership
Other insurances	Other investments		Distribution requirements

Some CRM programs go very deep into one or more of these areas, while others stay much broader and less deep. Many companies have customized their CRMs to their particular group of products and services. Soft data on clients includes the following:

- Names: Client, family members, business partners, key relationships
- Householding (connecting multiple individuals) of families or businesses
- Ages and dates of birth
- Addresses
- Phone numbers
- E-mail and Web site addresses
- Referral or other source from which the name was obtained
- Referrals received from the client
- Employer information
- Occupation and job duties
- Income and net worth
- Segment (A, B, C)
- Key advisors: Attorney, accountant, banker, broker, others
- Key upcoming personal, family, and/or business events
- Unique personal, family, and/or business circumstances
- Any potential "next sale" opportunity for the client
- Fields for personal information, such as those included in Figure 5.2

Figure 5.2

Client Information Included in the CRM Soft Data

Hobbies	Travel interests	Wine preferences	Cuisine preferences
Sports interests and participations	Health and exercise concerns	Favorite restaurants	Children's participations
Alumni affiliations	Volunteer activities	Artistic pursuits	Spouse's participations
Recreational interests	Charitable involvements	Clubs and organizations	Favorite retailers
Pets	Religious preferences	Team affiliations	Other

The ideal CRM will be able to produce reports that draw information from a variety of sources. For instance:

- List of all clients who have life insurance and a strong tie to a college alumni program (for charitable giving)
- List of clients who are involved with the Red Cross for an upcoming charity event being sponsored by the advisor's firm
- Holiday card list by religious affiliation
- Clients who have an insurance product but not an investment
- Clients who have exposure to a certain investment sector when the market takes a dip

A-Level Clients and Contacts

All three categories of A-level clients or prospects identify people who are — or could be—valuable to your practice. Consequently, it would make sense to foster strong relationships with them, stronger than with the C clients. Many advisors add a "likeability factor" to the mix—I often hear "They're not A clients unless I like them."

This is an important distinction. The segmentation process can identify clients who meet any or all of the A-level standards, but there may be some you just don't like or care to work with. Perhaps these are individuals who came aboard as clients in leaner times or over time have proven themselves to be less than honorable. The question to ask is whether or not they should continue to be your clients. Their reputation can affect the overall integrity of your practice.

This decision to "fire" clients is never an easy one. It is a characteristic of the Late Mature and Prime practitioners that their clients have complementary values. If you find that you are being held hostage by the purchasing power of clients you don't want to work with, it's time for a values gut-check.

If the issues are personality clashes, fire the clients by transferring them to another advisor who is more their style. If the issues are deeper, like dishonesty or ethics, sever ties with the clients by working with your compliance officer and helping to transfer their assets to another organization.

The remaining clients in the A-level group should be the main focus of the advisor's time and energy.

The top tier are the AAA clients. These people can truly be called advocates for your practice. They believe in you by providing you with a significant income stream, they have access to additional assets to be brought under management, and they promote you to others. Chris, an advisor in Tulsa, Oklahoma, calls them "triple-play" clients.

"I have 17 of these AAA clients," he notes, "out of around 1,200 total." Chris has been an advisor for 15 years and by surviving, has accumulated a book of assigned orphans from advisors who didn't make it. "Out of the 1,200, I'd say there are 750 clients that are mine—that I prospected for. The rest have been assigned to me over time.

"My AA clients number around 30. Those are mostly good revenue producers who aren't good referral sources, but they have access to additional sources of funds. Around 8 of those AA's are good revenue clients who give referrals, but I pretty much have all the assets of theirs that I'm going to get.

"And the number of single-A people," Chris continues, "changes as top prospects come and go. Right now there are about 40 A's, which breaks down to 15 good revenue-producing clients who don't give referrals and who don't have access to any more assets, 15 centers of influence who are good referral sources but are not clients and probably won't be, and another 10 who are prospects that I'm pampering until they tell me to go away."

Chris manages the relationships with the 87 AAA, AA, and A clients.

Where do you see your relationships with A-level clients heading?

"Ultimately, I'd like to be their legacy advisor. This means I'm their go-to guy for estate planning issues, coordinating them with their other professionals, like an attorney and CPA. I'm looking to manage their assets into the next generation, whether it's a family or a business. One of the special events I'm holding this year is a family retreat where we bring all of a family's members together for a seminar on strategies for inheritance. Mom, dad, kids, executors, beneficiaries—anyone involved in their legacy planning. My client actually asked for something like this to clarify why he has things arranged the way he does—trusts, annuities, long-term care. We'll discuss health-care directives and living wills. That's the sort of relationship I would like to foster with all my A-level clients."

For all of them?

"Well, I'm sure there will be some who won't want that sort of soul-baring openness. Maybe more than I think. But I want to offer it to the extent that they're comfortable. You can see these family transition planning tools on our opportunities checklist [Figure 5.3]. When a client passes away, I want to be the person the survivors turn to for comfort and advice."

These 87 A-level clients represent about 12 percent of the 750 Chris considers truly his own. His marketing assistant, Beth, helps with the routine functions of the A-level group: recording the contacts, updating client

Figure 5.3

Opportunity Inventory (Date to Approach)

Client	Insurances							Annuity		Investments						Planning					Other Services				
Opportunity	Term/Convert	Variable/Add	Disability	LTC	Health	Liability	Auto/Home	Fixed	Variable	Stock/Bond	Mutual Fund	Mgd. Acct	IRAs	Estate	Will/Trust	Fee Financial	Elder Care	Retirement	Charitable	Education	Tax Prep	Mortgage	Legacy Book	Budgeting	Benefit Review
Richards				2009	2012													2012							
Coleman	2009								2010																
Franklin															2009					2011					
Harding	2010																						2009		

information, and setting up appointments and calls for Chris to execute. They have devised an A-level service protocol that is a good model in a Mature practice. It includes the following:

- ASAP turnaround if an A-level calls in (by Chris or Beth)
- A formal quarterly contact protocol including the following:
  - Birthday cards (hand-signed) and/or lunches and market updates
  - Newsletters twice a year with follow-up calls and market updates
  - Formal annual reviews at six months from birthday (the "review date")
  - Wedding anniversary cards or business anniversary cards as appropriate
  - Holiday cards (Thanksgiving) or religious holiday cards as appropriate and possibly donations to the clients' favorite charities as holiday gifts
  - Acknowledgments of any public recognitions for the clients, the clients' families, or the clients' businesses
  - Acknowledgments of key personal and professional events for the clients, the clients' families, or the clients' businesses (These acknowledgment points are derived from client notes and supplemented by proactive Internet searches, local online media, and visits to the clients' Web sites.)
  - Invitations to "intimate" events

Each A-level client has a unique annual contact cycle based on the birthday of the person or head of household. This is managed by Beth.

Beth, can you give a good example of this cycle of contact?

"Here's Mark Richards. He's an AAA client, married to Pat, with three children, Brittany, Megan, and Bret. So it's a household. His birthday starts the ball rolling each year. Mark's is on August 11. Chris likes to take him to lunch on his birthday. So I put a reminder in a week earlier, on August 4, to call Mark and set up the lunch. This gives me some wiggle room if he's going to be away and we can schedule the lunch before or after the 11th.

"Once the lunch is held, Chris transcribes any notes, and I put them into SmartOffice (a CRM from the vendor E-Z Data). At that point, I schedule the newsletter to go out on November 11. We get a monthly newsletter, *Market Trends*, from our broker/dealer. We order around 100 a month to be sent to all of our A-level and B-level clients, with extras for the office. So Mark will get the newsletter from November, the three-month point from his birthday. If he'd like, we'd send one monthly, but our experience has been that newsletters become too routine and they never get read.

"I then schedule a call for Chris to make to Mark on November 12. That call will follow up on the newsletter, with Chris pointing out some articles that Mark would find interesting. For example, last month's newsletter had an article on long-term care. Chris has been after Mark to take a look at long-term care for the past two years. So it gave us an opportunity to reinforce the message. We keep a record of all these opportunities on a spreadsheet [Figure 5.3].

"Chris also does an update of Mark's holdings and the market. Once I get the call notes into SmartOffice, I schedule the formal annual review for the six-month-from-birthday point, February 11. Again, I put a note in for February 4 to set up the meeting with Mark and Pat, his wife. I do a lot of prep work for this review, using an agenda and assembling reports from SmartOffice and other sources. The annual review is the lynchpin of the client service cycle. It's very structured, and Chris insists on its being face to face with A- and B-level clients.

"The annual review happens, and I get the meeting notes entered. I will then set the next quarterly contact for the May 11 newsletter and follow-up call by Chris. Then we're back at the birthday again."

What does that annual review agenda look like?

"Here's the page from our best practices operations manual that describes it." (See Figure 5.4.)

So SmartOffice's calendaring system is fully integrated with Mark's records?

"Yes, it is. Each time I get a transcription from Chris on his digital recorder, I add to-do items that go on the calendar page and carry over from day to day until I mark them 'done.' Or he'll find out something about one of the kids, and I'll add it to the notes section. It's all integrated."

How about the rest of the family's birthdays?

"I run a monthly report on our A- and B-level clients, sorting by spouse and dependent birthdays. So they come up on that list, and we'll send them a hand-signed card. Chris wants the option of including a personal note. He takes the cards home once a month and writes them out while watching a ball game."

Client Annual Review Template

Advisor Objectives

- ☐ Keep clients satisfied and keep their business on the books.

- ☐ Identify or initiate any "next sale" opportunities for the clients or any assets the clients control.

- ☐ Obtain quality prospects.

Time and place

Approximately 1 hour, preferably in the advisor's office.

Attendees

Client, advisor, and advisor's associate. *Optional:* Other household members or client representatives.

Before Meeting

- ☐ Review notes from last client meeting.

- ☐ Review client holdings and financial goals.

- ☐ Assemble documents for use in meeting. See Supporting Documents section below.

Meeting Checklist

- ☐ Greeting and chitchat designed to connect with the client and uncover life events among important people in the client's world. These are events that might happen or are planned, such as pregnancy, job change, graduation, or retirement, in order to identify prospects, sales opportunities, and/or personal touches that can be made.

- ☐ Uncover any important issues on the client's mind.

- ☐ Update demographic information and gather additional details for the database to be used for proactive client contact (hobbies, interests, college affiliation, e-mail, contact preferences). Use a standard data-gathering form for this purpose.

(continued)

Figure 5.4

(Continued)

☐ Overview of the global, national, and/or local financial environment from the advisor's viewpoint and client's viewpoint. Examine the client's holdings within this broader financial environment.

☐ Discuss any recommended changes to holdings.

☐ Explain the scope of advisory products and services, including anything new.

☐ Identify and plant the seeds for the next step to secure the client's financial future (next opportunity).

☐ Identify any assets the client controls that might be up for a competitive bid.

☐ Ask how the client feels about the level of service and if they want any adjustments.

☐ Ask the client for help with the advisor's marketing plan, including quality referral names.

☐ Verbally summarize the key outcomes of the meeting.

After Meeting

☐ Communicate and/or provide staff the following:

    ☐ Demographic and personal information updates and notes for database entry. This includes a reassessed client rating as a result of the review and scheduling possible personal touches, as in an anticipated graduation or pregnancy due date.

    ☐ New prospects and/or referrals for the marketing assistant to schedule appointments and preferences for when and how to stay in touch.

    ☐ Anticipated sales opportunities, so the marketing assistant can schedule client follow-up contact.

    ☐ Client service requests and adjustments to be processed.

(continued)

Figure 5.4

(Continued)

☐ A review of the key points of the meeting, which are then included in a summary letter and thank-you note to the client.

☐ Schedule for the next quarterly contact.

Supporting Documents

☐ Prospect or client form to gather additional demographics and communicate action items to staff.

☐ Client holdings and performance information from CRM and other sources.

☐ Applications or service forms for client signature.

There are A's who are not clients, such as the COIs and prospects Chris is cultivating.

"Right. They're in the cycle too. The COIs get pretty much the same treatment: the birthday lunch is also a name-gathering meeting, as is the six-month date. So Chris meets with the COIs twice a year. Sometimes it's a phone conversation. They're on the quarterly newsletter mailing. The prospects also are driven by the birth date, which Chris is very good at getting. They get the newsletter quarterly with a follow-up call from Chris and an offer to sit down and talk business. The idea is to give the COIs and the prospects the sense of what being a client feels like. And we get good feedback from them."

Your protocols for A-level clients mention wedding anniversary cards and business birthday cards.

"We collect this information and store it in SmartOffice. Again, I run a monthly report on these dates, and we will send a card to some, flowers to others, bring some pastries to an office or send some balloons. Chris is pretty sensitive to marital situations and will back off if he senses that it would not be a good idea to celebrate what may be falling apart. But he strongly supports the family unit and the institution of marriage, and this is a way of reinforcing that commitment."

How do holiday cards fit in?

"We've gone to the Thanksgiving Day card because it is celebrated by pretty much all Americans. If we know the religious orientation of an A-level client, we may send an appropriate card for Christmas or Hanukkah. Chris likes to send a contribution to an A-level client's favorite charity toward the end of the year."

The section in the A-level protocols mentions acknowledging public and personal events and achievements. How do you accomplish that?

"Oh, that's the fun part of our Client Management system. Every time Chris meets or talks to an A-level client, he dictates notes about the conversation. In those notes he talks about anything of interest that's happening with the family or business. Like weddings, births, grandkids coming to visit, graduations—all that kind of thing. I'll plug those dates into the calendar, and they'll be available for Chris to use on the quarterly calls or to check in between quarters. Like yesterday. Chris has a client who is a real estate agent and has a test coming up for certification to be a relocation specialist. The test is scheduled for next week on Tuesday. So I have a note on Tuesday's to-do list for Chris to see how the test went. He may have me send a card or flowers if she passes since she's in an AAA household.

"For the A- and B-level clients, I also Google them every six months, as well as run their names through the local media searches like the *Tulsa World*, the *Oklahoman*, and the *Tulsa Business Journal* online editions. This is especially effective with families who have kids in sports, and we can track their progress through the season and use that as a discussion topic with the parents or grandparents. The Google searches sometimes turn up professional publications where a client has published an article or posted to a blog site. You can turn up some neat information. I just ran a search on the Martin family, and I found out that their high schooler, Jason, placed first in a science fair. His project was to determine how hollowing out and 'corking' a baseball bat with various substances will improve the hitting distance of a baseball. Chris is a real baseball fan, and he called Jason to discuss his findings. Contacts like that are hard to beat for cementing client relationships."

What kind of intimate events have you held?

"Chris tries to schedule four a year, on average, appealing to different groups. We're big OU [Oklahoma University] Sooner fans, so Chris has a football tailgating trip to Norman every year for a different home game.

Once we had a Fiesta Bowl party over the holidays—that wild Boise State game, a true classic, even though we lost in overtime. There were about 50 clients and guests at the local BBQ restaurant with the big screen, snacks, and the first couple rounds on Chris.

"We've done wine tastings, jewelry nights, cookouts, guest speakers like an FBI agent discussing identity theft and fund managers who are on tour for a fund family. We collect a lot of intimate information about the A- and B-level clients in order to tailor events to them. Chris will be taking eight diehard baseball fans to Arlington, Texas, to see the Rangers play the Yankees in June, chartering a plane and taking them out to dinner before-hand and getting back that same night. We're always on the alert for inter-esting new ideas for client events."

Are the client events a source of new prospects?

"Yes. For the larger gatherings, we'll ask that our clients bring a friend. We have a very good ratio of converting these friends into clients. They become single A's at first, and we stay in contact. We figured out that these A prospects usually become clients within nine months."

Do you have an event planning guide?

"Yes, we do. It's part of our operations manual, and it's a 10-page start-to-finish piece. It's actually very similar to the seminar guide we use from our vendor, Emerald."

B-, C-, and D-Level Clients

Our conversation with Beth, marketing assistant to Chris, continues. We dis-cussed managing B-, C-, and D-level clients.

OK, so now I'm a B-level client. What does my service cycle look like?

"You are either a new client or a selected C-level client we are determining whether to promote to A level. We have about 80 of you. So we want to give you the benefit of the doubt and as much as possible, treat you as an A level for the time being. We give the client a two-year cycle before reclassifying them to A level or back to C level.

"Chris has a junior advisor, Amber, who, along with me, does the B-level work. You would get these:

- Same-day turnaround for call-in requests from Amber or me
- Thanksgiving Day card

- Birthday contact for you and your family members
- Newsletter twice a year with a follow-up call from Amber
- Formal annual review at six months from your birthday (If you choose not to have a face-to-face review two years in a row, you will go into the C-level group.)

"Amber dictates the meeting notes, and I'll enter them in SmartOffice, plus do some search engine work prior to your birthday or review date.

"We will also invite some B-level clients to the intimate events so we can get a better feel for their potential as A-level referral sources or controllers of assets."

So there are 87 A-level and 80 B-level clients. Out of 1,200, that leaves a lot of C-level clients.

"Yep, we use that pun a lot: our bills are paid by those above sea level. But really, Chris is aware that there is a power to the mass of C-level clients. We have an administrative assistant, Mira, who handles the C-level clients, with Amber as the lead advisor. I get involved with some of the marketing. C-level clients get these:

- For a call-in request, same-day or next-day turnaround response from Mira or sometimes Amber
- Thanksgiving Day card
- An annual review offer in writing, and if the offer is accepted, the review will be held in the office or over the phone with Amber
- Cross-selling offers a couple times a year

"I'll do the last one with SmartOffice's reporting capability. I can bring up lists of people who have one product, like life insurance, but not another, like disability or long-term care. I'll do maybe four of these mail campaigns a year, and if there are responses, Amber gets back to them. It's all passive, so it's not too time-consuming. If there are other young advisors in the office who need some activity, they can do follow-up calls to these C-level cross-selling mail recipients.

"Mira's been with us a year now, and she's getting better at taking C-level service calls and alerting Amber to any sales opportunities that might arise from those calls. For instance, if there's an address or beneficiary change, she's learning to probe the 'why' behind the transactional request. A bigger house could mean more family members or a raise, beneficiaries can change based on changes in family relationships, and so on. That's led to a few sales."

And, finally, what about those D-level clients?

"The D clients are those who are C-level but take up way too much of our time. Once they are identified by name and isolated in the database, it is communicated to them that Chris has officially retired from their accounts. The letter goes on the say that his younger advisor, Amber, will be taking over and will be charging an hourly rate to work with them over and above one annual review and a quarterly market update. Amber is able to charge fees, and so far two people have taken their business elsewhere, and two are now paying the fees."

Client Management System Best Practices Checklist

The Client Management System Best Practices Checklist is shown in Figure 5.5. There are 61 specific steps in this checklist. It's the blueprint for the second section of your best practices operations manual.

In composing the checklist, I have assumed that the advisor is with a broker/dealer in a detached location, with a full-time administrative assistant and a full-time marketing assistant. The advisor is in a Mature life cycle stage.

Each practice is unique, of course, and the checklist can be modified for each advisor.

The resources referred to in the checklist are suggestions based on various best practices observed in the field. Any resource in italics refers to a piece that was reviewed or illustrated earlier in this chapter.

To put this checklist in perspective, the roles of advisor would be that of Chris and Amber, the marketing assistant would be Beth, and the administrative assistant would be Mira.

Figure 5.5

Client Management System Best Practices Checklist

Client Management Activities	Advisor	Marketing Assistant	Administrative Assistant	Firm	Resources
Client Segmentation					
2.1 Define criteria with which to segment personal clients, business clients, COIs, and top prospects (A, B, or C level).	X	S			*Segmentation Basics*
2.2 Mark each client with the appropriate segmentation.		X			Recorded in CRM
2.3 Identify key business-to-business partners, community contacts, friends, relatives, and other nonclients who impact the practice and with whom you'd like to maintain a contact.	X				*Project Brain-Dump, Mapping Exercise*
2.4 Record contact information about these key nonclients, and enter them in the CRM. Assign them a segment (A, B, or C level).	X	X			CRM
Client Contact Protocols					
2.5 Define a program of regular contacts, both proactive and passive, for each segment identified above.	X	S			*Service Protocols*

Note: X denotes primary accountability person, and S denotes shared accountability person.

#	Task				
2.6	Define a process flow for each passive contact: newsletters, birthday cards and/or calls, holiday cards and/or gifts, market updates, annual reviews.		X	S	Logistical checklists and materials
2.7	Schedule passive contacts based on this defined program.		X	S	CRM, calendar
2.8	Execute and record passive contacts.		X	S	CRM, calendar
2.9	Define a process flow for each proactive contact: annual reviews, appreciation meals, outreach calls, events, outings.	X	S		*Service Protocols*
2.10	Schedule proactive contacts based on the process flow for each contact.		X		*Service Protocols*
2.11	Execute proactive contacts.		X	S	
Client Reviews					
2.12	Draft a standard annual review agenda for A and B clients.	X	S		*Client Review* (Figure 5.3)
2.13	Draft variations of annual review agenda for C clients (used over the phone).	X	S		*Client Review* (Figure 5.3)
2.14	Outline standard materials and information to assemble for a review. Identify where and how each can be obtained: • Position statements • Performance information	S	X		

(continued)

Figure 5.5

(Continued)

Client Management Activities	Advisor	Marketing Assistant	Administrative Assistant	Firm	Resources
• Insurance status • Client information to be updated • Anticipated service or sales paperwork • Educational materials • Names to be fed for referrals					
2.15 Call to set review time and place (A and B clients).		X			
2.16 Confirm review time and place (A and B).		X			
2.17 Send C clients annual review reminder letter.		X	S		
2.18 Schedule appointments (phone or in office) with C clients who respond.		X			
2.19 Prepare and assemble review materials from 2.14.		X	S		
2.20 Establish a method to record and transcribe the annual review results and notes for CRM input.	X	X			CRM *update info form*
2.21 Conduct A and B client reviews.	X				CRM *update info form;* voice recording

No.	Task				Reference
2.22	Conduct C client reviews.		X		
2.23	Postreview: Input new and/or updated information into the CRM.		X		
2.24	Postreview: Send service, new business, and other requests to proper channels.		X	S	
Client Information					
2.25	Define hard data to be recorded in the CRM.	X	S		*Figure 5.1*
2.26	Define soft data to be recorded in the CRM.	X	S		*Figure 5.2*
2.27	Ensure that all hard and soft data can be sorted and retrieved for service and cross-selling campaigns.	S	X		
2.28	Be able to recover this information for client appreciation and intimate events.		X		CRM reporting capability
2.29	Make sure client account information is easily accessed by whole team.	S	X	S	Paper files and CRM records
Client Events					
2.30	Determine which client seminars or events will be held and if any will be an event for prospecting (clients bring a guest).	X		S	Approved vendors
2.31	Calendar: Set up an annual client event schedule.	X	S		CRM database, calendar

(continued)

Figure 5.5

(Continued)

	Client Management Activities	Advisor	Marketing Assistant	Administrative Assistant	Firm	Resources
2.32	Find a sponsor: wholesaler, fund rep, home office department.	X			S	
2.33	Create a budget.	X	S			
2.34	Create a timeline checklist for pre-event base, preparation: • Invitation selection and mailing • RSVP tracking and confirmation • Phone call follow-up for nonresponders • Food and beverage catering • Location, room rental, room setup and clean-up • Directions and parking • Speakers and presenters booked and prepped • Audio-visual equipment • Promotional materials, ads • Handouts, workbooks, feedback forms • Door prizes • Photographer	S	X			CRM data-calendar Follow suggested vendor steps (e.g., Emerald Publications) if available
2.35	Conduct the event: • Arrival procedure, check-in table • Agenda provided	X	S		S	Follow suggested vendor steps

	• Mingling, informal time, eat and drink • Presentation • Q&As • Postevent feedback forms completed and collected				(e.g., Emerald Publications) if available
2.36	Postevent: • Send thank-you notes, with photos, from approved material. • Send "sorry we missed you" notes. • Post additional information about clients and guests gathered at the seminar.		X		CRM database, calendar
2.37	Schedule follow-up phone calls to any prospects generated by the event.		X		CRM database, calendar
2.38	Make the follow-up calls.	X	S		Script
2.39	With warm responders, set initial appointment (go to Sales Process).	X	S		CRM database, calendar
2.40	Determine what to do with nonresponders: keep in database or eliminate.	X	S		CRM database
2.41	Track the success of the seminar; calculate ratios for the following: • Invites to accepted invites • Accepted invites to attendees • Attendees to prospects (if event is for this purpose)		X		CRM database analysis

(continued)

Figure 5.5

(Continued)

Client Management Activities	Advisor	Marketing Assistant	Administrative Assistant	Firm	Resources
• Prospects to actual appointments • Appointments to sales					
2.42 Add results to cumulative event experience.		X			CRM database
Client Service Requests					
2.43 Handle routine service requests.			X		Forms, processes, requirements and contacts for routine requests
2.44 Handle complex service requests.	S	S	X		"
2.45 Service: When client calls in with request, who takes the call for each segment?	X (A)	X (A/B)	X (C)		
2.46 Service: Processing insurance requests and changes.			X		
2.47 Service: Processing investment requests and changes.			X		
2.48 Service: Copies made as required for client files: insurances.			X		

2.49	Service: Copies made as required for client files: investments.	X			
2.50	Service: Tracking of progress on an insurance request.	S	X		
2.51	Service: Tracking of progress on an investment request.	S	X		
2.52	Service: Push notes to advisor as needed while action is taking place on a request.	S	X	S	
Promotion					
2.53	Reinforce that your best clients know how to promote you and what caliber of prospect you are looking for.			X	*Line Presentation*
Client Opportunity Management					
2.54	Track and monitor client "next step" opportunities.		S	X	*Opportunity Inventory (Figure 5.3)*
2.55	Prepare materials to support these opportunities.		X	S	
Client File Compliance					
2.56	Ensure that client files meet compliance standards and will stand up to an audit.	S	X	S	

(continued)

Figure 5.5

(Continued)

Client Management Activities	Advisor	Marketing Assistant	Administrative Assistant	Firm	Resources
Client Management Statistics					
2.57 Determine the average value of a referral-turned-client.	S	X			CRM records
2.58 Determine the percentage of referrals who become clients.	S	X			=
2.59 Calculate top referral sources in database.	S	X			=
2.60 Determine revenue these top sources have brought to the practice.	X	S			=
2.61 Determine the client retention rate.	X	S			=

6

Core Business System 3: Sales Process

The intent of the Sales Process business system is to quantify the steps that lead an advisor to successfully acquire new business or attract assets from either a prospect or an existing client. This is the sequence of events that culminates in the advisor's Inspiring People to Action genius. The best practices outline that follows is designed to take a new prospect from first contact through the placement of a product, agreement to do a financial plan, or initiation of a fund transfer.

With an existing client, the Sales Process may be abbreviated since the relationship is already established and the advisor can "get down to business" more quickly. That said, a warning must be issued about shortcutting the Sales Process. A strong Sales Process is what builds a solid client base in the first place. These clients will assume that any referral they give to the advisor will receive the same thoroughness that they experienced. Providing a diminished Sales Process to a referral just might end up affecting the client relationship.

Let's create a scale from 1 to 5, with 1 being a completely transactional sale, like searching for a term life insurance quote on the Internet, and 5 being a completely relational sale where the prospect is buying the advisor as much as she is buying the plan, product, or service.

Transaction	1	2	3	4	5	Relationship

In our best practices world, the best sale is one in which a strong relationship is created and fostered. If the product or service is fairly valued in terms of price, fees, charges, and historic performance, the advisor/ prospect relationship seals the deal; that's a 5 on the scale.

Many people prefer to do transactions based solely on price, fees, charges, and their own research. They aren't looking for a relationship, just the "best deal." That's a 1 on the scale.

There is plenty of material for transactional salespeople to study. But for our purposes in this book, we are unabashedly building the best practices of a relationship-based practice, not a transactional one.

Consequently, the warning is that shortcutting the breadth and depth of the Sales Process will tend to cheapen it in the long run. And the more transactional the advisor's client base, the more vulnerable it is. A consistent, methodical approach to guiding the prospect to the point of *inspiration to action* is our goal.

In the marketplace today, there are many fine sales systems. Bill Bachrach's Values Based Selling, Al Granum's One Card System, the Circle of Wealth, and the LEAP System are four that are very effective when properly implemented.

The best practices that follow are independent of these proprietary systems. However, they are consistent in terms of process and structure.

To help take us through these steps, we interviewed three advisors who have distinctly different practices. Jerry is an advisor with a large financial services company with a historic life insurance orientation. He survived the compliance-driven implosions of the 1990s and is in his nineteenth year. His practice is located in an office building near his local agency in Providence, Rhode Island. Jerry is a perennial Chairman's Club member and has two full-time assistants. He has had a successor advisor working with him for the past two years. His life cycle stage is Late Mature.

Profile 1: Jerry

Practice focus: Insurance-centered practice, mostly commission based, beginning to bulk up on assets under management

Personnel:
    Dale: Junior advisor, possible successor
    Millie: Marketing assistant and paraplanner
    Crystal: Administrative assistant

Lynda is a Certified Financial Planner (CFP) who prefers fee-based clients but is open to all qualified prospects. She's starting her seventh year and works out of Des Moines, Iowa. Lynda qualifies for the midlevel conferences with her broker/dealer and local firm. She's just brought on a full-time assistant to do a mix of marketing and administrative work. Her life cycle stage is Early Mature.

Profile 2: Lynda

Practice focus: Fee-based planning, transitioning from commission orientation

Personnel:
   Corinna: Hybrid assistant (both marketing and administrative)

Sal defines himself as wealth manager, and he has made a good living attracting, managing, and retaining assets. He's part of an independent broker/dealer group that outsources most of the product selling to a subsidiary LLC that he co-owns. Sal and his firm have $230 million under management after 11 years together. His life cycle stage is Mature.

Profile 3: Sal

Practice focus: Investments and assets under management

Personnel:
   Jenna: Hybrid assistant

Each of these advisors has a different take on the best-practice steps in the Sales Process:

- Initial contact
- Appointment confirmation
- Initial interview
- Discovery interview
- Discovery letter
- Presentation and close
- Delivery

Initial Contact

You have a brand-new prospect obtained as a referral or from another warm source. What does your initial contact look like?

Jerry: "If it's a referral from one of my centers of influence or from a top-tier client, I pick up the phone and call the prospect because he is expecting me to call. The COI or the client told him I would. I've got the COIs trained that way, you see. If it's a prospect from another source, I hand it off to Dale [junior advisor] to call. He has a script we put together that simply attempts to set the appointment to let the prospect see what we're all about. Dale's gotten pretty good at it."

Lynda: "First I send a letter with my brochure that gives an overview of what I do. When I can, I use the name of the referral source in the letter. In the letter, I say I'll be in touch to see about getting together for an introductory meeting. I wait a couple of days and make the follow-up call. I read somewhere that I should have my assistant make that initial call, but I can't let go of that. First impressions and all—it's me prospects need to talk to. After Corinna is with me a few years, I may change my mind, but not yet."

Sal: "We as a firm have only around 100 clients, so we're pretty picky about new prospects. They need to have at least $1 million in investable assets, and as a firm, we're only looking for 10 new investors a year. So when a person is recommended to us, I have a three-way call with the recommender and the prospect to set up a visit to the office and then lunch for the three of us."

Appointment Confirmation

Do you confirm the appointment and send the prospect anything in advance?

Jerry: "Once the appointment is set by either Dale or me, Millie [marketing assistant] sends an 'intro packet' that includes short bios of all four of us— Dale, Millie, Crystal [administrative assistant], and me. It also has a one-page checklist of various investment and insurance concepts—not products—that the prospect can use to indicate areas of interest. I've used that list for years, and it's a good piece to get us focused quickly. We also ask the prospect to complete a one-page 'vital statistics' questionnaire, with family information—you know, like the doctor's office has you do. There's also a map and directions to our office. The day before the appointment, Millie calls to confirm the time."

Lynda: "We have already sent a brochure, so all I have Corinna do is call and confirm and get or give directions if necessary. I'm still holding 40 percent of my appointments out of the office, so it's important to confirm especially if I'm the one doing the driving."

Sal: "I will confirm the appointment myself with both parties, often by e-mail. Our staff—Jenna in particular as my primary associate—has made the lunch arrangements and prepared the materials for the office visit. We're very much in a selling mode at this point—the prospect has the assets, and we're positioning ourselves as an investment option for her."

Having a Sales Process

The Sales Process, like the advisors who follow it, is full of nuances and idiosyncrasies. This is the "art" of the "art and science" industry legend Al Granum speaks of in his One Card System. Each advisor is an artist in that he carefully crafts a scenario in which the prospect will buy. Logic alone as a sales tool pulls the experience toward the transactional end of the scale. Inspiration alone as a sales tool, without structure, goes too far into the relationship end of the scale, resulting in a client who buys something because of the advisor's charisma.

This charismatic sale is solid only as long as the advisor is around to reassure the client. Without a structured Sales Process, the client will not really know what was purchased or why ... only that the advisor told him to. From a practice transition viewpoint, this will lead to client attrition after the sale or disposition of the practice. From a compliance standpoint, the charismatic sale is dangerous.

The insurance industry learned this the hard way in the late 1980s and early 1990s. Permanent life insurance products (whole life) were underperforming the stock market, and policyholders began to take a closer look at what they had purchased. Allegations flew:

- "I thought I bought a retirement plan, but it's just life insurance with cash value!"
- "I bought this to fund my kid's college education, but its value is not even close to this illustration I was given!"
- "I was told that the cash value is income tax free! I cashed it in and found out differently!"

Class action lawsuits against the deceptive sales practices of insurers and mutual fund (MF) companies ended up forcing the Securities and

Exchange Commission (SEC) and the National Association of Securities Dealers (NASD) to tighten the regulations concerning the sales of variable (market-based) products.*

"Tighten" is putting it mildly. Subsequent major compliance initiatives wracked the insurers, big and small, causing a huge hit to their credibility both from the consumer point of view and within their own agent and advisor ranks. Documentation of seemingly every detail in the Sales Process became the painful norm. Being mostly unsubstantiated, the days of charismatic selling were numbered as huge awards were paid out to clients for being misled by agents and advisors, whether real or perceived.

The investment industry hears from frightened customers every time the market drops 3 percent of its value:

- "Why did you put me in such risky stocks?"
- "You didn't tell me that mutual fund had such high volatility!"
- "Some of my money market money was in derivatives?"

Without a documented, systematic Sales Process, it's the advisor's word against the client's word, and guess who usually wins in a legal battle? With a clear, documented, systematic Sales Process, the ethical, honest advisor will prevail.

This documentation is even more critical as the turbulence of the entire economic system plays out.

The following steps in the Sales Process each have a set of best-practice results to achieve. Our three advisors agreed to a roundtable discussion about their approaches to each step. As you would expect with artists discussing their genius for inspiring a client to action, all three had distinct opinions and methods for getting at the core competencies.

Initial Interview

We discussed the initial contact with the prospect and the subsequent appointment confirmation. Let's look at the best practices in each part of the Sales Process, starting with the first time you meet a prospect—the initial interview. Here are the five ideal outcomes for this meeting:

1. You have had a true dialogue in which you have drawn out the prospect's wants and needs.

---

* In 2007, the NASD merged with the New York Stock Exchange's regulation committee to form the Financial Industry Regulatory Authority, (FINRA).

2. The prospect has explored with you what you do and why.
3. Together you have set expectations for the relationship.
4. You and the prospect have discussed compensation.
5. You and the prospect have segued into fact-finding.

How does your initial interview go?

Jerry: "Our initial interview can go either of two ways. We give all of our prospects a brief overview of our philosophy, and then we get right to the vital statistics and checklist of concepts that they have hopefully completed. We ask a lot of open-ended questions, and they tell us what they're looking for, so, yes, it's a dialogue. If it's not so much a relationship that they are looking for but more of a product or investment, we will segue right then and there to fact-finding; what you call the 'discovery interview.' If they are looking for a more comprehensive analysis, we discuss whether they want us primarily as a money manager or a full financial advisor."

Lynda: "Interesting. So you are flexible as to what the client needs. Are these initial meetings mostly with referrals?"

Jerry: "Most are. We do some seminars too."

Do you have a minimum standard for a referral?

Jerry: "That's something we need to work on. Really, no. Dale can't afford to be very picky at this point. He's still building his own networks and is learning his craft. You do that by seeing all sorts of people. As for me, my standards are whomever my referral sources send me. Usually, they are good quality, but I need to get better at educating my sources on some minimum standards."

Tell us a little more about the "brief overview" of your philosophy step.

Jerry: "It's a visual piece, a pyramid, with the Maslow's hierarchy of needs lined up with one's financial needs. It's very powerful, and we have fun with it. Once the person reaches over and touches the pyramid, we know she is engaged."

Sal: "Geez. How many of these initial interviews do you have in a week? We have maybe one."

Jerry: "Between Dale and me, it's easily four or five a week."

How many weeks a year does that entail?

Jerry: "With conferences, vacations, and study time, we calculated it to be 40 productive weeks where both of us are in the office."

Lynda: "When do you discuss compensation?"

Jerry: "Right at that segue point I was talking about. If it's a product or invest-ment, Dale will handle that, and we simply let the prospects know that this work will be on a commission basis and that we have chosen our products and carriers carefully for a fair blend of integrity and internal charges. If it's the money management direction we're going, we disclose that there will be an asset-based fee. If it's the financial plan, we review the three levels of planning and those prices."

So you get the agreement to go the money management route or the planning route. What's the next step for those two avenues?

Jerry: "If it's assets, we set the next appointment and have them bring all of their statements and other documents. We give them a detailed checklist of these to work from. We have the planning people sign the plan agreement and disclosure form (ADV) and collect the fee. Then we set a next appoint-ment, and again, we send them home with a checklist of what to bring to the fact-finder meeting."

Lynda: "One more question: when you first see the person, you have sent him a vital statistics page and a checklist of concepts. What if he doesn't fill those out or only partly fills them out?"

Jerry: "Immediate demerits! It's not a good sign, but we roll with it. Not surpris-ingly, the majority of those who do a half-assed job with the initial homework end up being product or investment people, not relationship people."

Let's turn to you, Lynda. How does your initial interview flow?

Lynda's Initial Interview

Lynda: "It opens with small talk and rapport building, and then I use the cover page of the fact finder that I work from to get the prospect's basic facts and figures. I'd like for the prospect to do more of that basic stuff up front, which is why I'm interested in seeing how Jerry's faring with it."

Jerry: "It saves time—in reviewing information that's already written down, we can go deeper faster."

Can you give an example?

Jerry: "Sure. Names are always nice to have already spelled for you. We got tired of asking how to spell 'Laurie' in its seemingly infinite forms. Now we can just say, 'Tell us about Lori.'"

Lynda: "Good point. Try spelling 'Brittany' sometime! After I get the information, I give a presentation on the process of developing a financial plan and lay out the fee structure. After that, we engage in a dialogue to determine what level of planning would be most appropriate. Sometimes it's not planning they're after but a product or investment. I just don't have enough of a client base yet to go for all fee-based planning clients."

Sal: "Is it a self-confidence issue, Lynda?"

Lynda: "... mmm. Somewhat. My centers of influence and other referral sources send me all sorts of people. My next step is to begin educating them as to the quality of prospect I'd like, which is the planning client, not the product client."

Jerry: "Yep, just like I need to do."

That's a critical step in your Client Acquisition system, the setting of some standards and educating your top clients and centers of influence about them.

Lynda: "I have a game plan for that outlined but not implemented. So after I see if they could be planning clients or not, we end the interview by scheduling the next one to do the fact-finding."

Jerry: "If they are, you don't get the check until next time?"

Lynda: "Correct. I quote them a fee, and I collect it at the beginning of the next appointment."

Jerry: "And how many stiff you?"

Lynda: "Early on, around 20 percent, but now it's not an issue. I just feel strongly that there should be some time and distance for the prospect before jumping into the process. That's why I always include an expectations talk in the initial interview."

Can you share that with us?

Lynda: "Certainly. It's a simple discussion, not requiring any documentation. It goes like this:

> *I appreciate your putting your confidence in my ability to handle your financial [investment, insurance] matters.*
> *My role is to listen to you carefully, obtain all the relevant materials from you, create a plan or solution that meets your needs and circumstances, and present that plan or solution to you.*

Do you have any additional expectations of me?
My expectation of you is that you have an honest dialogue
with me and permit me to access all the resources necessary for me
to do a thorough analysis of your situation. Is that fair?

"And then I quote the fee—if there is one—and set up the next appointment giving them a laundry list of documents they need to bring with them."

Sal, it sounds as if your first interview is somewhat different.

Sal: "It is, but you know, we manage to get all five of those outcomes you laid out. The prospect and the referrer come up to the office. We're in the Bay area and have four different locations, two on the East Bay and two on the San Francisco side. There's a tour of the physical office, meeting all the people who work in that particular location. Then we have a PowerPoint presentation of our asset base, allocations, styles, philosophy, risk management, fees, charges, and information about all of our affiliated companies.

"At that time, it's mostly us presenting to the prospect, but once the dog and pony show is over, her best interests come to the fore."

Lynda: "What does your referral source do during this time?"

Sal: "He is part of the show and tell, since he has been benefiting from our services. He tells his story about what we've done, the ups and downs and his overall experience. It's very powerful."

And then there's lunch?

Sal: "Yes. If the prospect has a favorite type of cuisine, we'll find a high-end eatery for that. If not, we have some nice restaurants near each location that have flexible menus."

Lynda: "What's the objective of the lunch?"

Sal: "It's an opportunity to give the prospect time to open up and feel comfortable with us. The conversation runs in many directions, but we end up with a pretty clear set of her priorities and goals. I take notes during the conversation and then dictate a more complete report afterward."

Lynda: "What sort of things do you dictate?"

Sal: "As I said, priorities and goals, plus family information, business relationships, hobbies and interests, favorite sports teams, and other information we can perhaps use down the road. The dictation goes to Jenna and into our Client Management system."

Discovery Interview

The next segment of the Sales Process is the fact finder, which includes questions about the prospect's feelings. As a best-practice piece, we call this the *discovery interview*. Like the initial interview, this also has five general outcomes to keep in mind:

1. The fact-finding tool that your practice uses consistently has been completed. This tool contains triggers to ensure that you ask the feeling questions.
2. You have gathered all necessary information to run illustrations, planning software, asset allocation models, and other Case Development resources.
3. It has been a dialogue although the prospect has done most of the talking.
4. The information you have gathered has allowed you to anticipate underwriting and/or issue complications.
5. The meeting has generated a good number of names to feed the prospect later for possible referrals.

The consistent use of the same thorough fact-finding tool is a best-practice necessity. Completing a fact and feeling finder, because it is a form that the advisor uses consistently with all clients, is a documentation of the advisor's interactions with them, and it ensures that all pertinent financial topics have been addressed.

Case in Point

Keith, an advisor with a large financial services company, holds himself out as a financial advisor. He does not have any designations such as the CFP, but he claims to do a "thorough analysis of a client's financial situation." His fact-finding tool is a yellow pad on which he records the answers to questions he's asked hundreds of times before—so often that he's jettisoned the company fact-finding booklet after convincing himself that it was "intimidating" to a prospect.

With one couple that he met as prospective clients, Keith took his fact-finding notes on his yellow pad, as he had always done, and afterward he went back to his office and ran his analysis. The prospects became clients after they purchased a variable life policy on Rod, a term policy on Rita, and two Roth IRAs.

A year and a half later, Rod, the primary breadwinner, suffered a permanently disabling head injury in a bicycle accident. His employer provided no disability coverage. Rob and Rita turned to Keith asking about that "disability coverage you sold us."

What Keith had sold them was a waiver-of-premium provision on the life insurance policies, which would pay the premium in the event that a policyholder was disabled. With cash flow getting tighter and tighter, Rod and Rita grew more desperate and they hired a lawyer to sue Keith.

In litigation, the claim was that Keith's examination of their financial situation did not address the possibility of loss of income due to disability, which was an "obvious gap" in their coverage. Keith's claim that he had suggested disability coverage was not upheld because there was no evidence that he had even asked about it. Nothing on the yellow-pad notes that were in the client file mentioned disability.

Rod and Rita were given an undisclosed sum as a settlement from Keith's company before going to trial. Fortunately, Keith's errors and omissions (E&O) coverage was paid up. He has since reverted to using the "intimidating booklet" during the fact-finding process with all new prospects, and he is updating his yellow-pad client files so that they are more complete documents when he meets with clients for their annual reviews.

Keith's experience leads to the question "What information should be part of a consistent, thorough fact finder?"

Figure 6.1 shows a best-practice sample of a discovery fact and feeling finder.

Sal's Discovery Interview

Sal: "Being more interested in the really high net worth clients, we have decided to focus primarily on where the assets are. I must admit that I use a legal pad for my initial fact finding. Sometimes, this happens during the lunch meeting. If it does, the information is part of the dictation for Jenna. But most of the information we gather comes from the prospects' accountants, lawyers, or benefits managers. It gets accumulated in a file for review and entry into the various programs."

Lynda: "Sounds impersonal to me. Where do you address all the other areas that are mentioned in the best-practice outline?" (Figure 6.1)

Figure 6.1

Fact and Feeling Finder

Immediate Concerns and Priorities

What brought the prospect to the advisor?

- ☐ Personal: Occupation, family, business associates
- ☐ Accumulation goals: Retirement, kids' education, big purchases
- ☐ Cash flow, budget, debt: How are these being managed?
- ☐ Life insurance, survivor needs, estate planning considerations
- ☐ Health, disability, long-term-care needs
- ☐ Liability, P&C needs

Financial Statements

Next, assemble financial statements and collect the facts in the following three areas:

1. Assets/liabilities:
   - ☐ Social Security
   - ☐ Nonqualified: Stocks, bonds, mutual funds, CDs, savings, annuities, managed accounts
   - ☐ Qualified: IRAs, SEPs, Roths
   - ☐ Health savings accounts (HSAs)
   - ☐ Employer programs: 401(k), 403(b), pensions, executive benefits
   - ☐ Cash value of permanent life insurance
   - ☐ Real estate, properties, time shares including any attendant mortgages
   - ☐ Personal use assets: Boats, collectibles
   - ☐ Consumer debt

2. Insurance:
   - ☐ Life insurance
   - ☐ Health
   - ☐ Disability

(continued)

Figure 6.1

(Continued)

- ☐ LTC
- ☐ Home
- ☐ Auto
- ☐ Liability

3. Relationships:

Who are the key people in the client's financial network?

- ☐ Family members involved in the client's financial decisions
- ☐ Attorney
- ☐ Accountant
- ☐ Executor
- ☐ Trustee
- ☐ Power of attorney
- ☐ Health care directive person
- ☐ Beneficiaries
- ☐ P&C agent
- ☐ Business relationships

Other Information

In addition to the facts, the discovery fact finder should record and reference the following:

- ☐ Current financial products and investments and why they were purchased
- ☐ Employer benefits
- ☐ Association benefits
- ☐ Government programs

The discovery fact finder should also uncover the prospect's sensitivity to the following:

- ☐ Taxes
- ☐ Inflation

(continued)

Figure 6.1

(Continued)

☐ Risk

☐ Liquidity

☐ Health issues

☐ Relationship issues

Other discovery considerations that represent the environmental aspects of the discovery appointment include the following:

☐ Time allotted for the appointment: How flexible is it? Did you schedule an hour, 90 minutes, 30 minutes? What can realistically be accomplished in that time?

☐ Where the interview is held: Your office, their home, their office? Is it conducive to real dialogue?

☐ The interruption factor: Are you a priority to the clients? Are the clients a priority to you? Will both of you put your cell phones on "silent"?

Sal: "If the prospects bring it up. Otherwise, we'll work to get their assets under management and then open them up to our subsidiaries. I'm not like that Keith guy—I hold myself out as a wealth manager, nothing more. That being said, let me look at how I do on the five best-practice outcomes of this discovery meeting. Use the same fact-finding tool consistently? No. Do I gather the necessary information to run the analysis? Yes. Is it a dialogue? Certainly. Do I anticipate underwriting or issue difficulties? Not necessarily underwriting, but issue, yes—bringing assets over can be tricky and time-consuming. Gather names? Not really. We get a lot of names, but they don't get posted anywhere. I can see that being an area to work on."

Sal, what about other discovery considerations such as length of time, place, and interruptions?

Sal: "Once the lunch meeting is over, we may or may not meet again. Usually it's handled over the phone, coordinating the transfer of information. If we do meet, I may go see them at their place of business or home, just to get a feel for their environment. The length of these face-to-face meetings varies. Some prospects want additional background on us; others just like to be hands-on talking about their money. I always make it a point to have the cell phone on vibrate only. I prefer the prospects to do the same, but half the time they don't."

Jerry's Discovery Interview

Jerry: "We have two fact finders, one for the product sale and a much more extensive one for the planning clients. For the product sale, Dale takes over and gets the information needed for the specific client need. The fact finder is in modules by product line: life, retirement, education, disability, long-term care, health, and such. We ask the prospects if they would like to have an analysis of each module. If they don't, we draw a line through it. We have the prospects initial the fact finder after it's done, so it's recorded what they did and did not want to discuss.

"Planning clients come in for a two-hour session. I start the meeting, review all the materials they brought, and get the major concerns and priorities on the whiteboard. Then I introduce Millie, our marketing assistant and paraplanner. Millie then takes them through the data collection using a more in-depth fact finder."

Lynda: "You don't personally do that?"

Jerry: "Nope. Millie's been working with me for seven years now, and she is very good at not only gathering the information but getting prospects to disclose all those important nonfinancial details as well, like the names of friends, relatives, coworkers, and the like. She also can sniff out a potential underwriting problem."

Sal: "How much time do you personally spend on this appointment?"

Jerry: "The first 20 minutes to a half hour. Then I stop back at the end to ensure that all went well and to send them off. Millie does the rest."

Where does all the information collected by Millie end up?

Jerry: "Millie uses the paper fact finder to update the clients' information in the Client Management system and also to enter the data into the planning software to produce the overall analysis. After that, it's permanently in the clients' physical file."

Lynda's Discovery Interview

Lynda: "Looks like I'm the most traditional of the three of us. My discovery interview is mostly held in my office, and it takes a couple of hours for a planning client. For the nonplanning clients, maybe an hour or less depending on the complexity. I have one fact finder that I use for everyone. I'm happy to say it covers all of the areas you outlined. I hold all calls and put the BlackBerry away. The clients are good about not taking calls. My conference room is very comfortable without a lot of distractions."

How are you at the gathering of names during this interview?

Lynda: "I'm like Sal in that respect. I do uncover a lot of names, but I haven't been very good at recording them and getting them into the contact management system. I recently empowered Corinna to keep me accountable for that after every discovery interview. She'll nag me."

The time between gathering the facts and feelings during the discovery interview and presenting the solution or the financial plan to the prospect is the *Case Development period*. Case Development is the fourth business system in the advisor's practice, and it is the topic of our next chapter.

During the Sales Process, however, this period of time provides a window of unparalleled opportunity for cementing the relationship and positioning a successful presentation. This interim step is the discovery letter.

Discovery Letter

The *discovery letter* is a document that summarizes where things stand. It's designed to arrive midway between the discovery interview and the presentation meeting. The timing is deliberate, to keep you top of mind with the prospect. Often, if there is no communication between discovery and presentation, the advisor drops off the prospect's radar screen. When this happens, the advisor needs to spend a good deal of time reconstructing the reasons for what he will be presenting and recommending.

The discovery letter provides a heads-up that you're working on the prospect's behalf and will be seeing him soon.

The elements of a best-practice discovery letter are these:

1. "I appreciate your time."
2. "Here's what I heard you say."
3. "These are your priorities as I recorded them."
4. "I'm working to use your available resources to address those priorities."
5. "If any of this is incorrect, please call."
6. "Here's when we'll be meeting again."

Figure 6.2 illustrates what a discovery letter looks like.

Figure 6.2

Sample Discovery Letter

Dear Prospect/Client,

We at [practice name] would like to take this opportunity to thank you for engaging us for your financial planning needs. We would like to assure you that we will continue to make every effort to fulfill your needs and exceed your expectations. It is our desire to provide you with a tailored experience that will leave you confident that you have made a wise decision to work with [insert practice name].

During our meeting last [day, date], we covered a substantial amount of information. While it may have seemed overwhelming at times, we believe it is crucial to take the time to gain a full and complete understanding of your needs, wants, and desires. To this end, below I have itemized your most important goals as I understand them:

1. Assure a comfortable retirement for Mary and Bill.

2. Minimize taxation during retirement.

3. Minimize expenses and taxes during the transfer of your assets to your heirs, Sarah, Emily, and Bill Jr.

4. Create a family foundation to support St. John's University, the American Red Cross, and the Center for the Arts.

If you have any additional concerns, or if you have reconsidered your priorities after further discussion and thought, please feel free to contact me. As we discussed, we will prepare a preliminary plan for your review at our meeting next [insert day] at [insert time], using the resources we identified.

Again, thank you for choosing [insert practice name].

Sincerely,

There are many reasons why the discovery letter is a best practice:

- It keeps the prospect involved while the case is being prepared.
- It's a professional touch.
- It gives the client a respectful opportunity to change her mind.

- It's a great piece to have in the file for compliance purposes.
- It can provide the agenda for the presentation meeting by addressing those priorities in sequence.
- It can be used to get a third party up to speed quickly. This third party is someone who didn't attend any of the other meetings but shows up at the presentation.

Here's what the roundtable advisors had to say about the discovery letter step:

Do any of you have something like a discovery letter to make contact with prospects between the discovery interview and the presentation?

Lynda: "For my planning clients I have a 'welcome aboard' letter with a refrigerator magnet that includes my office contact information. The magnet has been very effective as a constant reminder that I'm available. The letter I can probably do more with."

But nothing for the nonplanning clients?

Lynda: "No. We do call to confirm the presentation appointment, but that's about it."

Jerry: "Actually, we have a letter. It recaps the needs and priorities of the prospects and lays out the golden rule: 'In working with my clients, I shall, in light of all circumstances, recommend that course of action or provide that service which, had I been in the same situation, I would have applied to myself.'"

Lynda: "I like that. Isn't that the CFP pledge?"

Jerry: "I believe so. Millie slips the different priorities into the letter template and schedules a time for the letter to go out to arrive about a week prior to the presentation appointment."

Sal: "We don't have a letter like this. I think it's because we have multiple contacts with the clients and their representatives so one more communication would seem to be overkill. However, we do have an engagement letter once they decide we're the ones to manage their money."

How about if you send them to your subsidiaries? Do you have a discovery letter in place for those types of sales?

Sal: "We don't, as far as I know. But I can see the value of it, and I will be bringing it up at our next team meeting."

Presentation and Close

The advisor's genius in inspiring a person to take action culminates in the meeting where that action takes place. In traditional sales language, this is a *close* where the deal is secured, the check received, and the signature placed on the dotted line. This is the magical moment when the client solves a problem and the advisor creates a solution. It is also the magic moment when the client gets a degree of financial security and the advisor creates income.

The flow of the Sales Process system has led the prospect to this meeting. The relationship the advisor has been building with the prospect up to this point is the determining factor in whether or not they will agree to take action. This process of Relationship Building is the "inspiration" to take action.

Some call this ask-to-buy a "moment of insanity." Most advisors will agree that it's not a logical moment but one ruled by a leap of faith and trust in the advisor's intangible qualities. The danger, as we mentioned before, is that the sale will become one of charisma without any record of a logical sequence that led to the determination of what product or service was being sold. This logical sequence is what the new client will turn to for confirmation that his decision was the right one.

"Buyer's remorse" happens when the sale is made primarily on the charisma of the advisor. Once the client has left the advisor's sphere of influence, she looks rationally at the purchase. If there is no supporting material to turn to, the client may feel duped and renege on the sale. This is compounded by the reluctance of the client to talk to the advisor for fear she will be duped again. This fear leads to lapses, irate calls to management, and other passive/aggressive behaviors.

The presentation and close best practices are the following:

1. Making it crisp, clear, and as uncomplicated as possible
2. Having the solution well documented
3. Having the presentation well rehearsed
4. Anticipating most of the prospect's questions
5. Knowing when to ask for the business and being successful at least 75 to 90 percent of the time

Jerry's Presentation and Close

This would be the culmination of your mission: to create a client from a prospect or to deepen an existing client's relationship with you.

Jerry: "This is the moment of truth, when all of my efforts are put to a reality test. There have been times over the years when I've gotten lazy about this presentation and closing. There was no challenge in terms of whom I was seeing, and all the cases felt alike. This led to cutting corners in the presentations and assuming the clients knew more than I had told them. It wasn't long before I realized the relationships with these clients were not very strong."

What did you do?

Jerry: "That's when Pareto's principle began to make sense."

That's the 80/20 rule?

Jerry: "Yep. It means that 20 percent of my clients will generate 80 percent of my income. As it applies to presentations and closes, 80 percent are routine, and 20 percent are really interesting and different. So I decided to outsource to Dale and Millie the 80 percent that were routine."

And you said before that Millie is a licensed paraplanner. Does she do the routine presentations and closing?

Jerry: "Actually, yes. Often times she has the primary relationship with the clients after the discovery interview has been done. This is true with Dale as well. For each of our platforms—planning, product, and money management—we have a template presentation format that includes some educational pieces using the numbers for those particular clients. For my 20 percent of the cases, the interesting and challenging ones, I use the same templates but create some variations depending on the complexity of the situation."

What about the best practice of rehearsing the presentation and anticipating client questions?

Jerry: "Before handing off that 80 percent, I role-played with both Millie and Dale a number of times on videotape. We reviewed most of the client objections or questions that I've encountered over the years, and I was comfortable that they could handle them smoothly. I sit in on presentations every so often to keep an eye on quality control."

What about your own presentation skills?

Jerry: "I knew that was coming! I verbally run key ideas and concepts by another advisor I consider my mentor, and he's pretty good at peppering me with questions. We also have a good resource at our home office's advance planning unit who provides me with visuals and more sophisticated presentation tools. I definitely feel prepared when I go into a presentation."

Lynda's Presentation and Close

Lynda: "I'm looking forward to the day when I can delegate those routine cases, that's for sure. Let me go down the list. Crisp, clear, uncomplicated, and well documented. The software I use in the planning process does produce a snapshot summary that's two pages. Those two pages are what I go through with the clients, and then there's a 20-page planning booklet that they can take that includes all the details and calculations. I do use Kettley Backroom Technician to illustrate more complicated concepts such as trusts and taxation."

Jerry: "We use a similar set of presentation software pieces offered by our company. Very handy for clarifying the clients' understanding of tough concepts."

Lynda: "As for being rehearsed and anticipating the clients' questions, I guess I've done enough of these presentations to be pretty proficient, though I have not had an outside person take a look at what I'm doing. That would be a good idea to keep me sharp and honest. I haven't had any questions I couldn't handle."

Might that indicate that you aren't being stretched enough by your clientele? That's one reason I find a 100 percent closing ratio somewhat suspicious. It could mean that you just are stuck in a comfort zone.

Lynda: "That hits home! The referrals I'm getting are pretty much consistent, and none has been particularly challenging. This points to a referral-generating issue, it seems. Asking for the business and getting the product sale or investment money, that's a strength of mine—as you said, it's a natural outcome rather than something confrontational. I've been leading the clients through the process, verifying each step along the way, so the final transactions are expected and easy to execute. Corinna's learning the paperwork and has those signature arrows down pat!"

Sal's Presentation and Close

Sal: "I'll do presentations with maybe three or four people before we take over the assets of a client. Could be the CFO, CPA, attorney, then finally the client, who has the final say. Usually by that time, the others have given their approval—or not—and the clients and I agree to move the assets. Still, it's a scary moment—though I would never let on that it was!"

So it still comes down to the relationship?

Sal: "Yes. If there's no bond between us or it just doesn't feel right, the deal won't happen. Nor would I want it to. All signals must be 'go' before signing on."

What about if one of the clients' other advisors doesn't give approval?

Sal: "That happens but not very often. If the boss says it's a go, I try to meet with the dissenting person and come to an agree-to-disagree cordial understanding. I'll still put the clients on my Thanksgiving Day card list."

Are you rehearsed?

Sal: "You bet. Each of those meetings starts off as simply as possible, but they get into complexities pretty quickly. Tax implications, legal standings, stock discussions, allocations, investment philosophy, and performance history—we get drilled pretty thoroughly. So we have a dry run for each of these presentations beforehand."

Who's that with?

Sal: "We have a couple of investment managers who've been around the block for over 10 years and can do a good job of anticipating the questions. We're often in competition, and I'm proud to say we come away with the assets 75 percent of the time. I'm proud of that because we're not a national name but more of a boutique operation."

Delivery

The final step in the best practices Sales Process is the delivery. This brings the whole sequence of events to a satisfying conclusion. Where there was once a prospect there is now a client. Where once there was a prospect without a certain product, service, or investment, there is now a more financially fulfilled client with a deeper relationship.

This is a rite of passage that needs to be recognized in a formal way. Thus, the delivery appointment fills that pivotal role, and it has five elements:

1. Formal, face-to-face delivery agenda
2. Reinforcement of what the product, service, and/or investment is for
3. The planting of seeds to address the next sales opportunity
4. Discussion and acquisition of referrals
5. The covering of service expectations for the new client

A strong, consistent delivery process will enhance persistency and reduce attrition because of its professionalism and Relationship Building structure.

Lynda's Delivery Appointment

From all of my interviews in the past few years, I'm getting the impression that the delivery is becoming less and less of an event. Any thoughts on why this might be true?

Lynda: "The customer doesn't want it! In the financial planning process, we have a first meeting, a discovery process that might involve a couple of meetings and other contacts, then a prepresentation contact, and a presentation and closing appointment. That's a lot of time invested. Once I get the products underwritten or other business processed and transferred, I call to set a final delivery appointment and often will get a 'just put them in the mail' response."

Jerry: "How do you handle that?"

Lynda: "I find myself making client segmentation decisions: if they seem to have A-level potential, I'll stress the need to get together for a final tying up of all the loose ends. These would be people I feel strongly about developing a relationship with. If they tend to the C end of the scale—more transactional—I don't press too hard for the delivery appointment."

Jerry: "Do you usually get the appointment with the A's?"

Lynda: "Most of the time, yes. I sense some resistance because they know there will be a referral part of the agenda. I let them know that they will be spending 10 minutes 'helping me with my marketing.'"

What does that referral part look like?

Lynda: "In the setting up of the appointment, I ask if it's okay to set aside 10 minutes to discuss some marketing issues with them. I bring my list of names that have been accumulated from all my interactions with them and feed the names back."

Sal: "How do you do that?"

Lynda: "For example, yesterday I had a delivery appointment with a middle-aged couple, Chuck and Tammy, who have three young children. During the discovery process I had uncovered the names of their will's executor, Tammy's sister, Jodi. In the will, if there was a simultaneous death of both Chuck and Tammy, the children's guardian would be Chuck's brother, John. The secondary beneficiaries of their life insurance were the children, but until they reached the age of majority, they had chosen a person to receive the money on their behalf. That person was

Chuck's mother. All three of these important people to their estate were different individuals. During the planning, we rectified the situation, making the person who gets the children—the guardian—and the person who gets the life insurance money on their behalf the same person: Chuck's brother, John. However, there were three names that I could feed back: John, Jodi, and Chuck's mom."

Do you have a script for that feeding back?

Lynda: "It's not written down anywhere, but it goes like this: 'You obviously have a lot of faith in Jodi to appoint her the executor of your will. Do you think it would be prudent for me to get in touch with Jodi to review some of the basic responsibilities of being your executor and make sure that her understanding of your situation is current?'"

Jerry: "I like that."

Lynda: "It's the same for each person that has a fiduciary interest in the client's life."

Jerry: "And your success ratio in setting appointments with those people?"

Lynda: "About 50 percent, sometimes with the client in attendance. My clients like this part of my service. It gives them greater peace of mind to know that these key people are being contacted and educated."

How about setting the stage for the next sale?

Lynda: "Since I've done a financial plan, there's nearly always a next step that's been identified and a timeframe for implementing that step."

Jerry's Delivery Appointment

Jerry: "We follow the five elements you outlined. With the financial plan, I agree with Lynda that there is a planned next step. For the product sales, we do instill some ideas on the delivery as to what might be a future direction to take in terms of looking at their other holdings, but nothing concrete. We will spend time on the service expectations, which is when these future opportunities will arise."

How do you set service expectations?

Jerry: "We describe our cycle of service, which includes a newsletter twice a year, quarterly statements, an annual review, and a couple other touches during the year. We ask if there is anything else they would expect from us."

Lynda: "What usually comes up when you ask that?"

Jerry: "Oh, 'Get me 20 percent return on my money' is common. But some prefer fewer contacts, and others tell us not to bother with the newsletter because they get too many as it is."

Sal's Delivery Appointment

Sal, do you have a delivery process?

Sal: "Yes, actually, quite a complete one. Once all the transfers have taken place and the funds are under our control and any other business from the insurance side has been issued, we have a meeting with the clients and the principal advisors to pretty much review all of the steps outlined."

Lynda: "Even getting referrals?"

Sal: "Well, let's say we provide an opportunity for referrals by describing our ideal client profile and getting feedback from everyone on what his or her experience was like in dealing with us. It's nearly always positive. We leave it open ended, so I guess we discuss referrals more than we actually get them at that point."

What does "planting the seeds for the next sale" look like in your delivery model?

Sal: "There's always more assets to gather, estate planning to do, or executive benefits to pursue. These opportunities have come up during our discussions, and I usually suggest that as our relationship grows stronger, we might be a resource for these services as well."

Postsale Business Submission and Tracking

Once the new client has agreed to a course of action, the behind-the-scenes work of getting the product issued or transaction completed begins.

A thorough tracking process is certainly a best practice. The advisor normally has multiple lines of business available to him or her. The coordination of all of these products sold and transactions initiated should be centralized and monitored on a regular basis. Figure 6.3 illustrates those items essential to a submission and tracking system. It is not meant to be an exhaustive list; instead, it is meant to provide guidelines in the preparation of a best practices operations manual.

Figure 6.3

Submission and Tracking Checklist

At Submission	Client Name	Account Number	Date Completed
Screen paperwork for accuracy and clarity: Applications, supplemental forms, transfers, disclosures.			
Make or scan copies of forms and checks for filing.			
Set up new client files, separating insurance and securities.			
Handle money: Ensure that check is made out correctly. When one check covers multiple sales, confirm that the allocations are clearly noted.			
Order underwriting requirements for insurance.			
Log the application into the appropriate company tracking database.			
Set a follow-up date to view progress.			
Blotter securities transactions, money, and stock and bond sales.			
Submit variable/securities transactions to broker/dealer for suitability review.			
Submit variable/securities transactions by noon the next day.			
Mail insurance applications and forms.			
If it is a split case, specify the percent going to each advisor.			
Tracking			
Insurance: Medical requirements checklist by issuing company			
Insurance: Financial requirements checklist by issuing company			
Insurance: Other requirements checklist by issuing company			

(continued)

Figure 6.3

(Continued)

At Submission	Client Name	Account Number	Date Completed
Annuity: Issuing company tracking database			
Brokerage, securities account: Broker/dealer tracking database			
Mutual fund direct: MF company tracking database			
Expected compensation			
Actual compensation			
Insurance delivery requirements completion			
Annuity/securities: Transaction completion			

Sales Process System Best Practices Checklist

The Sales Process System Best Practices Checklist is shown in Figure 6.4. There are 65 specific steps in this checklist. It's the blueprint for the third section of your best practices operations manual. Subsequent checklists for the remaining five business systems will be in the same format.

In Figure 6.4, we have assumed that the advisor is with a broker/dealer in a detached location, with a full-time administrative assistant and a full-time marketing assistant. The advisor is in a Mature life cycle stage.

Each practice is unique, of course, and the checklist can be modified for each advisor. The resources referred to on the checklist are suggestions based on various best practices observed in the field. Any resource in italics refers to a piece reviewed or illustrated earlier in this chapter.

Figure 6.4

Sales Process System Best Practices Checklist

Sales Process Activities	Advisor	Marketing Assistant	Administrative Assistant	Firm	Resources
Initial Contact					
3.1 Hand-off from Client Acquisition system: Mail or e-mail any precall material to the prospect; set a time to make the first call for an appointment.		X			Advisor Marketing materials
3.2 Call for the appointment.	X				Script
3.3 If the response is a "no": Keep the name? If so, for how long? If a referral, inform referral source.	X	S			
3.4 If the response is "call back later": Schedule the future call. If a referral, inform referral source.	X	S			
3.5 If "yes," schedule initial appointment with prospect.	X	S			Record in calendar, CRM
Appointment Confirmation					
3.6 Determine what the prospect should receive prior to the initial meeting.	X				

Note: X denotes primary accountability person, and S denotes shared accountability person.

(continued)

Figure 6.4

(Continued)

Sales Process Activities	Advisor	Marketing Assistant	Administrative Assistant	Firm	Resources
3.7 Send materials.		X	S		
3.8 Appointment confirmation: Time, location, directions, material.		X	S		Script
3.9 Coordinate any joint work calendars.		X	S		Calendar, CRM
Initial Interview					
3.10 Receive back from prospect any requested preappointment paperwork: Checklists, census, documents, etc.		X	S		
3.11 Study requested prework; integrate into meeting agenda.	X				
3.12 Determine initial meeting agenda and objectives, and select materials to accomplish those goals. Elements of a best practices initial meeting: • It's truly a dialogue. The prospect's wants and needs are drawn out. • It explores what the advisor does and why. • It sets the expectations for the relationship.	X	S			

#				
	• It discusses compensation. • It leads naturally into fact-finding. • You agree to work together (formal or informal).			
3.13	Package materials for initial meeting; create file.	X	S	Initial meeting preparation and materials checklist
3.14	Conduct initial meeting.	S		
3.15	Give prospect "homework" to complete prior to next meeting.	S		
3.16	Record outcome of initial meeting: Next steps and additional information gathered; discovery interview appointment set.	X		CRM *info form.* Record for transfer of information and notes; calendar, CRM
3.17	Transfer information, appointment, and next steps into calendar and/or database and files.	X	S	CRM, files
Discovery Interview				
3.18	Discovery appointment confirmation: Time, location, directions, "homework."	X	S	Script
3.19	Determine discovery interview (fact/feeling finder) agenda and objectives, and arrange materials to accomplish those goals. Elements of a best practices discovery interview: • Use of a consistent fact-finding tool, with triggers to ensure that the feeling questions are asked	S		

(continued)

Figure 6.4

(Continued)

Sales Process Activities	Advisor	Marketing Assistant	Administrative Assistant	Firm	Resources
• Gathering of all necessary information to run illustrations, planning software, asset allocation models, and other Case Development resources • Dialogue, with the prospect's doing most of the talking • Anticipating underwriting and/or issue complications • Generating a good number of names to feed back to the prospect					
3.20 Package materials for the discovery interview.		X	S		Discovery interview preparation materials checklist
3.21 Conduct the discovery interview.	X	S			
3.22 Record outcome of discovery interview: Next steps, additional information needed, presentation appointment set.	X	S			CRM, calendar
3.23 Transcribe discovery information (profile info, details, names gathered, priorities) from fact-finding tool into CRM fields.		X			CRM
3.24 Image or copy prospect's personal and/or business documents and files.		X	S		

#			
3.25	Return original documents.	X	S	

(Go to Case Development system for analysis and preparation.)

Discovery Letter

#				
3.26	Proactive contact with prospect during Case Development: the discovery letter.	S	X	*Discovery letter*

The elements of a best practices discovery letter:
- "I appreciate your time."
- "Here's what I heard you say."
- "These are your priorities as I recorded them."
- "I'm working to use your available resources to address those priorities."
- "If any of this is incorrect, please call."
- "Here's when we'll be meeting again."

#				
3.27	Confirm presentation appointment (time, location, directions) and receipt of discovery letter.		X	Script

Presentation and Close

#				
3.28	Determine presentation appointment agenda and objectives, and select materials to accomplish those goals.	X	S	Based on priorities and discovery letter

Elements of a best practices presentation and close:
- Crisp, clear, and as uncomplicated as possible
- Well-documented solution
- Rehearsed presentation

(*continued*)

Figure 6.4

(Continued)

Sales Process Activities	Advisor	Marketing Assistant	Administrative Assistant	Firm	Resources
• Anticipating most of the prospect's questions • Knowing when to ask for the business • Successful at least 90% of the time					
3.29 Package the materials for the appointment.		X	S		
3.30 Prefill anticipated applications, gather prospectuses, transfer forms or other documents, and highlight signature spots.		X	S		Web site resource access for each product and/or company's requirements
3.31 Conduct the presentation appointment.	X	S			
3.32 Transcribe additional client information (profile info, details, names, purchases) into the CRM.		X			CRM, file
3.33 Image or copy new business; transfer or change forms as necessary.		S	X		
3.34 Distribute new business; transfer or change forms to proper channels for processing.		S	X		

Postsale Submission and Tracking

				Procedure manual by product and company
3.35	Life: New business/exchange issue procedures by product and company.		X	"
3.36	Life: Change/premium addition procedures by product and company.		X	"
3.37	Annuity: New business/exchange procedures by product and company.		X	"
3.38	Annuity: Change/contribution increase procedures by product and company.		X	"
3.39	Disability: New business procedures.		X	"
3.40	LTC: New business procedures.		X	"
3.41	Outside carriers' products: New business procedures.		X	"
3.42	Brokerage: New business/additional deposits/transfers.		X	"
3.43	Direct investments: New business/additional deposits/transfers.		X	"
3.44	Initiate security trades.	X	S	
3.45	Other product: New business and change procedures.		X	"

(continued)

Figure 6.4

(Continued)

Sales Process Activities	Advisor	Marketing Assistant	Administrative Assistant	Firm	Resources
3.46 Central tracking point for all insurance-related transaction status.				X	*Postsale business submission and tracking*
3.47 Central tracking point for all investment-related transaction status.				X	*Postsale business submission and tracking*
3.48 Proactive contact with prospect during issue period.		X			Letter or e-mail template, phone script
Delivery					
3.49 Set delivery appointment; alert prospect/client of any additional requirements to secure the transactions.		X			Phone script, calendar, CRM
3.50 Confirm delivery appointment: Time, location, directions.		X	S		Phone script
3.51 Determine delivery appointment agenda and objectives, and select materials to accomplish those goals.	X	S			

	Elements of a best practices delivery appointment agenda: • Reinforcement of what the product/transfer/exchange/deposit/investment is for • Planting seeds to address the next sales/planning opportunity • Positioning referral gathering • Covering service expectations for the new client			
3.52	Package the materials for the appointment.		X	
3.53	Prefill necessary placement paperwork; transfer forms or other documents; highlight signature spots.		X	S
3.54	Conduct the delivery appointment.	X		
3.55	Image or copy final documents as necessary; send paperwork to appropriate channels.		S	S
3.56	Complete and organize file anticipating the first scheduled review.		X	S	Paper files, CRM
3.57	Transcribe additional client information obtained during delivery (profile info, details, names, purchases) into CRM.		X	X	CRM
3.58	Place any referrals into the Client Acquisition system.		X		

(continued)

Figure 6.4

(Continued)

Sales Process Activities	Advisor	Marketing Assistant	Administrative Assistant	Firm	Resources
Sales Statistics					
3.59 Average case size by product tracking.		X			CRM, calendar
3.60 Average revenue by product.		X			"
3.61 Average revenue per client.		X			"
3.62 Total assets under management.	X	S			"
3.63 Ratio of initial interviews to discovery interviews.		X			"
3.64 Ratio of discovery interviews to presentations.		X			"
3.65 Ratio of presentations to successful closes.		X			"

7

Core Business System 4:
Case Development

The advisor's first area of genius, Relationship Building, is captured in the Client Acquisition system. The genius of deepening and maintaining those relationships supports the Client Management system. The advisor's third area of genius is the ability to inspire people to action, and it is reflected in the Sales Process system. This leads us to the fourth area of advisor genius: Solving Problems Creatively and Interpreting Information. Taken together, they form the advisor's Case Development system.

Why pay an advisor to prepare a financial plan, make an investment, or buy an insurance product? Some people simply don't. There are plenty of do-it-yourself money managers who create their own investment strategies, develop their own financial plans, and seek out their own products. The Internet and popular financial publications offer basic, sound tools with which to do simple stock, bond, and mutual fund research or comparison shop for brokerages, property and casualty companies, and term insurance purveyors. These are stand-alone analyses, and they don't provide much if any context for an investment or purchase.

Those who seek out an advisor are buying this context. Context in Case Development is found in the process, which includes the following:

1. Gathering all the client's pertinent facts and feelings
2. Entering them into analytical tools

3. Generating an overview of the client's financial position, studying the results, and providing recommendations based on the advisor's education and experience
4. Doing the due diligence in selecting the right product or service from the pantheon of offerings in the financial services universe
5. Preparing a presentation of findings for the client

We'll be distilling these steps into five best practices for creating a Case Development system later in this chapter.

Turning Chaos into Order

One of the simple joys of Case Development is in satisfying the primal human instinct to create order out of chaos—that is, the entropy prevailing over a client's financial life. *Entropy* is the tendency of all things in a given system to deteriorate into chaos if left to their own devices. The advisor is the force of *financial entropic reversal*. With an array of tools and techniques, the advisor pulls together all the financial aspects of a client's life and reorganizes them into a cohesive whole with a sense of purpose and direction. That is the science (reordering of the elements) and art (providing a guiding purpose) of case design.

In many cases this chaos has been created over the years by the client's listening to a variety of advisors, agents, bankers, investors, planners, and product peddlers. The client had a short engagement period with each person, presumably endured some specific fact-finding, and received an analysis that didn't look at the whole financial picture. The client came away with a purchase that seemed reasonable at the time but really addressed only a slice of his financial life.

The result is that the client now has an accumulation of financial instruments that don't reference each other. A common assemblage of this type may include an IRA, a variable life policy, mutual funds, an education fund, auto and homeowner's insurance, a mortgage protection policy, and an array of employee benefits, including health coverage, disability insurance, and a retirement plan. All of these were purchased or acquired separately without a unifying theme.

For example, the client's 401(k) money may be in conservative funds while his personal IRA might be invested in something highly speculative. Or both might be aggressive or both conservative. At the time of purchase, the chosen strategy may have made sense. The best practices advisor will ask: "In the context of all of your other holdings, does the strategy behind that single purchase continue to make sense?"

Let's next take a look at the various platforms an advisor might choose to pursue in helping clients create order in their financial lives. In the Client Acquisition system, I spoke of the iconic presentation as a way of communicating to prospects or clients the value an advisor brings to their relationship. There are many such icons, including the line presentation demonstrated in Chapter 4. The "Building a Financial House" in Figure 7.1 is another iconic presentation that can be useful in our discussion of the various business models advisors adopt.

Figure 7.1

Sample Iconic Presentation: Building a Financial House

The advisor can sketch a house or insert a clip art house showing the foundation, walls, windows, and the roof.

Building a Financial House

My work as a financial advisor is like building a financial house.

The construction of a house starts with an architect's helping you describe your goals and vision: what model of home you want, the features you're looking for, and any concerns you have in building that home. [You talk about your past experiences with homes, both good and bad.]

In building your financial house, we ask the same types of questions about your financial goals and vision. What have been your financial experiences, both good and bad? How do you feel about money and its place in your life? What does your picture of financial security look like? Who are the people involved?

After we've established your values and discussed your goals, I'll help you put together the blueprint outlining the necessary action steps and priorities.

(continued)

Figure 7.1

(Continued)

If you were building a house, you wouldn't start the walls until you had a solid foundation in place. That's also true of your financial house. So first we build the foundation of your financial home: savings habits, debts, insurance planning. We then build the walls with medium- and long-term savings planning. Next we put on a roof for retirement planning. And finally we help you furnish your home with basic estate planning tools such as wills and trusts. In building a house, you need to team up with qualified, experienced, professional contractors, builders, electricians, plumbers, cement layers, and painters. The same principle holds true in building a financial house, and I have access to all the professionals we'll need, such as investment specialists and advanced planning specialists.

Often I encounter people who have purchased the financial equivalent of windows, doors, and shingles without having the framework in place. Does this approach make sense?

Advisor Platforms

Advisors use a variety of approaches to address client needs. The following is a list of advisor platforms I've encountered most frequently. Most seek to develop relationships with clients, some more strongly than others. This relationship approach is distinct from a transactional approach that requires no emotional investment on the part of the seller or the buyer.

I also offer a tongue-in-cheek description of how a particular advisor platform might line up if we carried the financial house building metaphor a bit further.

Full Financial Planner

The full financial planner is the architect and general contractor of the whole house, inside and out, family or business; he subcontracts to proven, reputable vendors.

This category includes advisors who charge fees and examine all the financial aspects of a client's life. One may be a fee-only planner, providing advice and directing clients to purchase financial instruments, often no-load funds and low-margin products. Another may provide planning for an upfront fee and charge an annual retainer while also placing products that provide commissions and management fees. Yet another full financial planner may not charge a fee at all, preferring to make commissions and management fees the source of ongoing revenue. The emphasis is on the "full" financial planning—not leaving an economic stone unturned for the client.

Comprehensive Planner

The "comprehensive" planner is a general contractor who helps design and build the primary living spaces but directs the client to find his own subcontractors for the less important rooms and infrastructure systems. These advisors imply that they offer full financial planning capabilities, but in reality they focus on gathering assets and/or selling specific products—hence the quotation marks. Also known as "financial planning lite," fees may be charged up front and annually. In addition, there may be commissions and ongoing management fees, just as the full financial planners charge. This lite-planning advisor will often gloss over or ignore such things as property and casualty insurance, health insurance, budgeting, and debt structuring. It's a less-than-comprehensive analysis that is all too prevalent in the marketplace today.

Modular Planner

The modular planner is a good subcontractor who can build any internal or external component of the house (recreation room or roof) or infrastructure systems (electrical or plumbing), and she may or may not consult the client's blueprint before doing so. The modular planner goes conceptually wherever the client wants to go. This is a chameleon approach, with the advisor being able to change into whatever type of specialist is necessary. Various modules offered by these advisors include college planning, insurance planning, retirement planning, health coverage, benefits analysis, and investment analysis. Modular advisors are self-described "generalists." Their solutions do not provide a context for the client's entire fiscal situation, just a narrow focus on the particular concern of the client.

Investment Planner

The investment planner is a subcontractor who builds a strong roof with quality trusses, framing, shingles, flashing, and so on, hopefully *after* consulting the blueprint. The investment planner is primarily concerned with the securities side of a client's assets. The insurances are left for others to handle. Investment planners manage their client's portfolio for ongoing fees.

Wealth Manager

The wealth manager is the same as the investment planner, with the name suggesting that they do consult the blueprint before acting. This advisor is often an investment planner with a fancier moniker. The implication, however, is that they provide a more comprehensive look at the wealth of a client, which should involve life insurance, estate plans, and wealth transfers.

Financial Instrument Specialist

The financial instrument specialist is a purveyor of high-quality doors, windows, shingles, siding, and other necessary building products.

A specialist is an advisor who is generally called into a situation for his expertise with a particular line of insurance or investments. This could be in life, disability, property and casualty, long-term-care insurance, 401(k) plans, stock and fund analyses, or another financial services discipline. This specialist receives a piece of the action, whether it's a commission, a fee, or ongoing revenue.

Market Specialist

The market specialist helps the architect design the house inside and out for potential buyers in particular market segments. A market specialist differs from a financial instrument specialist in that the advisor has expertise with certain groups of people. These groups might be physicians, attorneys, chiropractors, construction managers, dentists, sports professionals, retirees, or employees of certain companies, among many, many others. Market specialists have learned the ins and outs of typical benefits packages for these groups, they know the challenges and issues faced by members of their chosen market, and they offer insights based on this knowledge.

Insurance Planner

The insurance planner is a subcontractor strong on the building of foundations and installation of the house's electrical and plumbing infrastructure. The insurance planning advisor is concerned with the protection aspects of the client's financial life. This includes a background in the insurances to include estate planning issues, life, disability, long-term care, property and casualty, health insurances, and annuities.

Benefits Planner

The benefits planner is a subcontractor and supplier of material to builders of business financial structures. The advisor who works with employee benefits is a benefits planner. This usually involves group insurances and group retirement plans with an emphasis on "group."

Executive Business Planner

The executive business planner is a subcontractor and supplier of material to high-end builders of business financial structures. The business planning advisor will be more involved with the executive level of the business world, across many markets. This includes things like deferred compensation, key employee insurance, buy/sell agreements, and other exclusive arrangements.

Now that these categories have been defined, you'll find that advisors wield multiple tools in the building of a client's financial house, not that you can tell from simply reading a business card. Federal, state, and company compliance requirements concerning insurance and investment nomenclature make it difficult to describe what an advisor does on her business card. In fact, if you examine a fully compliant advisor's card, there is precious little white space on either side on which to jot a note.

Our purpose here is to ensure that whatever platforms the advisor chooses, there are best-practice systems to support it. The sequence of best practices shared by all platforms in case development is the following:

1. Having a consistent discovery (fact-and-feeling-finding) tool, which is also a key component of Business System 3, Sales Process
2. Identifying and mastering the analysis programs and resources that produce the level of knowledge required for the chosen platform
3. Reviewing and selecting the suite of products and investment options best drawn upon to provide recommendations and solutions
4. Packaging the resulting materials in a consistent presentation format
5. Educating the client on the essentials of what is being proposed

Best Practice 1: Consistent Discovery Tool

How deep do you want to go? The depth of your fact-and-feeling-finding should mirror the analysis and presentation. We all know the computer maxim "garbage in/garbage out." Well, it's just as appropriate in the financial services arena. In this compliance-driven world, it's always smarter to err on the side of keeping too much information in the back room while keeping it simple in front of the client. As we reviewed in the last chapter, there are many possible elements of a complete discovery procedure. Once the discovery data has been collected, it needs to be transferred into the appropriate programs or software. The discovery tool should be aligned with the data entry screens for the analysis program. This is why a consistent discovery tool is a best practice not only for the completeness of data collection but also for the ease of transfer and entry by the advisor, assistant, paraplanner, or other associate.

I have encountered many experienced advisors over many platforms who have veteran support teams and use a yellow pad to record the clients' pertinent information. The advisor also collects all the clients' documents and turns the whole thing over to an assistant. The assistant sifts through the documents and with the yellow-pad notes, enters the appropriate information. This is extremely efficient and allows the advisor to maximize his face time with key people in his practice, a goal of Infrastructure Business System 5, Time Management, which is covered in the next chapter.

The yellow-pad discovery works for advisors who have a well-oiled Case Development machine to deliver plans or product recommendations. But there are drawbacks to using this discovery system even for these advisors because the system is apt to miss relationship discovery information. An example is Artie.

Artie, a 20-year veteran who is a self-described wealth manager, allowed me to observe his discovery process with a new client couple. The clients had complied with Artie's request to bring all the necessary documents via a checklist e-mailed prior to the meeting. Artie did a masterful job of yellow-padding, taking cryptic notes that his paraplanner, Jeanette, would know how to interpret. He spent 45 minutes with the clients, a husband and wife, building a wonderful rapport, exchanging stories, and eliciting their financial concerns and philosophy about money. After the clients departed his office, Artie popped open his digital recorder and verbally transcribed for Jeanette the clients' suggested asset allocation mix, risk tolerance preferences, and other case design requirements. She would be able to get the necessary facts from the accompanying documents. The next time Artie would see the case would be his initial review of the output prepared by Jeanette.

In our debriefing afterward, we reviewed the documents. For the purposes of the presentation, Jeanette had gleaned all the pertinent data. Looking over the life insurance, I noticed that the secondary beneficiary of the clients' $250,000 universal life policy was Catholic Charities. The primary beneficiary was the client's wife. The couple had three children—15, 21, and 25 years old—but none of them were named as either secondary or tertiary beneficiary on any of the four life policies. I brought this to Artie's attention.

"Interesting," Artie mused. "They never mentioned Catholic Charities in our meeting."

Does that affect the plan presentation?

Artie: "Initially, I don't think so. Right now I'm just gathering all their available assets into two managed accounts. Once they're established, we'll be doing some retirement income scenarios. At that point, when we talk about estate planning issues, this should come up."

Jeanette: "I enter the beneficiary information into the Client Management program."

Would you have brought this to Artie's attention?

Jeanette: "Not right away. I will eventually do a workup of the insurance holdings for an annual review. It would show up there."

Artie: "But I see your point. It's a relationship clue, one that might be good to know up front. It's obviously an important organization to the client, or at least was important once. It's a piece of information that may have slipped by."

As far as Case Development goes, Artie, what do you do if Jeanette is out for an extended period of time?

Artie: "Ah, yes. She does kind of read my mind, doesn't she? It would be difficult to replace her. I'd have to train a new person from scratch on how to interpret my yellow-pad code."

Which isn't very transferable.

Artie: "Touché!"

Until an advisor has a near-failsafe discovery process, much like Artie and Jeanette have developed, the best practice is to use a consistent, transferable discovery tool and not a yellow pad.

Best Practice 2: Analysis Programs and Resources

As you can see from the various platforms enumerated above, there is a great variety of needs to address in the financial services marketplace. From a

Case Development standpoint, this results in a plethora of analysis tools from which to choose, ranging from the comprehensive to the specific. Generally, they work within two conceptual frameworks:

1. *Target.* Beginning with the end in mind and planning to achieve specific goals. For instance, the advisor asks the client, "What would you like your income to be when you retire?" The advisor then proceeds to calculate what needs to be put away to get there.
2. *Projection.* Beginning with the current situation in mind and projecting possible outcomes. The advisor asks the client, "What are you currently putting aside for retirement?" The advisor then calculates what that would amount to in the future.

Each program has its advantages based on the advisor's particular style, background, and area of specialization. Many times, a mixture of the two is developed to compare and contrast where the client would like to be versus the trajectory the client is currently on.

Most parent companies have their own proprietary software programs to run specific product illustrations and basic asset allocations. For the investment-oriented advisor, there are portfolio construction and management tools. You have a choice of where the programs will reside. They can be installed on your stand-alone computer or on your local network, or they can be accessed remotely on the Web.

The search for the right program is not the purpose of this chapter. The analytical offerings are constantly evolving, and the best practice in discovering what fits your practice is to consider a combination of peer recommendations, affordability, vendor reputation, firm sponsorship, demo copies provided by the vendor's Web site, and reviews in professional publications.

Best Practice 3: Products and Investment Options

The universe of financial products and services is truly bewildering to the average consumer. An advisor is compensated for the ability to do the due diligence required to provide clients with the best possible solution for their unique situation. While that's a simple statement, there are many complications.

Access. For example, an advisor who doesn't have a Series 7 license is unable to provide equity trading. A captive non-7 advisor may be able to choose among only a specific set of funds or insurance products. Broker/dealers might have limited product and investment offerings. When an advisor moves from one firm to another, access to a greater variety of products is normally at the top of the list of reasons for doing so.

Pricing. What can the clients afford versus what do the clients need? A more expensive product might be the better option for a client's situation, but it may be less affordable. A less expensive alternative might be more affordable, but it may lack some features and benefits that the client needs. While the advisor can't normally control the pricing assumptions made by an issuing company, she can compare the relative merits of the products available in relation to the clients' needs and resources. To make those comparisons, she can obtain information on the pricing assumptions because those assumptions are usually available for examination upon request. For a variable product, the issuing company's prospectus offers a detailed accounting of the internal costs and pricing rationales.

Compensation. Another variable in the product and investment option choices centers on compensation. What is appropriate and fair? The best practice for compensation is transparency— that is, being up front with clients on how the advisor is compensated. If clients ask for additional detail, the advisor should willingly provide it. At that point, the advisor should be ready to show how the compensation is commensurate with the value the clients are receiving.

Performance. What has been the historical performance of a particular product or investment option? Good overall performance can lessen the impact of the pricing and compensation issues. Conversely, leaner returns foster more questions about pricing and compensation.

Better mousetraps. What is the shelf life of a particular product or investment option? Certainly, term life insurance rates have gotten cheaper over time, and replacement of an old policy with a new one would be a prudent choice if the client is still insurable. That's an easy one compared to studying each successive generation of fixed and variable annuities, mutual funds, and variable life policies. When is it in the best interest of the clients to move money? I've always enjoyed the phrase "new business" as it applies to the financial services profession. Much, if not most, of the so-called new business is actually money being moved from one account to another, from one company to another by replacements, rollovers, transfers, or exchanges. This money movement is often prompted by the introduction of a new product with a "new and improved" feature or benefit. While there is a lengthy ethical discussion possible around these issues, suffice it to say that there are appropriate and inappropriate times to suggest moving clients' money into new products. Most companies require replacement paperwork that includes the reason for the change and a suitability check on its appropriateness.

Once the strategy has been decided upon and the products and services are selected to accomplish the clients' objectives, two steps remain in the Case Development system: the packaging of the presentation and the education of the client.

Best Practice 4: Consistent Presentation

All parts of the Case Development presentation should have a uniform look and feel. Rather than a hodgepodge assembly of product illustrations, hypotheticals, asset allocation models, graphs, and charts, the packaging of the final plan or proposal should conform to a certain template that reflects the advisor's image and platform, and it should be presented in a binder or folder with a consistent design, color, and logo.

The presentation package should also be consistent with the discovery letter, if one is used (see Chapter 6). In the discovery letter, the advisor outlines the clients' priorities. Assuming the clients agree with the list, the packaging and presentation ought to reflect those priorities. This is best covered in a one-page executive summary.

After the executive summary, a limited number of charts and graphs may be presented, with plenty of backup material off to the side to be used only as necessary. This initial presentation to the clients should also be a template for revisiting and updating the plan's performance at annual review time. Looking at something familiar will provide the clients with a memory bridge, a familiar work-in-progress continuity, over the years.

Best Practice 5: Client Education

An area of the advisor's Case Development genius is the ability to simplify the complex and chaotic world of money and risk management. There are a number of core concepts to which clients should be exposed to ensure (to the best of their ability) an understanding of how their case will be developed and presented:

- Historic fixed and variable investment index trends
- Historic trends in inflation
- Historic trends in taxation: Federal, state, estate
- Types of income: Taxable, tax deferred, tax exempt
- Review of government-sponsored health and retirement plans
- Review of life expectancy trends
- Review of health-care costs in later years (for retirement planning)

Depending on the Sales Process an advisor uses, there are three opportunities to provide clients with basic education about these financial concepts, specific products, and/or other financial ideas: (1) up front, (2) during discovery, and (3) as part of the presentation.

Up front is using an educational process to segue potential clients into a fact-finding appointment. The advisor provides an educational experience, usually a presentation on a particular topic. These educational endeavors include one-on-one presentations, group seminars, and classes. In these events, the prospects learn about a specific product (long-term care, disability, and/or mutual funds); a strategy (estate planning, tax strategies, and/or retirement planning); or general financial overviews (Financial Planning 101, "Stewardship of Your Wealth," "Steps to Successful Senior Living"). The purpose of this upfront education is to instill a sense of urgency about addressing a particular issue and then to offer the prospects a chance to do so. From these educational experiences, the advisor follows up with offers for one-on-one consultations as an entry into the Sales Process.

An example would be an advisor who does a presentation on college education planning to a group of grade school parents. He offers charts on the spiraling cost of private and state colleges, with specific examples. The inflation rate of tuition outpaces the consumer price index (CPI) and is showing no sign of slowing down. Getting an early start on college funding is a wise move. Next, he presents a variety of possible investment options. He closes with a Q&A session. Attendees are given a feedback form that includes an option to have the advisor contact them for an appointment.

Education *during discovery* occurs when the advisor integrates it while gathering information face-to-face with the prospects. Using the college planning example, the advisor would open to the education section of the fact finder and ask if a college education is important to the prospects and their young children. If the answer is affirmative, the advisor might pull out some fact sheets showing that college graduates out-earn their nongraduate counterparts, tuition inflation numbers, and how a 529 plan works. He will then continue gathering the facts.

Education *as part of the presentation* is designed to explain to the prospects the rationale for what the advisor is proposing based on the facts and feelings previously recorded. In this scenario, the advisor is presenting a $100-a-month contribution to a 529 plan as part of an overall financial strategy. He may suggest the $100 figure after studying the prospect's cash flow and ability to save. In presenting the tuition inflation and cost of private versus state college materials at this point, the advisor is presenting a rationale for getting the prospect to agree with the $100-a-month suggestion.

Placement of this education component of the Case Development system will be affected by the number of meetings the advisor utilizes in the Sales Process. The advisor who has a one-interview close will educate the prospects with the intent to ask them to buy while the iron is hot. This approach takes advantage of the prospects' willingness to make a quick decision. The disadvantage of the single-appointment sale is that buyer's remorse might set in and the clients might subsequently cancel the deal. A multimeeting Sales Process allows education to be sprinkled in over time and allows the prospects time to absorb the impact of what the advisor is presenting.

Client education in general often treads a fine line. The advisor can't assume the prospects know the statistics concerning the issues in funding a child's college education. There is the danger, however, of overeducating the prospects. The more material that the advisor dumps on the prospects, the more information they have to think about and absorb. This can postpone a decision to buy or even bring the prospects to a state of information overload where they are unable to ever make a buying decision. In addition, there is the trust-me factor. After providing education, the prospects can choose to trust the advisor or not. They may be asking themselves, "Is this advisor giving us good information, or has he spun the facts to make a sale?"

The answer to that question can be in the transparency of the information sources used. As we suggested in the Sales Process, advisor compensation should be transparent—that is, open and honest. The same is true for resources used in Case Development and client education.

Offer the clients access to the same resources used to create the need. The cost of college education materials, in our example above, should be available for the clients or prospects to view online. Copies of source material used by the advisor can be left with the prospects if requested. The method used to calculate the amount of money needed to be put away to provide a child's college education should also be available to the clients. Many company Web sites offer a number of these calculators, some proprietary, some generic.

Along the same lines, product comparisons, investment returns, performance history, and other resources used in creating a proposal should also be open for the clients to access. This is not to say that the clients should be privy to all the programs used by the advisor in building a plan and presentation. This would be overkill and infringe on the advisor's turf. The best-practice point here is for the advisor to be able to openly demonstrate how and why she arrived at a particular conclusion.

Artie, our wealth manager, brings his clients into his office for the presentation. He has a conference room set up with a large, flat screen monitor, and the clients' case is up on the screen. He presents a one-page summary of what he's recommending to the clients. A multipage, bound copy of the more comprehensive plan is available. During his presentation, he will often do what-if scenarios at the request of the clients. I observed one presentation during which he took Social Security out of the retirement income projection and then adjusted the inflation rate up and the rate of return down on the suggested portfolio. He did all this on the computer, with the results showing immediately on the wide screen.

"I like to show clients the different scenarios," Artie says. "The clients like it too. They don't need to see how I put the whole car together. But I let 'em kick the tires and change some of the options before they buy."

Competition and Compliance-Proofing

When competition is present, it is a good idea to gauge your chances of getting the case. A good attorney will prepare the prosecution side of a case before she prepares the defense.

First and foremost, keep in mind what the prospects want to accomplish. Don't ever lose sight of this; you may need to leverage it during subsequent meetings. As advisors are often good conversationalists, occasionally a meeting can get off the subject. While building a relationship is certainly important, it is imperative to see that prospect meetings remain on track and stay focused. What do the prospects want to accomplish after all is said and done? The decision to do business with you or the competitor ultimately will come down to who the clients perceive will get them to their goals most efficiently and effectively.

Second, learn as much as you can about the competition. Consult with others—such as experienced advisors, sales managers, wholesalers, and company competition units—who can help you position the competitors' products. They can also address issues around a company's rating if that becomes an issue. (A.M. Best, Moody's, Standard & Poor's, Weiss Research, and Duff & Phelps are five major insurer rating services.) For investment comparisons, Morningstar is the leading resource for mutual fund and variable annuity comparisons.

Third, study the relationship: How strong is the relationship between you and the prospects, and how strong is the relationship between the prospects and the competition? Can the prospects be truly objective? A strong ongoing service relationship might be a critical factor. Would having the prospects contact existing satisfied clients help your case?

Fourth, verify the criteria the prospects have stated that must be met to get the case. Most companies provide a suitability document for advisors to use in gathering the prospects' preferences. Clarifying the prospects' risk tolerance, need for guarantees, ability to pay, investment experience, and time horizon are important for ensuring that the competition stays on a level playing field.

In most competitive situations, you have a gut feeling about the case. Don't be afraid to act on your feelings. Take a pragmatic, logical look at the case as well. Once you understand the competition, put together an outline of comparative strengths, weaknesses, and any other pertinent information that will help you succeed.

After the Sale

Potential Landmines

Once a case is developed, accepted by the clients, and put into action, the concern turns to keeping the business on the books. We discussed the Client Management system in Chapter 5. However, there are some key elements of client satisfaction that belong squarely in the Case Development system. These are retroactive in nature, causing the clients to question their decision and the advisor's integrity after the case has been placed.

Ambush by a Competitor

There are many salespeople who are compensated on the amount of assets that they can "roll" from an existing product to one of their own products. This compensation system encourages the sharks of the financial service world to sniff out and attack underserved clients of well-meaning but perhaps overstretched (or naïve) advisors.

It's not difficult to point out the negatives of a particular investment or insurance product. As we all know, numbers can be manipulated to serve anyone's purpose. Common themes include a slam against the company itself ("Have you seen their ratings lately?"); the rate of return ("That's a lousy return compared to what we've been getting on our product."); the loads ("They're charging you so much it's a wonder you can make any profit at all."); and the advisor who sold it ("When was the last time you heard from him?"). If your clients have been victimized by a predator's ambush and suddenly their assets disappear from your book, it's too late. Your chances of retrieving them are slim to none.

Integrity Questions

Many a good advisor has been called out on the carpet by having her firm or company caught in a compliance action. If the XYZ Insurance Company has been subject to a class action lawsuit, suddenly all of its advisors and products become suspect. The predators from competing companies begin nipping away, using XYZ's black eye as a reason to switch products. Recent examples include states suing large insurers for improperly selling indexed annuities to senior citizens.

An advisor might have clients who decide for whatever reason they they've been wronged. Whether the claim is warranted or not, these clients might decide to create a stir and poison other client relationships the advisor might have.

Lacey, a CFP in central California, has a horror story in this area. A top-tier client sued her because she felt she was repeatedly "abused" on the telephone by Lacey's assistant. The client demanded a published apology by Lacey and her assistant plus a brand-new financial plan paid for by Lacey with another advisor in a competing company. The client knew a number of Lacey's other top clients, and she started calling them in a smear campaign. Lacey eventually (and painfully) won a cease-and-desist order when it was determined that the client had experienced a breakdown after her only child filed for a divorce and attempted suicide. Lacey was grateful that her company's attorneys responded strongly to the client. "They might be a pain on the compliance side," she said of the legal department, "but they really came to my rescue."

Media Attention

Mass communication venues such as newspapers, magazines, and Internet sites are full of reasoned articles and well-meaning columns about financial planning topics. There are also product-bashing pieces and screeds about consumers who have been ripped off by advisors and financial services sales-people in general. Clients who have read some of this material might well question their own advisor and products. While most single pieces don't arouse suspicion, the cumulative effect might cast a pall over an advisor's best efforts.

Response

For all three of these issues, the best defense is a strong offense. You've heard it over and over at compliance meetings and in ethics continuing-education classes. Documentation is the strongest line of defense.

Document each step in the Sales Process and Case Development. Why did you suggest that particular investment strategy? What was the reason for placing that type of life policy? Did you discuss long-term care, and why did the clients decide not the pursue it? Did you document that decision?

Documentation is the legal defense. But that's after the damage is done—if you're in court defending an action, you've already been sued. The cloud of suspicion has enveloped you. Clients who have already moved their money to a predator are not interested in your documentation. Were they swayed by the media, another salesperson, or questions of integrity? The best defense is your clients' ability to articulate what they bought and why.

Think about it. If clients of yours are approached by a predatory sales-person who questions the product or strategy you put in place, are they armed with the ability to defend their position? The job of the advisor is to provide this defensive coaching to the clients. The best practice is to ensure that your clients, especially the top-tier clients, understand what value you have brought to them. They should know enough about the products they purchased or the strategies they initiated with you to rebuff any predator attempting to cast aspersions on your work. At the very least, the clients should ask that the predator call you before they take any action. Few, if any, actually have the guts to take your clients up on that suggestion.

The crowning strategy in the Case Development system is to make the case bullet-proof so it will stay on the books. There are three best-practice elements to this:

1. Ensure that new clients are able to *describe* (to the best of their ability) what product or service they have purchased.
2. Ensure that clients can articulate *why* they chose that particular product, service, or strategy.
3. *Document* the clients' understanding and decision process along the way.

Collaboration and Joint Work

Case Development often requires an advisor to collaborate with other professionals, both internal and external to the practice. Garland in Meridian, Idaho, has an expertise in the area of money management. He also possesses a particular genius in helping landowners convert their acreage into transferable wealth. In doing so, he consults with a select group of professional experts including an estate planning attorney, real estate attorney, 1031 exchange specialist, CPA, land sale expert, developer, and real estate broker.

Garland describes his role as "the coach for these players in getting the best deal for the client. My payoff is to manage the wealth that is unlocked." His team members meet individually and collectively with each other and with Garland to exchange ideas, research, market conditions, and prospecting leads and to hold each other accountable in their respective roles with a common client.

How does that work for compensation purposes?

"We all have our hourly fees that accumulate on speculation that the deal will go through. If it falls apart, we're out of luck. But when we do hit pay dirt, the rewards are uncommonly good. [He smiled.] When the real estate market tanks, we are wise to have other clients."

What has been the result of the credit crunch and subprime loan debacle?

"You see it. [He motioned around his office. The whiteboard where he tracked the progress of land deals was blank.] We did only one deal in this year. So I've resurrected the financial planning part of my practice. We all still meet and share leads and prospects. Most of my income this year will be from planning fees and assets under management."

Sharing fees and commissions with outside professionals is usually not permitted unless the collaborator is properly licensed. Some CPAs, for example, have become licensed for this very purpose. They don't want to become experts in insurance or investing, but they would like to share in any business placed with a referral by an advisor. Lacey, our California CFP, has used her internal resource people to build cases.

"I'm in a firm where we have some excellent senior specialists," she said. "We have an estate planning guru, an investment department, a long-term-care specialist, and other insurance experts."

How's the compensation handled?

"The investment department does all the work around the research and development of the investment part of the clients' plan. Their services are part of the overhead, and I pay a fixed amount every month as part of being a member of the firm. Gladly: they do a bang-up job. The others I work with are advisors, and we generally work the MDRT split."

What's that?

"The Million Dollar Round Table (MDRT) is an international organization for financial professionals that provides a wealth of support for its members. I'm not sure where the term 'MDRT split' originated within the MDRT, but it's a nifty way to break down the sale.* It's five 20 percent splits. The first 20 percent goes to the person who provided the lead. Then 20 percent goes to whoever does the discovery, gathering the information and feelings. The next 20 percent goes to whoever prepares the case. The fourth 20 percent is for the person who presents and closes the deal. The final 20 percent is for whoever will provide ongoing service for the account."

The "MDRT split" is a best practice. It takes the guesswork out of 50/50 arrangements, where one person can easily be perceived as doing the lion's share of the work for only half the case. It rewards the key elements of the Core Four business systems:

1. The Client Acquisition system is served by the 20 percent going to the lead generator.
2. The Client Management system is rewarded with 20 percent of the ongoing service.
3. The Sales Process system gets 20 percent for the discovery and 20 percent for the presentation and close.
4. Finally, the Case Development system gets its 20 percent for analysis and preparation.

---

* The Million Dollar Round Table (MDRT) is an international sales organization of life insurance salespeople. Membership is attained by sales success, and in times past it was the mark of having "made it" in the insurance industry. The influence and popularity of MDRT has waned considerably with the demise of the career agency system and the subsequent integration of insurance and investment products. However, the MDRT is still the industry standard for many sales concepts and team selling arrangements.

The MDRT split is an excellent starting place for discussing collaborative compensation sharing.

Lacey also refers clients to a property and casualty agency in which her firm has an ownership interest.

"I'm not P&C licensed, nor do I ever want to be!" she declared. "They get to keep all their commissions. But they do send me their clients who check off an interest in financial planning on their annual renewal mailers. It works out nicely."

Case Development Personnel

Before looking at the best practices checklist for the Case Development system, let's look at the people who may contribute to a successful Case Development team.

Paraplanners

An advisor should consider a paraplanner once he has a solidified his Case Development process and is beginning to attract a steady stream of clients. A good rule of thumb is that a paraplanner should be hired once the advisor's case load consists of 80 percent routine plans that, with individual client variations, are cookie cutter in nature. In other words, someone else can process them—the advisor doesn't need to spend valuable time on routine cases. Instead, he can be using the time to do some rainmaking, working on the 20 percent of the cases that are challenging or on other high-dollar-value activities. The fully licensed paraplanner accomplishes the following:

- Gathers client statements and documents, copies them, and returns them after inputting the data into the analysis program.
- Organizes and updates client files.
- Sits in on the client meetings and takes notes with the advisor. The advisor will focus on the client relationship and bigger-picture issues, while the paraplanner homes in on information and data gathering.
- Transcribes those notes and creates the clients' priorities for inclusion in the discovery letter. The paraplanner will also prepare the discovery letter for the advisor's signature.
- Has telephone contact with the clients when calling to follow up on documentation issues (statements, tax returns, wills).
- Enters all the data into the analysis programs and creates initial drafts of plans, illustrations, projections, asset allocations, and the

like for the advisor to review. The paraplanner has the latitude to create investment scenarios in line with the advisor's philosophy.

• Can earn $30,000 or more depending on the volume, incentives, and markets provided by the advisor.

An advanced paraplanner:

• Has achieved or is in the process of achieving a designation such as Registered Paraplanner (RP) or Certified Financial Planner (CFP).
• Is capable of deeper analysis and more complex issues.
• Can receive a share of the plan fees, investment fees, or commissions.
• Helps with the case presentation and product placement.
• Is part of the ongoing Client Management process, assisting with quarterly and annual reviews.
• Can earn a base of $40,000 with incentives and participation in fees and commissions.

Marketing or Administrative Assistants

Whereas a paraplanner is dedicated solely to Case Development, an assistant's duties are spread throughout all eight of the business systems. Many assistants, whether wearing a marketing or an administrative hat, do some minor Case Development work for the advisor. Most commonly, an assistant might collect and copy documents from clients, organize case files, do some basic illustrations for insurance products or run generic investment scenarios.

The duties of an assistant in the Case Development system will also be affected by the licensing they have acquired. An assistant who has a Series 7, for example, can execute trades for an advisor's clients, saving the advisor with a heavily investment oriented practice a good deal of time and energy.

Specialists

The case specialist has expertise in a particular niche in the financial services world. It might be a particular product expertise, like long-term care, or a deep knowledge of estate or executive benefits planning. The advisor is wise to assemble a cadre of these specialists in order to offer higher-end prospects and clients a complete array of services. The advisor can then be the point-person for all the clients' needs rather than be forced to send clients elsewhere because "we don't do that."

Case Development Units

A Case Development unit is a service that will take all of the clients' information and independently produce a plan to the advisor's specifications. They are staffed by financial planners, investment and insurance specialists, and paraplanners. Case Development units are offered by some firms and companies as a benefit of being part of their organizations; these companies usually charge a modest fee per plan or integrate the fees into an advisor's monthly fixed payment. Their interest may also be in proposing a particular family of funds or proprietary insurance products. There are also independent Case Development services—more expensive, less proprietary.

Wholesalers and Advanced Sales Support

Don't overlook the help that is offered by insurance companies and investment firms. Many internal and external wholesalers are well equipped to help you with case design, illustrations, hypotheticals, product materials, third-party materials, and point-of-sale support. Many companies and firms offer advanced sales support as well that can save you time and money.

Case Development System Best Practices Checklist

The Case Development System Best Practices Checklist is shown in Figure 7.2. There are 34 specific steps in this checklist. It's the blueprint for the fourth section of your best practices operations manual.

In Figure 7.2, we have assumed that the advisor is with a broker/dealer in a detached location, with a full-time administrative assistant and a full-time paraplanner/marketing assistant. The advisor is in a Mature life cycle stage. Each practice is unique, of course, and the checklist can be modified for each advisor.

The resources referred to on the checklist are suggestions based on various best practices observed in the field. Any resource in italics refers to a piece reviewed or illustrated earlier in this chapter.

Figure 7.2

Case Development System Best Practices Checklist

Case Development Activities	Advisor	Paraplanner/ Marketing Assistant	Assistant	Firm	Resources
Analysis Software					
4.1 Research case analysis software necessary for the chosen financial service platform: • Comprehensive • Modular • Investment • Insurance • Group Research case analysis software for the following: • Client education materials • Client need calculators • Presentation suites	X	S		S	Peer recommendations Affordability Vendor reputation Firm sponsorship Demo copies provided by vendor's Web site Write-ups in professional publications
4.2 Evaluate necessary software.	X	S		S	
4.3 Purchase and install necessary software.	X	S		S	
4.4 Learn the capabilities of the software.	X	S			
4.5 Establish a training process for teaching the software to others.	X	S		S	

Note: X denotes primary accountability person, and S denotes shared responsibility person.

4.6	Create a Case Development progress flowchart based on the chosen financial service platform: • Case name • Checklist of discovery items normally collected and the date received • Date: Exploratory underwriting started for insurance case rating • Date: First draft • Dates: Revisions • Date: Completed case ready for presentation • Dates: Case presentation by type of meeting (education, consultation, ask-to-buy) • Implementation: Products placed, assets transferred (Refer here to specific product and investment issues and/or underwriting checklists as in the Sales Process system.) • Anticipated compensation • Actual compensation paid out	X	S	S	

Assemble Material

4.7	Collect discovery material into a client file: Advisor's notes and fact finder.		X	S	CRM
4.8	Collect discovery material into a client file: Clients' statements and documents.		X	S	CRM
4.9	Copy documentation as needed, and return originals to clients.		X	S	

(continued)

Figure 7.2

(continued)

Case Development Activities	Advisor	Paraplanner/ Marketing Assistant	Assistant	Firm	Resources
Data Transfer					
4.10 Data transfer: Into comprehensive financial planning analysis program.		X			Financial Planning software
4.11 Data transfer: Into investment hypothetical scenarios.		X			Portfolio construction and management software
4.12 Data transfer: Into asset allocation/ reallocation program.		X			"
4.13 Data transfer: Into life insurance illustration program.		X			Proprietary software
4.14 Data transfer: Into DI, LTC, other product illustration programs.		X			"
4.15 Data transfer: Into group retirement or benefits programs.					"
4.16 Request and assemble quotes from vendors: • Individual health • Group health • Group retirement • P&C: Auto, home, liability		X	S		"
4.17 Create presentation from assembled vendor quotes.		X	S		

Research and Analysis

				Specialists Wholesalers Home office Firm Planning Unit
4.18	Research clients' current holdings.	X	S	
4.19	Analyze clients' current holdings; provide recommendations.	X	S	
4.20	Creative input into case solutions: Outline analysis direction and objectives: • Form for advisor to record particular case prep preferences • Voice instructions for transcription of particular case prep preferences	X		
4.21	Research tax, investment, and compliance implications.	X	S	
4.22	Consult with strategic partners/joint workers.	X	S	
4.23	Product, investment vehicle selection.	X	S	
4.24	Create what-if scenarios.	X	S	

First Draft

4.25	Complete first draft of case analysis output.		X	
4.26	Make initial review of output.	X		
4.27	Make revisions in case analysis.		X	

Final Draft and Packaging

4.28	Create case summaries to include the following: • Possible objections	S	X	

(continued)

Figure 7.2

(continued)

Case Development Activities	Advisor	Paraplanner/ Marketing Assistant	Assistant	Firm	Resources
• People who will need to buy into the solution for it to be placed • What-if variations					
4.29 Make final review of case output prior to packaging for presentation.	X				
4.30 Package presentation: Executive summary.	S	X			Presentation template
4.31 Package presentation: Support analysis output.		X			
4.32 Package presentation: Support paperwork: • Prospectus and other compliance paperwork • Prefilled applications, rollovers, transfers		X	S		
Connect to Sales Process System					
4.33 Implementation: (Refer here to the specific product and investment issues and/or underwriting checklists in the Sales Process system.)		X	S	S	
4.34 Prepare issued policies for placement and signatures as needed: (Refer to the delivery section of the Sales Process system.)		S	X		

158

8

Infrastructure Business System 5: Time Management

When I called Steve for our second scheduled practice management consultation, I got his voice-mail. This happens occasionally when an advisor is finishing up a call with a client. So I left a message and waited for his call back. Ten minutes passed. Still no call from Steve. This was unusual. Steve was in his third year as an advisor. He had joined a financial services firm in North Carolina, and he wanted to eventually move from being an insurance and investment generalist to a fee-based financial planner. He had originally contacted me earlier in the year to assess his practice and help in the transition.

Another five minutes passed. So I called back, hoping nothing dire had happened to him. He picked up right away.

"Sorry," he began. "I've just gotten so far behind. I haven't worked on last month's action items, and I'm not prepared today."

"OK, let's take a step back," I answered. "Where are you at this moment?"

"At my desk."

"Describe your desk."

Steve laughed. "It's a mess. Stuff piled everywhere, with some additional piles on the floor. There's the need-to-do-now pile and the need-to-do-tomorrow pile and a nice-to-do pile."

"At least you have a system." I said.

"Yeah, right. Stuff is slipping through the cracks, and if I screw up a piece of paperwork, it comes back to haunt me!"

"Sounds like we need to get a handle on your time before we do any other work on your practice."

"Yes! I'm getting really frustrated," he sighed.

Steve is not alone. Of the hundreds of advisor practices I've assessed and studied over the years, the one business system in which advisors consistently score themselves the lowest is Time Management. Advisors, like the general population, never seem to have enough time to "get everything done."

This is somewhat baffling. Enter "time management" into Google and there are 98 million hits. Plug it into Amazon's search engine and you get 270 suggested products and an invitation to join a Time Management discussion forum. My own library of materials collected over the years contains more than 50 Time Management articles, books, audiotapes, manuals, and scribbled notes. There is no shortage of resources.

My purpose in this chapter is not to revolutionize or rewrite the Time Management canon. We'll simply take a look at some tools and perspectives that have worked for advisors in their practices. Steve will be our focal point. Steve has made solid progress, though not without some bumps and bruises. Looking back over that span of four years, we identified two overarching goals of managing an advisor's time: (1) maximize the advisor's genius time, and (2) delegate the rest.

Maximize the Advisor's Genius Time

In the course of studying advisor practices, I've been able to assemble some statistics that can guide us in our Time Management journey.

The median workweek for advisors in Emerging and Mature practices is 50 hours. There are those who are less ambitious and work a 30-hour week. On the other end are the workaholics who put in an 80-hour week. The median—those in the middle of the sample—is 50 hours. New advisors who survive into their third year work an average of 62 hours per week in their first two years.

We have identified the four areas of the advisor's genius:

1. Relationship Building
2. Relationship Maintenance and Growth
3. Inspiring People to Action
4. Solving Problems Creatively and Interpreting Information

In a perfect Time Management world, the advisor would be spending all of his time in those four activities. Everything else he will have delegated away to a support team. In fact, a practice that has achieved the Prime life cycle stage would even have the routine aspects of the four genius areas outsourced.

Sound farfetched? The Core Four business systems have been created around that very notion. By breaking down all the elements of the Client Acquisition, Client Management, Sales Process, and Case Development systems into best practices operations checklists, we are able to see what tasks have the potential to be outsourced. These activities—the advisor's genius time—include the following:

Client Acquisition
- Meeting with centers of influence and top clients to gather introductions
- Networking in business, public, or personal groups
- Calling on the phone or meeting in person with top prospects

Client Management
- Reviews with top-tier clients, annually or more frequently

Sales Process
- Initial interviews
- Discovery meetings
- Presentations
- Closes (ask-to-buy meetings)
- Delivery meetings

Case Development
- Studying first drafts and making recommendations
- Researching and preparing cases

A Prime practice advisor will spend 30 to 35 hours a week in these genius activities. An advisor in a Mature practice should be spending 25 to 30 hours in this genius zone. That's half (or more) of the 50 that comprise an average workweek. The advisor in an Emerging practice should aim for 20 to 25 hours a week in these Core Four activities, while a new advisor in her Developing stage might only manage 15 to 20 hours a week, mostly in the Client Acquisition and Sales Process systems.

These are the hours for which the advisor is highly compensated. There is a saying from a seasoned veteran to the young advisor: "In your early years, you will be severely underpaid. In your later years, you'll be severely overpaid." As the advisor grows in experience and wisdom, an hour with a client becomes more and more valuable.

Steve's practice was initially assessed in our first year together with a score of 428, placing it in the mid-Emerging range. We began with a target of 20 hours per week in balanced genius activities. It is necessary to maintain a balance. An advisor who spends most of his 20 hours in the Case Development world is not out proactively seeing anyone. A healthy blend of all the core activities is desirable.

We began with the fact that there are 168 hours in a week. Steve agreed that we could schedule 50 work hours in an ideal week. So we put together a grid to account for all 168 hours. We took a look at his calendar and broke the work hours out into the activities he was doing most often. Finally, we highlighted the "gray" time, which consists of the hours spent in his genius pursuits, those directly producing revenue for his practice. The result was Figure 8.1. We agreed that there were 45 weeks a year that we would measure, not all 52. With holidays, vacations, company conferences, and family considerations, we were willing to see 7 of those weeks be fragmented.

There were 8 genius hours identified in the Sales Process, 6 hours in Client Acquisition, 2 in Client Management, and 4 in Case Development. We would shoot for a mix of these 20 each full workweek in year 1. Let's compare this with Steve's year-3 model week (Figure 8.2).

As his practice matured, Steve began shifting his time to encompass more genius time while keeping the same 50-hour week. Notice that there are now 28 hours devoted to core activities. This would coincide with the Mature practice's goal of 25 to 30 genius hours. Some of the differences from year 1 to year-3 in Steve's practice include the following:

> *Personal.* Family time increased as his children entered preschool and kindergarten. This time was gained from stealing some time from physical and spiritual maintenance and community activities.
>
> *Sales Process.* An additional 3 hours for face-to-face meetings aimed at inspiring people to take action.
>
> *Client Acquisition.* This took 1 hour less due to a stronger referral process.
>
> *Client Management.* An increase in client reviews from 2 hours to 7 was a natural result of the growth of his client base from 120 to 250 during the intervening three years. The time is taken from the client service area as a result of bringing on a marketing/ administrative hybrid assistant. Within a year and a half, Erika reached a proficiency level to enable her to take on nearly all the service work.

Figure 8.1

Steve's Model Week for Year 1

Category	Hours to Allocate	Day(s) Preference
Personal		
Sleep	45	All
Recreation: Nonphysical	20	All
Family commitments	33	All
Physical maintenance	10	T Th Sa
Spiritual maintenance	5	W Su
Community commitments	5	M W Sa
Total	118	
Sales Process Face-to-Face Appointments		
Initial interviews	2	T W Th
Fact finders/discovery	3	T W Th
Other sales process follow-up	3	M-F
Presentations and closes	2	T W Th
Deliveries	1	T W Th
Total	11	
Client Acquisition		
Centers of influence	1	M-F
Network groups	1	M-F
Prospecting: Phone	4	M-F

(*continued*)

Figure 8.1

(Continued)

Prospecting: Research	1	M-F
Total	7	
Client Management		
Client (quarterly or annual) reviews	2	T W Th
Service work: Phone	3	M F
Service work: Paperwork and research	3	M F
Total	8	
Case Development		
Case preparation: Analysis and research	4	M-F
Case paperwork; data entry	8	M-F
Total	12	
Other		
Regular supervision sessions	0.5	F
Regularly scheduled meetings	3	M W F
Study and education	3	M-F
Administration	2	M-F
Staff meetings and staff development	0.5	M
Travel time	3	M-F
Total	12	
Week total	168	
Gray genius hours	20	

Figure 8.2

Steve's Model Week for Year 3

Category	Hours to Allocate	Day(s) Preference
Personal		
Sleep	45	All
Recreation: Nonphysical	23	All
Family commitments	37	All
Physical maintenance	7	T Th Sa
Spiritual maintenance	3	W Su
Community commitments	3	M W Sa
Total	118	
Sales Process Face-to-Face Appointments		
Initial interviews	2	T W Th
Fact finders/discovery	4	T W Th
Other sales process follow-up	3	M-F
Presentations and closes	3	T W Th
Deliveries	2	T W Th
Total	14	
Client Acquisition		
Centers of influence	1	M-F
Network groups	1	M-F
Prospecting: Phone	3	M-F

(*continued*)

Figure 8.2

(Continued)

Prospecting: Research	1	M-F
Total	6	

Client Management		
Client (quarterly or annual) reviews	7	T W Th
Service work: Phone	0.5	M F
Service work: Paperwork and research	0.5	M F
Total	8	

Case Development		
Case preparation: Analysis and research	5	M-F
Case paperwork; data entry	5	M-F
Total	10	

Other		
Regular supervision sessions	0.5	F
Regularly scheduled meetings	2	M W F
Study and education	3	M-F
Administration	2	M-F
Staff meetings and staff development	1.5	M
Travel time	3	M-F
Total	12	
Week total	168	
Gray genius hours	28	

Case Development. This time decreased from 12 to 10 hours. While Steve still does most of this work himself, he has begun to see that the majority of his case work is fairly routine and he delegates it. Eventually, Steve would like to have just 4 hours of case analysis, devoting the difference, 6 hours, to networking into a target market and allowing for family time flexibility.

Other. In the last category, not much has changed. He is now spending an hour and a half meeting with Erika per week, and he has one less meeting to go to in his firm as he has gained seniority.

Tracking Steve's actual income dollars tells a strong story. In compensation discussions, as we'll see in Chapter 11, things can get rather convoluted and even unintelligible. With Steve, we took his actual reported earnings for the three years from his tax returns. This included income from his primary company, outbrokerage, and W-2 earnings. In the first year, his gross income from these sources was $59,100. Year 2 yielded $73,455. Year 3 it had increased to $136,800. That's an increase of $63,345, or 87 percent, from year 2 to year 3.

We can compare those income figures to the number of genius hours Steve had been putting in. He averaged 16.5 of these hours per week in year 1, with no Erika. In year 2, with Erika in a steep learning curve for six months, it rose to 22. Year 3, with Erika fully engaged, he held an average of 28 genius hours per week.

The following table summarizes Steve's growth. Note that we assumed that there were 45 complete workweeks in Steve's average year taking into account holidays and fragments of weeks away due to conferences, family vacation, and illness.

Steve's Progress	Year 1	Year 2	Year 3
Gross income	$59,100	$73,455	$136,800
Average genius hours worked per week	16.5	22.0	28.0
Total genius hours worked per year (45 workweeks)	742.5	990.0	1,260.0
Productivity per genius hour (income/annual genius hours)	$79.60	$74.20	$108.57
Erika's status	None	6-month learning curve	Full time

It is interesting to note that Steve's productivity per genius hour in year 2 dipped from year 1. This was expected as he was spending time finding, hiring, and training Erika in year 2. Once up and running, however, the productivity per genius hour soared in year 3.

I have been assembling statistics as to how much an assistant is worth to an Emerging practice that grows into its Mature phase. As a working number, I was telling Steve that an investment in a full-time hybrid marketing/administrative assistant, once up to speed, should increase revenues by a factor of two times that investment. This was with the very important caveat that the advisor was to use the hours freed up by the assistant for core genius activities and not for personal time. Steve, an avid golfer, pushed back on that.

"If I golf more with the right people like clients, centers of influence, and prospects—that qualifies, right?" He had me on that one.

"I'll need names and results," I challenged. "We need to know how successful these rounds are." So we began tracking Steve's golf index, pitting rounds played versus prospects gained versus income generated.

Erika's compensation in the third year we tracked was a $25,000 base with $4,000 in quarterly bonuses for a total of $29,000. Steve was hitting his quarterly goals, so the company paid half of Erika's bonuses. Steve was out of pocket $27,000. That investment resulted in $63,345 of additional income, or 2.3 times his investment in her. This was consistent with my research. Erika received a raise going into the following year, to a $30,000 base plus quarterly bonuses. Steve's production has continued to grow as he's been migrating to a financial planning platform.

As for Steve's golf index, between July of the first year and July of the second year, he played 24 rounds of 18 holes that could be considered business related. Of the 24 rounds, he generated an average of two new prospects each time. These 48 prospects so far have resulted in 13 meetings and 10 new clients. Each new client has generated $5,120 in revenue through fees and commissions. So Steve's golf index is $213.33, the amount he makes each time he plays a business round. His goal for the next 12-month period is to get the index to $250.00.

Back to Steve's model week. His success at hitting the 20 hours of gray genius time each week in year 1 didn't fare as well as we had hoped. On average, he scored 16.5 hours a week in year 1, falling short mostly in the Sales Process area. This had the net effect of convincing him that he could not avoid hiring an assistant.

But Steve is hardheaded, and he wasn't about to invest in anything that didn't come with a prospectus. So for the first three months of the second year, we plotted what we should have this new person do and the quickest, most efficient way to do the training that would be necessary. We used the prototypes of the best practices operations manual checklists found at the end of each business system chapter. By the time he pulled the trigger and hired Erika, he had a comprehensive job description for her. He understood that for the balance of the second year, she would have marginal impact on his productivity. The payoff was to be in the third year, when he would actually execute the 28 genius hours to their fullest. And indeed, Steve averaged 28 genius hours in year 3.

Delegate the Rest

Steve understood that his Time Management system would never be possible without an assistant. Remember that growth from the Emerging life cycle stage into Mature requires a conversion from an independent mindset to interdependence. Interdependence requires support and interaction with people.

Some companies and firms provide a good deal of support, usually on the administrative side. This can replace the need for a dedicated assistant up to a point. These support people are usually pooled to work with a group of advisors. Sometimes the advisor's production is such that a full-time assistant is provided by the firm. As we have been working through this book, each business system has a checklist in which there are columns for both a marketing assistant and an administrative assistant. The following Time Management system pieces are best practices that can be implemented in whatever configuration you are operating within.

Telephone and E-Mail Screening

One of the most time-consuming areas in an advisor's practice is dealing with unwanted and unproductive phone calls and e-mails. An issue faced by an advisor making an outbound call to a busy prospect is how to get through the gatekeeper. From a Time Management perspective, let's turn that around: who's *your* gatekeeper?

Do you want to be constantly interrupted? We know that each time someone is distracted by a phone ringing or ring-toning, that person loses productivity. The advisor looks at the caller ID and makes a decision to pick up or not. If he doesn't pick up, he thinks about the caller for a moment before refocusing, which takes an additional minute. If he does pick up, he ventures into a conversation. We all know that most advisors enjoy talking and one conversation thread leads to another and suddenly 15 minutes is gone. Yes, it's a good client who needs some hand-holding. Yes, you need to talk to the service person at the home office. However, you also need to know how to balance those decisions.

Key Issues to Consider

There are many issues to consider when setting up a phone and e-mail system, including the following:

- The phone systems in use around the country vary widely technologically—some are advanced, some are impersonal, and some are broken and awaiting repair.
- The need for having a receptionist varies according to the phone system. Having a live voice answer the phone is great, but it's cheaper to read caller ID or have the caller punch in an extension after consulting a menu.
- Cell phones, PDAs, iPhones, or land lines? Each advisor and client has a preferred way of communication. My own advisor, Mike, seems to call me on a different line each time—work number, home number, or cell phone. Personal and business e-mail addresses can be similarly juxtaposed.
- The skill levels of all the associates involved in the advisor's world vary. It seems that just when a person gets proficient and things are running smoothly, that person is replaced and the learning curve starts up all over again.
- Privacy issues are compounding the simple phone call. Who's a do-not-call person and who isn't? Defining that fine line at the state and federal levels and in the company compliance departments can be confusing.
- How willing is the advisor to allow someone else to access his business inbox?
- Trust levels and politics can affect the decision about a phone system. A person who is able to direct calls might have a bias for one advisor or another, be on a power trip, or simply have a quirky personality beloved by some and reviled by others.

The following gatekeeping process will reflect those and perhaps other factors. It all begins with segmenting your client base, first discussed in Chapter 5. Once segmented, the following suggested flow is for a Mature practice.

The point person, an assistant, or combination of receptionist/assistant receives all incoming calls and e-mail on behalf of the advisor, thus becoming the gatekeeper.

C-Level Clients

Calls and e-mails from C-level clients should not be initially dealt with by the advisor. On the call, the point person asks if he can help and takes care of the issue or hands it off to someone who can. If the caller insists on speaking to the advisor or has a strong personal relationship with the advisor, a message is taken (not sent to voice-mail) and passed on to the advisor to take care of when convenient. If the caller would like investment advice or another action requiring specific licensure, a designated person should be assigned to pick up this work. Otherwise, it falls back into the advisor's lap via message. In an e-mail from a C-level client with a request, the point person deals with it or passes it along to someone who can. If the sender continues to insist on the advisor's attention to the matter, the e-mail thread can then be sent to the advisor for follow-up.

B-Level Clients

Calls and e-mails from B-level clients should primarily be dealt with by the marketing assistant who is empowered by the advisor to cultivate these clients to possibly grow to A-level status. On the call, the point person asks if she can help and takes care of the issue or hands it off to someone who can. If the caller insists on speaking to the advisor or has a strong personal relationship with the advisor, the caller is sent to voice-mail for the advisor to take care of when convenient. If the caller would like investment advice or another action requiring specific licensure, a designated person may be assigned to pick up this work, or the advisor might want to do it as an opportunity to deepen the relationship. In an e-mail from a B-level client with a request, the point person deals with it or passes it along to someone who can. If the sender continues to insist on the advisor's attention to the matter, the e-mail thread can then be sent to the advisor for follow-up.

A-Level Clients

The best-practice definition of an A-level client includes clients but can also mean a prominent center of influence or a decision maker representing a potential client. For the most part, the advisor should handle these calls and e-mails. On an A-level client call, the point person asks if he can help and takes care of the issue or hands it off to someone who can if there's no need for the advisor's input. The advisor is informed of what transpired. If the caller prefers speaking to the advisor, the call is sent through if the advisor is available. Otherwise, the caller is sent to voice-mail for the advisor to take care of as soon as possible. An instant message heads-up might also inform the advisor that an A-level client message is waiting. Advisors who give their private cell number to top clients are taking a risk of the client abusing the privilege. In an e-mail from an A-level client with a simple request, the point person deals with it or passes it along to someone who can, copying the advisor all the way. Otherwise, the A-level client's e-mails stay in the advisor's inbox.

Calendars

Let's start with the ideal, best-practice calendaring system. In our technologically sophisticated world, we can expect to achieve some semblance of integration among all the necessary tools for the financial services trade. In this integration, we will find all manner of time efficiency. Witness the perfect client database that contains all of our clients and prospects:

- We are able to input personal (soft) information about them into our system. This soft information can be retrieved to find sets of people with common interests and belonging to similar organizations. Clients can be householded, with relatives linking to each other. There is also a link to other nonfamily interested parties that form the clients' contact networks.
- There is a business side to the database that is integrated with the personal information. People in a particular business are connected and viewable on the personal side.
- Our database also has all of our clients' product and investment information (hard data). Product values are updated daily, and investment values are available in real time. Again, this information can be cross referenced, sliced, and diced to find opportunities and common characteristics.
- A calendar function exists in this database. Each scheduled activity links to the person it concerns and is recorded in their history. This calendar insists that each scheduled activity be completed by posting an outcome and next activity. By completing an activity, the advisor can post follow-up notes, transcribe client information, and schedule the next client contact. The calendar also synchronizes with the advisor's PDA and Microsoft Outlook.

- The calendar contains a to-do list, with activities that roll over until they are dealt with. Once dealt with, the results are posted to the client's record.
- E-mail can be sent to the client's file and attached as a record.
- Documents can be scanned and saved, as well as attached to the client's record.
- The entire system is backed up continually because it's Web based and utilizes mirrored servers.

Got one of those? If you do, congratulations! The closest I've encountered off-the-shelf is from E-Z Data. It's called SmartOffice, and it's been successfully adopted by companies and independent advisors I've worked with.

The best-practice calendar is linked to client hard and soft information, a to-do list, and other team members' calendars. The calendaring should be in real time to permit on-the-fly changes from remote locations and on the road.

That said, there are many successful, Mature practice advisors who prefer a paper calendar. Franklin Planners, Time Tactics, At-a-Glance, DayRunner, and many other organizers have their loyal subscribers. These are also to-do list repositories. A good paper system plus a strong database can complement each other quite nicely. Other advisors are PDA addicts, with particularly strong advocates for the BlackBerry, iPhone, and by the time you read this, the next greatest tele/calendar/organizer tool. Again, these may not be linked to a database, but they can be synchronized in some way to provide continuity with client records.

In an advisor's practice, it's usually a good idea to have a calendar point person who regularly ensures that all calendars are coordinated. An advisor's next workday should be planned out, preferably the day or evening before. This gives the day structure and purpose, making it less likely that distractions will occur.

In order to prevent dates from "sneaking up" on the advisor and team, a master calendar should integrate all the following:

- Client, prospect, other key business contact appointments
- Seminar and other planned prospecting or client events
- Birthdays for clients and key contacts
- Holidays
- The local firm's calendar of training, educational, and marketing activities
- The parent company's calendar of deadlines, conferences, and promotions

- Advisor and team vacations and important events
- Continuing-education and other compliance-driven dates

It's also a good idea to keep a year-at-a-glance calendar posted to keep a longer-range perspective in mind.

Dealing with Time Wasters

Steve, you will recall, had a cluttered desk with piles of paper and files all over the place. It took him two years and Erika's organizational skills to finally have a "pretty clean" desk.

"It is powerful," Steve admitted. "Coming in to a clean work environment is psychologically positive. I feel proactive. The clutter always made me feel like I needed to catch up before moving on—dragging me down."

Other issues we faced in our battle to get Steve more genius time included the following:

> Free advice. Steve's door was always open. At first, he actually had no door, being in a cubicle in the firm's bullpen. It was easy for other advisors to stop by his desk and ask questions, get his opinion on a case, or simply to chat. When he was given a small office in year 2, Erika took over his old cubicle. Steve had more control over his interruptions with the addition of the door. For his case analysis and telephone prospecting times, the door was shut. Otherwise, he kept it open and kept his reputation intact as being "friendly and accessible," as he put it.
>
> *Firm meetings.* These meetings were inevitable and usually had some substance. While Steve managed to show up on time, others did not. Politely but firmly, he set a policy of showing up on time and leaving on time. After it happened a few times that Steve, a good producer, left at the scheduled end time but before the meeting was over, management slowly adapted. Meetings, both required and optional, are still two hours of his time a week, but just two hours.
>
> *To-do list.* Keep the to-do list under 50 items at all times. We started with an unwieldy rolling-over-daily to-do list of over 150 items, from people to call, service work, follow-ups on client paperwork, to responding to requests from home office and firm personnel, his wife's car's mechanic, and his church's youth minister. He'd get a few tasks done each day and added a few more. Once Erika was aboard, we triaged the to-do list. All personal items were moved out and kept separately. Items for

Erika to handle went next, and what was left required Steve's personal attention. There were 70 of those. By later in the year, his business to-do list had cracked the 50 barrier. Erika's was similarly at 50, and his personal life to-do list was under 15.

Monotasking. Steve rediscovered the art of monotasking. A requirement of his genius time was to unplug his Bluetooth ear piece and put away his BlackBerry. All genius activities got his full attention. "Once I really implemented that rule," Steve said, "the people I'm with seem to reciprocate and I got their undivided attention. The pressure is lessened without the potential distractions of a ring-tone or e-mail beep."

E-mail one-touch. Steve has adopted a one-touch approach to handling e-mail. As he opens each message, he determines the nature of the message, using Stephen Covey's definitions from *The 7 Habits of Highly Effective People.* If a message is deemed "urgent and important," Steve deals with it immediately and deletes it. Otherwise, it stays in the inbox. If it's "important but not urgent," he transfers it to the to-do folder or forwards it to Erika for handling. "Urgent but not important" messages are dealt with immediately if they can be responded to in two minutes or less and then deleted. Otherwise, they go into the to-do folder or they are forwarded to Erika. "Not urgent and not important" messages are immediately deleted or sent to appropriate folders.

Procrastination

Prior to Erika's arrival, Steve was a self-admitted procrastinator. Part of this had to do with the clutter in his cubicle and the sense of dread he had upon sitting down in the midst of it all. He eventually got that fixed but only with Erika's assistance. Another factor in Steve's tendency toward procrastination was that he "worked best under pressure."

To be sure, the tyranny of a deadline is a strong motivator, yet it rarely produces one's best efforts. With Steve, it had become commonplace to get a presentation together just in time for the appointment to present it. He would run around printing out illustrations and hypotheticals at the last minute. He'd quickly assemble the necessary paperwork for the sale and would often find something missing at the presentation. After completing the appointment, he'd return to the office and realize he'd missed a required signature. Back he went to obtain it. While this was frustrating, it was also rewarded.

His sales success was hailed in the office. Steve's name was constantly in the top two or three of the under-five-year advisors at the firm. He was held up as a role model for his consistency and sales statistics.

Despite the acclaim, Steve knew he wasn't doing as thorough a job as he wanted to for his clients. However, the thrill of being at the top outweighed the duty to his clients, and he continued to procrastinate on case prep, frantically preparing for appointments and missing opportunities. He rationalized that "any money being left on the table today I'll be able to get tomorrow."

But his to-do list continued to grow into a monster. He was chronically late for appointments. After blowing a sale because he rushed a presentation, we regrouped. We developed a case preparation checklist that had to be completed the day before a presentation. In his preoffice days, he bought a roll of masking tape and put a strip across the entrance to his cubicle, creating a metaphoric door when he wanted to focus on case work. His fellow advisors respected his boundary. Steve's best work is now "done when I'm *not* under pressure."

Accountability

Accountability is perhaps the most important ingredient in one's Time Management. Like dieting, when left to one's own devices, it's short lived and marginally successful. Join a Weight Watchers group where the scales are viewed by your peers and the weight tends to stay off longer.

Steve really began to take control of his time when he empowered Erika to run his calendar. He asked that she be firm and call him on it if he was getting sloppy in returning calls in a timely manner or letting Case Development opportunities slip by. "She really does keep the machine humming," Steve said. "She holds me accountable."

Time Management System Best Practices Checklist

The Time Management System Best Practices Checklist is shown in Figure 8.3. There are 23 specific steps in this checklist. It's the blueprint for the fifth section of your best practices operations manual.

In Figure 8.3, we have assumed that the advisor is with a broker/dealer in a detached location, with a full-time administrative assistant and a full-time paraplanner/marketing assistant. The advisor is in a Mature life cycle stage. Each practice is unique, of course, and the checklist can be modified for each advisor.

The resources referred to on the checklist are suggestions based on various best practices observed in the field. Any resource in italics refers to a piece reviewed or illustrated earlier in this chapter.

Figure 8.3

Time Management System Best Practices Checklist

Time Management Activities	Advisor	Marketing Assistant	Administrative Assistant	Firm	Resources
Telephone Calls					
5.1 Call screening: A-level clients, A-level prospects, centers of influence, or other practice VIPs.	X	S			*Screening*
5.2 Call screening: B-level clients, prospects, or others.	S	X			
5.3 Call screening: C-level clients, prospects, or others.		X	S		
5.4 Call screening: Identify criteria for other types of calls that the advisor can take "live," delegate to others, go to voice-mail, or be ignored.	X	S	S		
5.5 Cell phones: Set criteria for business use.	X	S	S		
E-Mail					
5.6 E-mail screening: A-level clients, A-level prospects, centers of influence, or other practice VIPs.	X	S			
5.7 E-mail screening: B-level clients, prospects, or others.		X	S		
5.8 E-mail screening: C-level clients, prospects, or others.		X	S		
5.9 E-mail screening: Identify criteria for responding, filing, forwarding, or deleting.	X	X	S		

Note: X denotes primary accountability person, and S denotes shared accountability person.

Calendar

#	Task				
5.10	Coordinate and monitor a master calendar to avoid conflicts. It can integrate the following: • Client Acquisition functions • Client service functions • Firm events • Marketing events • Joint work with advisors • Company events • Professional events • Key personal and family events • Holidays • Vacations • Education and CE events • Testing for designations • Community events • Bonus and recognition deadlines	S	X	S	S
5.11	Produce an in-advance daily calendar for the advisor with the following: • Activities • Appointments • To-dos	S	X		
5.12	Determine who has access to whose calendars among the team.	X	S	S	
5.13	Coordinate time to synchronize team calendars.		X		

(continued)

179

Figure 8.3

(Continued)

Time Management Activities	Advisor	Marketing Assistant	Administrative Assistant	Firm	Resources
Delegation					
5.14 Determine what can be delegated.	X	S	S		Communication System chapter, Figures 9.2 and 9.3
5.15 Develop delegation skills ("letting go").	X				
Model Week					

5.16 Develop a prototype model week that allows for 25 hours in the following genius activities:
 	
• Client Acquisition:
  ○ Meetings with centers of influence and top clients to gather introductions
  ○ Networking in business, public, or personal groups
  ○ On-the-phone or in-person meeting with top prospects
• Client Maintenance
  ○ Reviews with top-tier clients, annually or more frequently
	X	S	S		

- Sales Process
  - Initial interviews
  - Discovery meetings
  - Presentations
  - Closes (ask-to-buy meetings)
  - Delivery meetings
- Case Development
  - Studying first drafts and making recommendations
  - Case research and preparation

5.17 Communicate model week to team members.	X	X	S	

CRM Database Integration

5.18 CRM should synchronize the following: • Hard data for personal and business clients • Soft data for personal and business clients • Calendar • To-do list • E-mail postings • Document images • Backing up daily	X			

Time Wasters and Procrastination

5.19 Set open-door policy and limit free advice.	X			
5.20 Minimize firm and company meetings.	X			X

(continued)

Figure 8.3
(Continued)

Time Management Activities	Advisor	Marketing Assistant	Administrative Assistant	Firm	Resources
5.21 Limit to-do list: Create a maximum number at any one point.	X	S	S		
5.22 Establish periods of "alone time" for focused projects.	X	S	S		
5.23 Address procrastination issues with team and accountability partners.	X	X	X		
5.23 Conduct a time log exercise to determine time usage patterns.	X	X	X		
Time Management Statistics					
Hours spent per week in genius activities = 25.	X	X			CRM, calendar

9

Infrastructure Business System 6: Communication

The genesis of the Communication system started with a seminal event when I was a training director. In this role I was interviewing all the new and experienced advisors in the firm, which spanned three states, looking for their best business practices to incorporate into the training curriculum. An area I was struggling with was how to help advisors best utilize their assistants. At the time, we had few resources for advisors who wanted to hire, train, and supervise staff. The advisor was on his own to navigate these waters as best he could.

One day, my managing director pulled me into his office and closed the door.

"I have a mission for you," he said in his best *Mission Impossible* voice. "Should you decide to take it, it's confidential."

"All right, what is it?" I asked, intrigued.

"Have you had a chance to visit John Corkoran over in Denton?" John was a senior advisor in a far-flung detached location, easily 200 miles from the Minneapolis office.

"Not yet."

"Good. I want you to arrange to do one of your two-day visits to his office. His production has flattened over the last couple of years, and the new business area is telling me his applications have gotten sloppy."

"So you want me to examine his sales systems?" I assumed.

"Yes, but the important part is for you to dig in and find out about his working relationship with Marge."

"His assistant?" I'd never met her, but I knew Marge had been with John for nearly two years.

"Yes. I'm getting word through the grapevine that she might be planning a harassment lawsuit. Before that happens, I'd like you to explore the situation, take notes, observe their interaction."

I took the assignment. I arranged for a two-day training and development trip to Denton, during which I would interview both John and Marge, possibly suggest some tweaks to their systems, study John's marketing plan, and prepare a "best practices report."

All seemed calm as I set up shop. Both John and Marge greeted me warmly. I set up the individual meetings and then the joint meeting with both of them the next day.

John and I met first. We discussed his prospecting, referrals, markets, and production year-to-date. Then I asked about the reported "sloppy paperwork."

"Ah!" His eyes widened. "Yes. I think Marge may be getting dumber. This is confidential, right?" he quickly added.

"That comment certainly is. But the bigger issues aren't," I responded.

John paused, pondering this. "Yes, well, she used to be very good at catching all the little things I missed or forgot. I sell it; her job is to get it issued. Now she's missing things all the time, and new business is on my ass, and that will probably trigger a compliance unit audit, which I do not want." He huffed. "I think I'll fire her."

"Fire her?" I echoed. "For what reason?"

"Incompetence, for one. I hate to think of bringing in a new girl, but I've done it before and will do it again." He sighed. "What do I do to deserve this?"

I waited a moment, then asked: "How many assistants have you had in your 22 years?"

"Hmm," John started, gazing up to mentally count them. "Lucy was the first when I was five years in the business. Then Audrey, Ann, Connie, uh, Janet, Brenda, and now Marge."

"Who was the best of them?"

"Connie lasted the longest, three years."

"Why did she leave?"

"They had a baby, and she decided to be a stay-at-home mom."

I did some quick math. "Seventeen years, seven assistants. About two and a half years each. Sounds like a high turnover to me. Any common threads in their reasons for leaving?"

"What can I say," John replied. "Good help is hard to find out here. They all left for different reasons. Better pay, better hours, moving, getting married, babies. You name it."

"And Marge? I asked.

"Regressing, like I said. She doesn't seem to care about the quality of her work anymore. Once I break them in, they leave. It's all very frustrating." John then proceeded to give me a laundry list of complaints about her, from phone etiquette ("too snippy") to service work ("it took her three weeks to process an address change!").

We wrapped up his interview. Marge was next. As soon as the door closed behind her, she flared up.

"I don't know what you can do, but I'm ready to snap."

"How so?"

"Him," she pointed toward his office. "How he treats me is unacceptable."

"In what way?"

"Verbal abuse. I mess up, and I get yelled and screamed at, and berated. Calls me 'Margie' and I specifically told him I'm 'Marge.' I'm 'his girl' when he talks with clients about me. I won't bend over anymore to pick up something on the floor when he's nearby. Chances are I'll get a wolf whistle."

"So why don't you quit?" I asked.

"That's too easy. I've talked with other assistants he's had, and they have had similar experiences. They chickened out and quit, I want more." Her anger was palpable.

"Suing him?"

"Yes, for verbal abuse. I have some people next door who will testify to his outbursts at me."

I pondered what I was hearing. On the outside, John was a type-A personality, to be sure. He tended to be impatient and to micromanage. He was in his late fifties, and he had a reputation at firm meetings for being opinionated and disrespectful. His production, while it had flattened, was also the third highest in the entire firm. This earned him the right to be demanding and arrogant. He exercised that right often.

None of the support staff at the main office wanted to deal with him.

"You've been here almost two years," I continued. "Is this behavior new?"

Marge thought for a few seconds. "It's been building. For the first year, he was fine. He can be kind of a jerk, but tolerable. In the past six months, though, he's gotten downright nasty and mean."

"Any idea what's caused this to happen in the last six months?"

"Nothing specific. He's 20 percent behind last year, and that's frustrating him. He lost a big case a few months back that he hasn't recovered from. He's more stressed out than ever."

"So you've pulled back on checking his paperwork before it goes in?" I asked.

She seemed surprised. "I ... well, yes."

"Sort of a subversion—undermining him," I suggested.

She stared at me and simply smiled.

How did this toxic relationship develop? I've seen this dysfunctional advisor/assistant interplay in many practices. John and Marge were on the negative end of the relationship scale, to be sure. What I was witnessing at the time was the logical outcome of not having a system in place to bring an assistant on board. Looking deeper, I was caught in a classic trap of triangulation.

Triangulation happens when two parties (Marge and John) refuse to talk to each other about the real issues they are encountering in their relationship. Instead, they turn to a third party (in this case, me) to vent and do the communicating for them. Triangulation can occur anywhere, any time where two or more people are unwilling to share honest feelings. Often, that third party will relish the role and proceed to play the other two off of each other. It's like a child's manipulating her separated parents for her own ends. Triangulation keeps the psychiatrists, negotiators, and marriage counselors in business. It has a firm hold in the financial services world, from advisors to firms to home offices.

Our goal here is to address how to avoid triangulation in the advisor's practice.

John's serial hiring of assistants and having them quit was a case of chronic triangulation. I was learning a big lesson in being the third party: I didn't like being in that position. As I would discover the following day when the three of us met in the conference room, the failure to communicate stemmed from a particular demon. The demon that we needed to exorcise was unexpressed or poorly expressed expectations. This was the essential cause of our hot-tempered, volcanic, and ultimately unsatisfying meeting. Suffice it to say that in our three-person group encounter, John angrily made a point by breaking an arm on his swivel chair, and after that Marge threw a notebook at him, hitting him in the chest. I survived unscathed.

She did quit that day. Marge began a harassment lawsuit shortly thereafter. I was interviewed by her attorney, and I gave statements to our law department. After that, it was hushed up, and I didn't find out what had happened until a year later. John remained in business but had paid a substantial sum to Marge to convince her to not defame him publicly. When John did eventually hire another assistant, she was from a neighboring town. Marge had poisoned his name as an employer in Denton. His clientele was drawn from a large region, so the overall impact on his practice was diluted.

Preventing unexpressed or poorly expressed expectations from occurring became a best-practice mantra of mine ever since. From this seed grew the concept of a Communication system, rather than a staffing system. The Communication system envelops the process of creating a strong team. In addition, it examines how the advisor communicates with clients and important nonclients.

Communication with Administrative and Marketing Assistants

Hiring and Selecting

The Mature practice advisor has need of two full-time resources: one for marketing and one for administration. Sometimes these are two distinct people. Often, the advisor's firm provides the equivalent of a full-time administrative resource. The advisor will then need to hire only a marketing person. When an advisor is in his Emerging life cycle stage, growing into Maturity, a normal first step is to hire a hybrid marketing/administrative person.

Many practices have one or more assistants composing their staff. The staff performs multiple duties for the advisor in both the marketing and administrative sides of the business. The Prime performer has gone beyond staff and has surrounded herself with a team of advocates. Staff members perform tasks. Team members are advocates of the advisor and the practice.

Certainly team members must complete tasks and routine duties. But for an advocate assistant these tasks and duties are done with a proactive mindset. For example, a staff person would take a service call for an address change, gather the appropriate information, thank the client for calling, and process the change. The team advocate member would take the same call and probe the client on why she moved, ask about the new neighborhood, collect new demographic information to help determine if there might be a need to adjust her financial profile (growing family, larger mortgage), and initiate a housewarming card. The advocate assistant then will post a to-do on the advisor's calendar to make a follow-up call after the move.

Team advocates are dedicated to deepening client relationships, uncovering new prospecting opportunities, and enhancing the reputation of the practice. These advocates are empowered to hold the advisor and his team accountable for implementation of plans and achievement of objectives, a power that is particularly useful in our discussion of team meetings.

Before beginning, two important notes:

1. We will be covering compensation for an assistant in Chapter 11 on the Financial Management infrastructure system.
2. The information below is not meant to be a replacement for a human resources (HR) department. It's offered in addition to the resources to which you already may have access.

The best-practice sequence of events in the hiring process that addresses the past, present, and future of the candidate is shown in Figure 9.1 and includes the following steps:

1. Creating the job description
2. Creating the ad copy
3. Finding the sources for candidates
4. Screening the candidates
5. Face-to-face interviewing with the candidates
6. Checking the references and testing the candidates

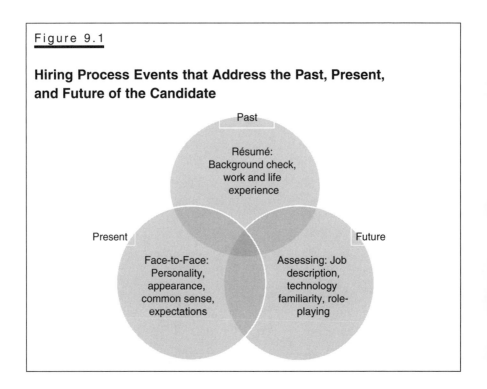

Figure 9.1

Hiring Process Events that Address the Past, Present, and Future of the Candidate

Past

Résumé: Background check, work and life experience

Present

Face-to-Face: Personality, appearance, common sense, expectations

Future

Assessing: Job description, technology familiarity, role-playing

7. Making the offer

8. Creating the personnel file

We will cover Step 1 next. (For best practices, sample material, and guidance on Steps 2 through 8, contact us online at www.praticetools.net.)

Creating the Job Description

There will be a constant theme in the assistant Communication system: clear expectations will carry through the hiring, selecting, and supervising of the assistant. Clear expectations will allow for a strong review process and provide a track for the assistant to grow from being a staff person into an advocate.

Begin with the end in mind: What would you like the assistant to do? What are those tasks that can be delegated in order to free you up to focus on your genius time? The best practices operations manual pages at the end of each of the business system chapters have been designed to do just that. Broken down into small activities, the advisor can choose who should be held responsible for each one.

To speed that process, I have put together two job description checklists, one for marketing (Figure 9.2) and one for administration (Figure 9.3). These distill all those activities into general categories. With these checklists, you can create a unique job description that is based on your practice's needs.

Figure 9.2

Sample Job Description Checklist for a Marketing Assistant

Marketing Assistant Job Duties

Time Management/Calendar

1. Fills advisor's calendar with the following:

   - Client annual reviews

   - Sales Process appointments: Initial, discovery, presentation, and delivery appointments

   - COI and networking meetings

2. Coordinates and updates advisor's calendar:

   - To-do lists

   - Appointments

   - Forward planning

(continued)

Figure 9.2

(Continued)

Client Relationship Management (CRM) Software

  3. Maintains database for the following:

- Client hard product information

- Client soft information

- Prospect tracking

- Client segmentation

  4. Postappointment:

- Transcribes client notes and discovery materials into CRM database

- Fulfills any follow-up

- Creates unique client correspondence

Client Management

  5. Cultivates top clients by way of proactive interaction and client appreciation events

  6. Executes contact protocols for each client segment (newsletters, cards, and so on)

  7. Maintains physical client files to be compliance ready

  8. Culls through C-level clients to determine if they can grow to A or B level

  9. Prepares annual review materials and manages client opportunity inventory

Client Acquisition

  10. Researches and provides advisor with prospect names and names to feed during referral-gathering appointments

  11. Plans and executes seminars and other marketing efforts (campaigns) and manages the follow-up

(continued)

Figure 9.2

(Continued)

Sales Process

12. Creates the discovery letter

13. Tracks activity and sales statistics

14. Executes and tracks trades

15. Packages appointment materials

16. Prefills application information

17. Reviews applications for submission

Case Development

18. Data input

19. Creates routine illustrations, hypotheticals, asset allocations, quotes, and other case prep work

20. Assembles presentation materials

Figure 9.3

Sample Job Description Checklist for an Administrative Assistant

Administrative Assistant Job Duties

Client Management

1. Handles all client service requests

2. Manages routine filing, copying, processing correspondence, and other administrative types of work

3. Helps assemble routine client review materials

4. Helps manage the CRM

(continued)

Figure 9.3

(Continued)

Sales Process

5. Proofs, submits, and monitors new business underwriting/issue requirements and tracking

6. Helps package routine interview/appointment materials

7. Greets visitors

8. Executes routine investment sales transactions and logs incoming securities checks and correspondence (blotter)

Time Management

9. Manages telephone coverage; is the gatekeeper

Communication

10. Manages personnel issues, including hiring, training, and supervision of staff

11. Manages routine mail and e-mail correspondence, incoming and outgoing

12. Keeps the practice's best practices operations manual

13. Is the go-to person in the day-to-day operations of the office

Case Development

14. Helps run back-office routine sales and Case Development functions (illustrations, templates)

Financial Management

15. Manages the practice's budget and cash flow; handles billings and financial records

16. Does internal bookkeeping and accounting for tax purposes

General Business Environment

17. Acts as the practice's compliance officer

18. Manages technology support, software, and hardware

19. Manages licensing issues

20. Orders supplies and forms; manages inventory

Once you have compiled the tasks for the new assistant, ensure that you have a training plan for him to learn these tasks quickly and effectively. This will be covered in more detail in the next chapter on the Education system.

Supervising and Reviewing Performance

Supervising

Now that the assistant is on board, the training process starts (see also Chapter 10). Once the assistant has learned enough and is into the day-to-day flow of the practice, the advisor should have a process for supervising the new assistant. Supervisory styles vary across the board, but they are usually one of three types:

The *micromanager* has a tough time letting go of a task and is constantly checking up on an assistant's progress. This can result in an assistant's feeling suffocated and insecure, not to mention annoyed.

The *abdicator* doles out a task to be done and assumes it gets done, checking back only if something goes haywire. The abdicating advisor risks the results of unclear expectations, as with John and Marge at the beginning of the chapter. The assistant working with this type of advisor often creates her own systems. This is fine if the systems are recorded and transferable. The assistant may also have too much freedom and sometimes can become a compliance risk.

The *monitor* falls in the middle. Stephanie, an advisor in the Bay Area in California, is a proponent of this supervisory style.

"Yes, it took a while to develop," she told me. "I was loath to let go of top client communications. I mean, I grew my practice with them, they know me, and to transfer those relationships to an assistant was difficult. But once Maria was with me for six months, I began to get over it. She was so personable on the phone, and clients would compliment her. Once I decided she was a good fit, we arrived at a good supervisory system.

"We meet daily for 10 minutes or so and review the key events of the day, setting priorities. I make sure she knows how to do the tasks assigned to her or where to go for resources. Then I go off on appointments. I'll check in regularly during the day to see if there any problems or to reprioritize the tasks. At the end of the day, we review the to-do list, either by phone or in person. So that's my supervisory style: assign, monitor, and follow up. Maria responds well to it—she has independence to get the work done but has a sense of urgency because she knows I'll be checking in and expecting results by day's end."

To facilitate strong communication, the best practices are to have daily briefings, as with Stephanie and Maria. But they have one more key element to their Communication system: a weekly, formal meeting. In addition to Maria, Stephanie also has a junior advisor she's mentoring, Samantha, and another assistant, Phil, who does case preparation and splits marketing and administrative duties with Maria. Stephanie, Maria, Sam, and Phil have a weekly, formal meeting throughout the year. Generally, they are held on Friday over the lunch hour. Stephanie shared her agenda, and I've annotated it for general use, as shown in Figure 9.4.

Figure 9.4

Elements of the Formal Team (or Staff) Meeting Agenda

Guiding Principles

1. "Seek first to understand, then to be understood." (Stephen Covey)

2. Ensure that each team member's voice is heard.

3. Keep the big picture in mind—this is a time to focus on strategy and direction as a group.

Time: Thursday, Friday, or Monday, early morning or working lunch. 45 minutes maximum.

Place: Away from the immediate work space.

Who: Anyone who makes regular, significant contributions to the business practice. Have a notetaker record the general points of the meeting and prepare a brief summary at the end.

Topics (Suggested Order)

- Ask the team members for any specific discussion issues that need addressing. Put the issues on a whiteboard or separate list to be addressed at the appropriate time in the agenda. Avoid jumping in and going off on a tangent before the meeting really begins.

- Review previous two weeks' production results and overall progress toward stated goals.

(continued)

Figure 9.4

(Continued)

- Set production expectations for the next two weeks.

- Ensure that calendars are coordinated for next two weeks. Review the specific appointments that are scheduled, and discuss any preparations needed.

- Evaluate model-week expectations for the next period: Is it working? What adjustments need to be made? For example, is the mix of the types of appointments that are actually held meeting the expectations? Is the advisor being freed up to maximize her face-to-face time with clients, prospects, centers of influence and networking opportunities? The rule of thumb is to aim for 25 of these genius hours per week.

- Identify production priorities.

- Review the pending business. Are there any underwriting issues or delays in processing rollovers or trades? Who is the accountable party for taking action?

- Review the anticipated sales to prepare for. How much paperwork can be filled out beforehand?

- Review the prospecting flow and activity, especially referral goals. Get updates on current and projected marketing efforts, such as seminars, mail campaigns, client events, and other community initiatives.

- Review client service issues.

- Review reactive issues (calls-in, stalled service work).

- Review proactive issues (annual reviews scheduled, regular contacts updated, newsletters, birthdays, special outreaches, events, and so on).

- Address technology and/or database issues.

- Address Case Development issues.

- Address financial issues.

(continued)

Figure 9.4

(Continued)

- Identify team training and development needs.

- Discuss any personal issues affecting the team.

- Summarize the key meeting points.

- Assign a deadline for any actions that need one.

- Review who's responsible for any to-do items discussed.

Who facilitates the meeting? Usually, that would be the advisor's role, but explore having another team member rotate through taking charge of the agenda. This could be valuable growth experience for stronger associates. Stephanie usually has Maria lead their weekly sessions. "She is a strong driver," Stephanie reported. "She keeps us on task, whereas I would jump all over the place. We always get to the core issues and spend the necessary time to deliberate them. No time is wasted."

As with a good discovery meeting with a prospect, there are parallel skills for the execution of a successful team meeting. To stimulate discussion among the team members, the meeting facilitator should review the following techniques and strategies to ensure that there is open and honest communication and that all the issues that need to be addressed are brought to the table. Sitting in on two Maria-led meetings with Stephanie's team, I recorded the following statements and questions:

> *Ask for feelings and opinions.* "What is your reaction to … ?" "Why do you say that?"
> *Paraphrase for clarity.* "Let me see if I understand your question." "What I'm hearing is …"
> *Encourage participation.* "We haven't heard from Phil yet. Phil, how do you feel about … ?"
> *Ask for examples.* "Sam, can you give an example of what you mean?"
> *Test for consensus.* "Before we go on to the next topic, let me make sure that we all have agreed to …"
> *Initiate action.* "Stephanie, how would you suggest we proceed on this?"

Explore an idea in more detail. "Are there other things we should consider?"

Share your feelings. "I'm frustrated. Let's take this issue up next week after we do a little research. How do the rest of you feel?"

Reflect on what you think someone is feeling. "Maria, I get the impression you're not satisfied with that answer. Is that right?"

Be supportive. "Let's give Phil a chance to tell it the way he sees it."

Question assumptions. "Your objection assumes that home office will continue to stall on a decision. Is that a good assumption?"

Reverse roles. "Pretend you're an A-level client. How would you perceive this course of action?"

Focus on action items. "We've talked about it; now let's settle on a course of action."

There are a few meeting situations that the team should be aware of and agree to avoid. The facilitator is in the position to recognize and put an early end to them:

- Allowing one person to dominate the discussion
- Encouraging heated arguments
- Tolerating side conversations
- Allowing personal communication devices to be accessed during the meeting
- Getting off on tangents

All of this may sound daunting. There is an art to running a good meeting, and like any artistic endeavor, it takes practice to perfect. "It took us six months of meetings to get it to what you saw," said Stephanie. "But this team is as tight and effective as it's ever been."

Reviewing Performance

The final piece in the Communication system with an assistant is to provide her with a formal feedback meeting at least annually. While it's true that there is daily interaction between the advisor and team members, it's informal communication and doesn't usually address the development of the assistant. As you saw in the weekly meeting agenda, there is a place for addressing training and development needs. This keeps the assistant's progress top of mind. Still, it doesn't provide a one-on-one dialogue with the assistant and advisor on longer-term goals and growth opportunities.

The new assistant will prove himself fairly quickly. If it's not working out, all parties will know within a month and the search will begin anew.

Survival for three months is a good sign, and the new assistant should have a formal 90-day performance review. This represents a generous learning curve for the essential job duties of the position. At this 90-day point, reviewing the job description from the hiring process would be prudent. Taking the duties one by one, check the assistant's progress in mastering each one. In all likelihood, he will have accelerated on one duty (setting appointments) while having difficulty with another (learning the database). It's a good time to revamp the training materials or provide additional resources.

The 90-day point is also normally a point where the assistant's pay gets its first bump for making it that far. Each annual review should then be a point at which compensation is discussed. We will explore this in more detail in Chapter 11.

The annual performance review for the assistant has best-practice elements. Performance feedback is critical because it accomplishes the following:

- Assures that the employee knows exactly where he or she stands and what is expected
- Helps keep performance on track, resolving problems before they become a crisis
- Allows you to support and reward positive outcomes and achievement of goals
- Helps you and the assistant establish a shared vision and objectives
- Avoids loss of time, productivity, and profitability for your team
- Reduces job stress and increases job satisfaction for the assistant

Jay, an advisor in El Paso, Texas, has a format that works well. He has two assistants, Jorge and Venita. They divide up administrative and marketing duties, with Venita skewing more to the administrative side and Jorge to marketing. I spoke to Jay about his performance review process.

"My goal is cross training," Jay states. "I want both of them to be flexible, and if Venita's kids have an issue with school, she can take off and Jorge can handle the day's workload. She doesn't abuse this privilege. We're into our third year as a team, and I've done my second round of annual reviews."

Jay uses a single-page worksheet with numerical evaluations on one side and developmental issues on the other, as shown in Figure 9.5. On the anniversary of the assistant's hiring date, Jay takes him or her to a coffee shop and covers the performance review. "The reviews last an hour and change," Jay relates. "The coffee shop has some nice nooks to secure privacy, and the owners encourage patrons to hang around and buy more lattes. I usually have a couple of refills, actually," he laughed.

Figure 9.5

Sample Performance Review Form

Front of Document

Annual Assistant Performance Review				
Subject	**Assistant Score**			
	Advocate ————————————————— Staff Person			
	5 **Exceptional**	**4** **Above average**	**3** **Meets standards**	**2** **Below average**	**1** **Unacceptable**
Attendance: Punctuality, control of absences				
Quality of work: Consistency and reliability of results; follows systems				
Job knowledge: Review of job duties list expectations				
Organization: Time management, prioritization, multitasking				
Client interactions: Phone etiquette, client problem solving, proactive contact				

(continued)

Figure 9.5

(Continued)

Annual Assistant Performance Review					
Subject	**Assistant Score**				
	Advocate ————————————————————— Staff Person				
	5 **Exceptional**	**4** **Above** **average**	**3** **Meets** **standards**	**2** **Below** **average**	**1** **Unacceptable**
Teamwork: Relationships with advisor, assistants and office personnel, flexibility					
Initiative: Self-starter, accepts responsibility, anticipates opportunities					

Back of Document

Accomplishments in past year versus stated goals:

Picture of assistant's role in one year versus role today:

Goals for next year with time frames:

Other issues to be addressed and considered:

Assistant's comments for the record:

First, he works on the front of the review form. Here is where the two of them agree on a numerical score on seven topics.

Why seven topics?

"That's the result of doing this for two years. I started with this awful three-page thing from the home office. It was way too much, and it seemed to be designed to find faults. So I pared it down to seven topics that will result in our having a proactive discussion."

So the scores are a consensus? Not like "you rate yourself, and I'll rate you, and then we'll compare scores?"

"Yes. I hated that in grade school, and I hate it now. I'm not playing 'gotcha!' I want to grow an advocate. So we agree that a 5 is truly an advocate for the practice. That is, the assistant is contributing to the growth of the business by providing sales and relationship opportunities for me."

And the 3 is for?

"The assistant is doing just what's expected and not much more in that area."

You agree on an overall average and then what?

"A 3 to 3.9 average gets the assistant a cost-of-living raise. A score of 4 or more provides a raise of 5 times the cost-of-living increase. So if the consumer price index (CPI) is 2 percent, the raise would be 10 percent for a score of 4."

This is on the base pay, correct?

"Yes, that increase is on the base pay. There are also bonuses based on production, assets under management growth, and self-development goals being met." (More on this in Chapter 11.)

You chose those seven topics with a method in mind?

"Why, of course I did! Actually, they seem to flow nicely. Attendance is an easy one, pretty obvious. Quality of work is my perception as the end user at the point of sale, say, versus Jorge's as the creator and packager of the presentation. Expectations are tested with each item. Is he sticking to the systems manual or taking shortcuts? Is he adding his knowledge to the best practices manual?"

This leads to job knowledge.

"Nice segue. This is where we spend most of the time. We review his job description that started back when he was hired and has been morphing ever since. We'll discuss each item, remove some, add some, adjust some."

After that is organization.

"Right. How he uses his time and prioritizes his work. Then come the two sections on client interaction and teamwork. These rate his communication with our clients and within our team. I get feedback from clients on Jorge and Venita all the time. There's not a lot of room to hide, especially with our A-level clients."

And finally, initiative.

"Here's where we review how he has contributed directly to sales and prospecting. We have an opportunities inventory that Jorge manages. We figure it's worth $30,000 in income each year, just converting 60 percent of the opportunities. We look at those numbers."

And on side 2 of your performance review form?

"Goal setting for the coming year and other items affecting his work and personal life. Jorge, for example, is studying for his Series 7 license and would like to begin working on a paraplanner designation. We put deadlines on steps to achieve those goals. These will provide us with his personal growth factor in the bonus equation. His wife is pregnant, and we took some measures to free up a week around the due date. We also strategized for the contingency of a problem with the pregnancy. Venita is ready to take over his duties in that case."

And you talk money, of course.

"Of course. The four elements of his compensation are broken down: benefits, base pay, productivity bonus, and personal growth bonus. He gets the bonus check at once or he can have it spread out over the year. His wife prefers the spreading out method for her peace of mind."

How do you end the meeting?

"The assistant adds any comments, like things we agree to disagree on, and we both sign off. Then it's in his personnel file forever."

Jay, what's an example of something you agree to disagree on?

"We have a top-level client, who just rubs Jorge the wrong way. I say he should learn to work with her, but he won't have anything to do with her. He feels there's an underlying prejudice on her part. I'm not sure I see it. She's a pain, very demanding, with everyone. So he'll never get a perfect 5 in client interactions."

Do you score only in whole numbers—5, 4, 3, 2, 1?

"We have fun with that. I told Jorge that since he won't deal with her, he'll only be able to aspire to a 4.8! We do 4.5 and 3.5 and 0.75s occasionally."

Observing Jay in his performance review with Venita, I witnessed some essentials in communication between them. Here are some guidelines for giving effective performance feedback during reviews:

> *Be direct and honest in your communication.* State what you believe to be true based on facts and feedback from others. Don't try to smooth over difficult messages with indirect statements; they can confuse the employee.
> *Be factual.* Focus on patterns of behavior that demonstrate performance problems or strengths, not isolated incidents of behavior. Control your personal biases. Collect facts to build any generalizations.
> *Have a helpful and constructive attitude—show your support.* Your role is to help the employee grow so he or she can achieve desired goals for position and salary.
> *Create an environment that promotes two-way communication.* Performance discussions must be a dialogue, not a monologue.

As is evident in the above dialogue, Jay is very good at keeping the review interactive.

Make sure the employee leaves the performance discussion with an understanding of what is expected of him or her, when it is expected, and the consequences of unsatisfactory improvement.

When the meeting ended, all Venita's goals for the coming year were clearly spelled out and set into a timeline. Jay asked if she had any questions or needed clarification before signing off on the document. She had none. Clarity of expectations had been achieved!

Harassment

The story of John and Marge at the beginning of this chapter ended with Marge's filing a harassment lawsuit. John, as you might have inferred, was a "male chauvinist pig" in Marge's opinion. As with many things in life, perception becomes reality. John had no documentation of his frustrations with Marge. He had issued no warnings. He hadn't initiated any disciplinary action. As far as a court was concerned, John was guilty of harassment.

The advisor/assistant relationship is first a business relationship. It may evolve into a friendship over time. The advisor and assistant will face challenges together, endure highs and lows, and emotions will often run high. Naturally, a strong bond will form between the advisor and an assistant. The fine line is to not allow the relationship to go out of bounds. Harassment occurs when the bounds are crossed, often inadvertently. With this in mind, let's take a quick look at harassment, a danger that has ruined many a supervisor.

Harassment is defined as follows:

> *Behavior, language, jokes, or requests for sexual favors that are unwelcome, personally offensive, demonstrate a lack of respect for the rights of others, and create an intimidating, hostile, or offensive working environment.*
>
> *Deliberate, careless, or repeated unwelcome sexual contact or verbal abuse that is of a racist, bigoted, or sexual nature, that is made by a person (advisor or assistant) within the scope of his or her employment, and that adversely affects the terms or conditions of another person's employment.*
>
> *Coercive sexual behavior (implicit or explicit) used to control, influence, or affect the career, salary, or job of an employee.*

For legal purposes, *harassment* is simply another form of discrimination. It is illegal just like other forms of discrimination, and it carries the same penalties. Both your company and members of management can be held personally liable for harassment that occurs in the office. Prompt reporting and handling of any harassment issue is extremely important, and it is the law.

Discipline and Termination

Unfortunately, there will be assistants who will, for a variety of reasons, just not work out. As a supervisor of assistants, you are responsible to maintain a productive and positive working environment. Sometimes, this means that you must address problems by taking corrective action. All of the proactive communication discussed thus far in this chapter combines to form the single most important factor in preventing assistant discipline problems. Treating your assistants with respect, dignity, and honesty promotes positive business results, greater client satisfaction, lower absenteeism and turnover, and higher performance and productivity. It also creates true advocates in your practice. In the event that there is a discipline problem, it is important for you to address it early, use a positive approach with open communication, conduct a thorough investigation, and develop good documentation.

If a problem arises, it's important to carefully analyze the situation and determine a course of action based on objective and documented facts to ensure fair treatment of your assistant. If an assistant perceives that he has been treated fairly—he feels that expectations are clear and feedback is timely and honest, he has had an opportunity to give his side, he has received fair warning of problems, and he has had an opportunity to correct them—your chance of a lawsuit is greatly diminished.

There are several laws that affect the fair treatment of assistants as employees. Become familiar with the Equal Employment Opportunity (EEO) laws outlined below, and when in doubt, consult legal counsel. These laws are, naturally, also applicable in the hiring process:

> *Title VII: Civil Rights Act of 1964.* This federal law bans discrimination in employment due to race, color, religion, sex, or national origin.
>
> *Age Discrimination in Employment Act, 1967 and 1986 Amendments.* This act forbids discrimination in employment due to age, and it applies to people 40 years and older.
>
> *Americans with Disabilities Act (ADA).* For an office with 15 or more employees, you are required to comply with the provisions of the Americans with Disabilities Act. The ADA prohibits discrimination against any qualified individual with a disability. It also requires that reasonable accommodations be made for qualified disabled persons.

Progressive discipline is a process used when you believe that a performance problem can be rectified by a positive change in the assistant's behavior. There are four steps to progressive discipline that encourage employees to change unproductive behavior: (1) verbal warning, (2) written warning, (3) probation, and (4) termination.

The philosophy behind progressive discipline is that the discipline should be corrective rather than punitive and positive rather than negative. Your goal is to improve and shape behavior. Your course of action should be based on the severity and nature of the problem. The steps in progressive discipline need to be clearly documented and kept in the assistant's file. When a problem occurs that goes beyond the weekly meeting or annual performance review, the following is a best-practice sequence of events:

- Establish clearly what the specific problem is before taking action:
  - Do not discuss the problem with other individuals unless they have a "need to know." Employee privacy is the law, and as we saw before, we want to avoid triangulation from rearing its ugly head.

- o Find out the viewpoints of those involved, including the assistant.
- o Rely only on statements of fact or written documentation.
- o Do not take personal feelings, biases, or hearsay into account.
- Consider the cause of the problem:
  - o Did the assistant have clear expectations of the job?
  - o Did he or she know how to do what was expected?
  - o Was he or she able to do what was expected?
  - o Why else would he or she not do what was expected?
  - o Did the assistant receive adequate training?
  - o Is the problem tolerated by others? Consistent treatment of employees in similar situations is critical.
- Validate your information:
  - o Listen to the assistant's side of the story.
  - o Investigate all sources of information.
  - o Conduct interviews privately.
- Consider the following factors in deciding on disciplinary action:
  - o What was done in similar cases at your company?
  - o Did you let personalities, personal feelings, or biases influence your decision?
  - o What was the nature of the violation?
  - o What was the severity of the damage or gravity of the offense?
  - o What was the assistant's perspective?
  - o What is the assistant's previous work record?
- Select a course of action:
  - o Verbal warning
  - o Written warning
  - o Probation
  - o Termination

Verbal Warning

The progressive discipline process begins with a discussion between you and the employee and a verbal warning. Avoiding confrontation by just "dropping hints" instead is counterproductive, confuses the issue, and simply postpones the inevitable. Meet with the employee in a private place, and inform her that you are putting her on notice and want to encourage her to evaluate the situation and take steps to remedy it. Handle all discipline matters honestly, accurately, directly, and reasonably based on validated information. Timing is crucial. Always address the problem quickly—don't wait until it becomes overwhelming for the practice. Document the verbal warning discussion.

When documenting such a meeting with an assistant, be sure to note the following:

- Date of the incident
- The behavior that was exhibited
- Consequences of this performance
- Expected performance (be specific)
- The result of your discussion

Documentation of performance problems and discussions doesn't have to be lengthy. Keep it short and to the point. A brief, dated, handwritten account of the incident or discussion is all that is necessary.

Written Warning

If there is little or no improvement within a reasonable time frame after the verbal warning, prepare a written warning memo. Meet in a private place to discuss the warning with the assistant. The memo should inform him that failure to improve on the noted deficiencies will result in further disciplinary action, such as probation or termination. A sample written warning is available upon request. This warning ensures that the employee understands exactly what the problem is and what is expected.

You and the assistant should both sign the warning as proof that it was discussed. If the employee refuses to sign, ask him to draft a memo explaining why and note any differences in opinion about the written warning. Attach that memo to the written warning.

Probation

If the improvement expected in the written warning is not made within a reasonable time frame, probation is the typical next step. If you determine that probation is necessary, develop a probation memo.

A written probation memo is similar to a written warning memo, but it incorporates the actions that have taken place since the written warning was issued. The probation memo should state that if expectations are not met, termination of employment will result. Deliver it in a private meeting to discuss your actions and to ensure confidentiality.

If the problem becomes more serious during the probationary period, you may interrupt the probationary process and consider termination of employment. Be certain that you have reasonable and good cause and that you review the Equal Employment Opportunity laws to ensure that you are applying fair treatment.

Termination of Employment

If during or at the end of the probationary period, improvement is inadequate and the problem remains, termination of employment may be necessary. Prepare a termination memo outlining the reasons for the termination. A sample termination letter is available upon request.

Deliver the memo when you inform the assistant that you are terminating her employment. Again, meet in a private place to ensure confidentiality. Be prepared to present the detailed reasons for your decision. The meeting should be brief and nonargumentative.

Your purpose is to inform the assistant that her employment has been terminated, not to argue the reasons. If you do not have sufficient time to prepare a termination memo prior to meeting with the assistant, you can verbally discuss the termination and present any facts or documentation of the performance problem causing the termination. You can then follow up the discussion with a summary termination memo sent through the mail to the assistant's home.

At the end of the termination discussion, make arrangements for the assistant to return any company property. Inform her as to how the last paycheck and any benefits administration will be handled.

Progressive discipline is the preferred course of action. There are, however, times when immediate termination may be appropriate and necessary if the assistant's actions pose a serious threat to disrupt or impair your business. Some examples of such actions include the following:

- Unusually disruptive actions or attitudes
- Damage of property or reputation
- Using employment-related information for personal benefit or gain
- Gross inefficiency or neglect of work
- Fights
- Theft of property or misuse of funds
- Falsifying records, including the employment application
- Failure to maintain confidentiality of information
- Harassment of coworkers or clients
- Consuming drugs during working hours

Communication with Key Nonclients

There are many people who have a significant impact on your practice who are not currently clients. In the Client Management system, we designated these folks as single A's:

- High-potential prospects
- Centers of influence

- Business partners
- Home office personnel
- Local firm personnel
- Family and friends

The idea behind identifying these key nonclients is to be sure they are in your client relationship management (CRM) database and are receiving a series of contacts throughout the year. Why? All should be getting a sense of what it would be like to be a client of yours. A positive impression will go a long way toward their mentioning you in a favorable light should there be an opportunity to make a referral.

Brooke, an advisor in Schaumberg, Illinois, has used a proactive process in this aspect of her practice's operations.

"There are around 30 people who get an A-level touch from me every quarter," she said from her downtown corner office. "I have a favorite underwriter, for example, who has helped me with difficult cases. He's on my newsletter list and gets a birthday card or call from me on March 24. I try to get birthdays for everyone. I'm bullish on birthdays!" She smiled.

Other examples?

"Of course. There's a real estate agent who is a COI for me. She and I have lunch every month or so. I keep her on my mailing list for newsletters, and I receive hers. I invite her to client appreciation events and to participate in Web seminars. Sometimes she does, usually not. But the invitation's the thing. And her birthday, of course, is cause for a silly card."

Do you have a prospect on that list?

"A number of them. Those are prospects who have given me permission to stay in touch. So they receive the newsletter and a birthday note. There are a couple of small businesses that have a 401(k) coming up for bid in the next few months, so I drop by their offices just to touch base. I'll bring some bagels and cream cheese for the staff. A small investment that will eventually pay off."

Small businesses don't have birthdays!

"No, but they have anniversaries. I use the date they opened shop as the birthday of the business. That's the day I bring the goodies by. I do this for all of my small business clients. This gives a prospective client a sense of my service philosophy. It works. I convert over three-quarters of these into clients."

The Communication System
and the Client Experience

In the chapter on the Client Management system, I discussed in depth how to stay in communication with your clients. I reviewed a method for segmenting the client base, and then, for each segment, I gave an ongoing contact sequence that can be implemented. Part of the best practices annual review is to ask for the client's opinion of the service you and your team have been providing.

The purpose of this section of the Communication system is to give the clients an opportunity to step back and provide more detached feedback about the practice. This is done through the use of a client survey.

A best practice is to have your top-tier clients surveyed every two to three years. The advisor can initiate the survey or can have an outside company conduct it to get a more impersonal response from the clients. I've found that clients tend to be straightforward in either scenario. The point is to give them a forum to assess the quality of their experience as clients of yours.

Melissa, an advisor outside of Milwaukee, Wisconsin, uses an outside group every two years to do the survey. "It's always eye-opening," she said. "Our service is 98 percent positive, which has been consistent over the past six years. This year's survey pointed out that the majority of our top clients would feel good about referring us to others if we would ask, so we have instituted a referral section to our annual reviews. It also pointed out that 45 percent of them are interested in family legacy planning, something we haven't formally addressed. We will now!"

What were the numbers on your survey?

"We submitted our top 150 client households. Of those, 78 responded, roughly half, which is great. Of the 78, 28 preferred to respond anonymously. So we feel that we have an excellent picture of our clientele."

Hank, in the Miami area, is an advisor who does his own survey. He patched one together 10 years back, and he has been refining it ever since. A copy of this survey is available upon request.

"Our team has been using it every year. You'll see that there are seven parts to it, with client information having two of those parts. We don't send all seven out at once. One year we'll send three to the A-level clients, and two sections each to the B- and C-level clients. That way we're having a constant flow of input in all seven categories."

Do you use mail-in surveys, or do you have clients access the surveys online?

"We put all of them on a survey service on the Internet and send paper copies to those whose e-mail addresses we don't have. After sending a link to a client's e-mail address, we'll wait three weeks. If we see that the client hasn't done the survey online, we call to see if the client received the link or was having trouble opening it. If the client had a problem with it, we'll send a paper copy."

What's your response rate?

"We have about 75 A-level clients, 175 B-level, and 750 C-level. The A's respond 80 percent of the time, half right away and half after we make a follow-up request. Using the same process with the B-level clients, it's more like 50 percent. We don't do any follow-up on the C-level clients. They have a 20 percent response rate in a good year."

What's the biggest take-away from your use of a survey?

"A couple of things. It shows our clients that we care about their opinions and they can have an impact on the quality of service they get. It certainly keeps us sharp. Three years ago, the survey told us that our office location was a mix of 'acceptable' and 'unacceptable.' Our office was in a growth corridor, and it was difficult to reach for the clients over 60. We have since relocated to a less stressful office building. Lastly, it keeps our opportunity inventory full. The 'products and services' section gives us areas of future interest to follow up on. That alone is worth the effort. I calculate next year we'll do $100,000 in revenue from those opportunities."

The Tools of the Communication System

A discussion of a Communication system for an advisor's practice would be remiss if we didn't address the tools that can be utilized in its creation. We'll take a look at each medium and touch on some of the highlights. The communication playing field is constantly evolving. Mobile phones are now minicomputers as well as cameras, calendars, and to-do lists. Or is it that computers are now phones, cameras, calendars and to-do lists? Compliance departments are running to catch up with all the online venues for communication with the goal of keeping client information secure.

Postal Mail

What is the role of the U.S. Postal Service in your practice? Considerations here include understanding the flood of communication that flows to your clients from the home offices of insurance and investment companies. These mailings are often invisible to the advisor: prospectuses, statements, updates, solicitations, proxy voting information, invoices with stuffers, to name a few. Do your clients know how to opt out of mailed material and have it e-mailed? This might be a service to provide after a client survey says it's all too much. Using the mail for cards, invitations, and more intimate forms of communication is still a good idea. Lisa, in the Boston area, keeps a supply of new first-class stamp commemoratives on hand to liven up the envelope when she sends personal correspondence to her top-tier clients. "The Marvel Superheroes were among the most popular," she reported. "The kids in the households thought I must be pretty cool to send mail with the Iron Man on it. Parents were duly impressed."

E-Mail

More and more communication is being handled via e-mail. There are e-newsletters, e-cards, e-statements, and e-prospectuses. As the Internet has become more accessible and stable, clients of all ages are converting much of the routine mail to electronic delivery. The danger is that mailboxes are crammed with all manner of spam, junk, solicitations from mailing lists you joined inadvertently, forwarded items, cc's someone thought you should be aware of, and updates from the home office. I am sure that an e-prospectus or e-newsletter is just as unlikely to be read as a paper one. It's easier on the environment to delete an e-prospectus.

On the other hand, many company filters inadvertently block legitimate communications, which can result in confusion and lost opportunities. I use an AOL address that is sometimes blocked and a client wonders why the report I promised hasn't arrived.

Blast e-mails can be useful when a big event, like the stock market's crashing, occurs. These messages, however, tread a fine line between "useful" and "annoying." Judicious use of blast e-mail is suggested.

An e-mail that provides an alert can be popular. Peggy, in Torrance, California, sends an e-mail alert for the time change twice a year. "My clients love it," she told me. "I also use an e-newsletter. But I always send birthday greetings by U.S. mail." Another advisor, Forrest, has his top-tier clients' wedding anniversary dates in his contact management system. "I'll send an e-mail reminder to the husband a week prior to his anniversary," he said. "I have clients who own floral shops, restaurants, and jewelry stores. I put links to their businesses in the e-mail. I'm a hero."

E-mail used for one-on-one communication with clients, service providers, and home office people is quite effective. Sending a link to an article on fishing to a client who's an avid angler is usually okay with most compliance departments. It's also an appreciated, unique touch.

Advisors I've worked with are divided on the topic of having their e-mail screened. Many have expressed the desire to keep it confidential. Others are happy to have an assistant delete the junk and forward the relevant e-mails. Either way, there is a constant flow of e-mail to the advisor's computer or PDA. The biggest issue here is when the advisor is constantly looking at the inbox and is perpetually distracted when each new e-mail hits. We all know that during conference calls, most of the participants are multitasking, including "doing their e-mail" while the host rambles on. As we suggested in the last chapter, restrict the times you check your e-mail.

And, by the way, there's nothing more annoying and dismaying to a presenter in front of a group than attendees' always glancing away at a device. I've sat in the back of enough presentations to feel sorry for the person trying to lead a discussion or conduct a class. Be polite—that's also a best practice.

The generational divide between older and younger advisors isn't as distinct with e-mail. There are few holdouts, I'm finding, under age 65. Even my Uncle Umberto, who passed away recently in his midseventies, became an avid e-mailer and Internet maven. As with the postal mail, the best practice is to keep in mind how your communication will affect your client's inbox and regularly ask if it's too much.

Personal Digital Assistants (PDAs)

Earlier in this book, I suggested that the ideal client relationship management program would unite four things: (1) client hard data, (2) client soft data, (3) an interactive calendar, and (4) a to-do list. The next generation of iPhones and BlackBerries will, with compliance oversight, effectively combine the four while adding the e-mail, cell phone, and browser functions. The client data will be stored on the Web and be retrieved via the Internet-enabled device. The calendar, e-mail, cell phone, and to-do list are already well established as entry-level PDA features.

Security is and will continue to be the biggest issue, but I see this as a good thing. It slows down the adoption process and allows the advisor to pace the integration of technology into the practice. Due diligence must be done around issues such as how the technology will affect the other team members and clients. Also, privacy issues arise: who has whose personal and business numbers, addresses, and access to Web sites? The best practice here is to have patience. Don't rush into new technology that needs to be vetted by the technology people for compatibility and by the compliance folks for security.

Phones

I do enough telephone consulting to feel confident in declaring the land line still alive and well. For on-the-fly communication, cell phones are certainly the best thing since sliced bread. For longer talks, maybe not so much. If both parties are in static locations and both phones are charged up, there may well be clear contact. But I'm not ready to dump my land line just yet.

Truth be told, I guess I already have—as of this writing, I make my business calls via our cable company, which is a form of *intra*net service. I tried an *Inter*net telephone provider for a while, but the quality was too inconsistent on the laptop I was using. Others swear by services like Skype and Vonage. When there's a "money call" on the line (so to speak), like a top prospect, a negotiation, or an hour-long consultation that the advisor is paying for, all participants usually agree on a land line connection, at least for now. It's a fact that a growing number of households are abandoning land lines and have gone all cellular or all Internet. This is mainly a phenomenon of the postboomer generation and seems to represent a small fraction of most advisors' client bases.

Voice-mail, caller-ID, and other services are endowing the modern phone user with gatekeeping power. Games and countergames can be played by selecting phone numbers with made-up area codes, generating false caller-ID names, and instantly capturing a caller's phone number for future use.

Do-not-call lists for both land lines and cell phone users are in place but tricky to enforce.

Is there a best practice around the use of a phone? Only one: if a top client has an issue and would like to talk to you—the advisor—having a live voice picking up the phone is a breath of fresh air.

Internet

Cyberspace is packed. The resources for an advisor are seemingly endless. Type "financial planning" into Google and you receive 55.4 million results. Being a science fiction fan, I looked back on the futures imagined by my favorite authors, such as Isaac Asimov, Arthur C. Clarke, and Robert Sheckley. None of them envisioned the ubiquity of personal computers. Some posited a global knowledge base but presumed it would happen through some technology of the future. That technology is right in front of us every day and saturates the air around us. The PC and the Internet have been embedded in our lives and your practices. For the financial advisor and her team, some specific best-practice uses of the Internet I've encountered include the following:

- *Accessing up-to-the-minute values of the clients' holdings.* This is a two-way street in that the clients can also access their values any time they wish.
- *Accessing real-time market information, research, and news.*
- *Accessing the enhanced communication capabilities available through all the above-mentioned devices that utilize the Web.*
- *Looking up information about clients and prospects.* Todd, in Hartford, Connecticut, has his assistant Google new prospects to gather intelligence about them. "Rose, my assistant, doesn't go overboard, but we do Google new prospects. We find out all sorts of things that I can use in my initial approach to them. If I know their employer, I'll try to find the prospects on the company Web site. We also run their names through the local newspaper Web site. It has a search engine, and just yesterday, I discovered that a prospect was honored a year ago by the local chamber of commerce for his work teaching English to adult immigrants. The person who referred the prospect didn't include that information. Now it can be a conversation topic. Small business owners usually have Web sites of some sort. Rose gives me an overview of what the business does and who the key personnel are, and she prints out any fact sheets that are available. Again, we don't dig too deep. Every year, before the annual review, we'll run our top clients through Google and the newspaper to see what comes up." He coughed. "Um, then there's the client we ran through the newspaper site only to learn that he had been convicted of a DWI. Glad I don't have his auto policy!"
- *Taking advantage of some of the networking opportunities that are available over the Internet.* Compliance units usually have reservations about advisors' joining online communities, such as Facebook, LinkedIn, and Plaxo. Many of these communities eventually disappear due to low membership or poor maintenance. However, I've heard some success stories, usually around gathering names of "business contacts" on a client's network and feeding them back to the client as referral possibilities. Dan, in North Carolina, has had success in this area. "My LinkedIn profile is gathering a number of new connections, and I'll recommend the services of a client who also has a page set up. I've been recommended several times, and that's powerful.

When I meet with prospects that are connections of mine, it opens up all their connections. I'll use these to bring up the topic of referrals. If a person is a connection of one of those prospects, I can hopefully get an introduction. My LinkedIn profile led to my establishing five new clients this year."

- *Accessing educational resources (many of which are covered in the next chapter).*

The Internet can pose a major distraction to a financial services practice. "I'll admit," said Jim, an advisor in Virginia, "to spending an hour a day on my fantasy football league. There are some fellow advisors throughout our company across the country who are in it with me. I don't want to know what that costs me in lost productivity—just don't tell my manager!"

Another case is that of Regina, an assistant to an advisor in the Seattle, Washington, area. After consulting with the advisor, I worked with Regina and found she was running an online business writing and proofreading term papers. Good entrepreneurship, but she was using the advisor's time for about two hours a day in small chunks for her "other job." If we teamed up Jim and Regina, not much financial services work would get done. And did I mention all the solitaire that gets played and the Web surfing that's done in the course of a business day? Part of an advisor's supervision should be to monitor the use of the Internet by all members of the practice.

Communication System Best Practices Checklist

The Communication System Best Practices Checklist is shown in Figure 9.6. There are 56 specific steps in this checklist. It's the blueprint for the sixth section of your best practices operations manual.

In Figure 9.6, we have assumed that the advisor is with a broker/ dealer in a detached location, with a full-time administrative assistant and a full-time paraplanner/marketing assistant. The advisor is in a Mature life cycle stage. Each practice is unique, of course, and the checklist can be modified for each advisor.

The resources referred to on the checklist are suggestions based on various best practices observed in the field. Any resource in italics refers to a piece reviewed or illustrated earlier in this chapter.

Figure 9.6

Communication System Best Practices Checklist

Communication Activities	Advisor Assistant	Marketing Assistant	Administrative	Firm	Resources
Assistants: Hiring and Selecting					
6.1 Create a job description.	X			S	*Marketing assistant duties, administrative assistant duties, Figures 9.2 and 9.3*
6.2 Create ad copy.				S	
6.3 Identify sources: • Recent graduates from business schools or programs • Interns in business schools or programs • Online • Job fairs • Local newspapers, both print and online • Family and friends	X			S	
6.4 Screen applications.	X			S	
6.5 Application for employment completed by candidate.	X			S	
6.6 Prepare questions and materials for personal interview.					Interview template questions; résumé

Note: X denotes primary accountability person, and S denotes shared accountability person.

(continued)

217

Figure 9.6

(Continued)

	Communication Activities	Advisor Assistant	Marketing Assistant	Administrative	Firm	Resources
6.7	Face-to-face interview(s).	X	S		S	Notepad
6.8	Reference checks.	X			S	
6.9	Background checks.	S			X	
6.10	Prepare offer letter.	X			S	
6.11	Prepare "no" letter.	X			S	
6.12	Send "no" letter.	S	X		S	
6.13	Send offer letter.	S	X		S	
6.14	Prepare personnel file.	S		X	S	
6.15	Confidentiality agreement signed.	X			S	
6.16	Establish training process (see Education system).	X	S	S	S	
Assistants: Supervision						
6.17	Supervisory style: • Micromanager • Monitor • Abdicator	X				

6.18	Set criteria for daily informal interaction: • Open-door policy • Daily briefings	X	S	S	
6.19	Set a day and time for a formal team meeting.	X	S	S	Calendar
6.20	Create an agenda for the formal team meeting.	X	S	S	Team meeting agenda, Figure 9.4
6.21	Conduct formal, regular team meetings.	X	X	X	
6.22	Send a follow-up note with the formal team meeting's key points.	X	S	S	
Assistants: Performance Evaluation					
6.23	Set dates and times for formal performance reviews.	X	S	S	Calendar
6.24	Create an agenda for the formal performance review.	X		S	
6.25	Create a formal performance review form.	X		S	Performance review form, Figure 9.5
6.26	Conduct the formal performance review.	X	X	X	
6.27	Send a follow-up with action steps and goals discussed during the performance review.	X	S	S	
6.28	Put review in personnel file.	X		S	
Assistants: Harassment, Discipline, and Termination					
6.29	Discuss any behaviors, language, or situations that might be considered harassment.	X	X	X	

(continued)

Figure 9.6

(Continued)

	Communication Activities	Advisor Assistant	Marketing Assistant	Administrative	Firm	Resources
6.30	Document problem.	X			S	Personnel file
6.31	Research and validate the issues.	X			S	Personnel file
6.32	Define verbal warning issues.	X			S	Verbal warning language
6.33	Define written warning issues.	X			S	
6.34	Define probation issues.	X			S	Probation letter template
6.35	Define termination issues.	X			S	
6.36	Recover materials from terminated assistant.	X			S	
6.37	Ensure the security of practice, firm, client, and company confidential materials.	X			S	
	Key Nonclients					
6.38	Identify key nonclients: • Prospects • Centers of influence • In the community • In the firm and company • Family and friends	X	S	S		

#	Task				Tools
6.39	Enter these key people into the CRM.		X		CRM
6.40	Establish and program the passive and proactive contacts with key nonclients.	X	S		CRM
6.41	Execute passive and proactive contacts with key nonclients.		X		CRM
Client's Experience					
6.42	Develop a client survey.	X	S	S	
6.43	Identify whom to survey and means of delivery.	X	S		
6.44	Schedule the survey.	X	S		
6.45	Send the survey.		X		
6.46	Make follow-up contact.	X	S		
6.47	Tabulate results.	S	X		
6.48	Determine action steps from the results.	X	S		
Communication Tools					
6.49	Set up ongoing field-to-office messaging system among team members. Coordinate all devices for the following: • Scheduling appointments • Adding and deleting to-dos • Synchronization requirements • Priority communications		X	X	CRM PDAs Phones Faxes E-mail

(continued)

Figure 9.6

(Continued)

	Communication Activities	Advisor Assistant	Marketing Assistant	Administrative	Firm	Resources
6.50	Confirm consistent methods and media for transcription of case notes, data, and updates from advisor to staff.	X	X	X		Core Four business systems checklists
6.51	Conduct proactive Internet searches about prospects to feed Client Acquisition system.		X			Internet search engines
6.52	Create feeder lists from Internet resources to use with COIs.		X			"
6.53	Conduct proactive Internet searches about top clients to acquire information about them to be used in the Client Management system.		X			"
6.54	Confirm telephone and e-mail filtering and screening protocols.					Time Management system checklist
6.55	Evaluate mail and overnight delivery services periodically for reliability and cost-effectiveness.	X	S	S	S	
6.56	Evaluate communication tools periodically for reliability, upgrades, and cost-effectiveness.	X	S	S	S	

10

Infrastructure Business System 7: Education

Once upon a time, all knowledge was kept in the realm of a select few. Throughout most of human history, the flow of information to the majority of average citizens was tightly controlled by tribal leaders, monarchies, papacies, and governments.

In 1450, Johannes Gutenberg made his first printing press that eventually led to mass literacy. The classic works were reprinted, and the average person was soon able to access, read, and exchange opinions about them. Newspapers and periodicals began to flourish, challenging those who held the traditional financial, political, and spiritual knowledge. Every significant communication tool that was invented and assimilated into society from that point on provided more ways to wrench knowledge away from the few and share it with the many. The personal printing press known as the typewriter, the telephone, telegraph, copiers, and fax machines all served to further disseminate knowledge among the citizenry.

The knowledge base of the financial services business was no exception. Yet, into the mid-1980s, the knowledge of the inner workings of financial products was still tightly controlled by brokers, agents, home offices, and Wall Street. It wasn't until the confluence of three events that the average person was able to wrest product and performance information from these gatekeepers.

The first event was the growth in the 1980s of small, nimble mutual fund companies that were able to take advantage of the soaring interest rates. The newly popular mutual funds allowed their burgeoning number of small investors to see holdings, assets allocations, and the manager's investment philosophy spelled out in the prospectus. The same kind of transparency was soon expected and demanded from all insurance and investment company products, much to the industry's collective chagrin.

The second event contributing to the dissemination of financial information was the spread of the personal computer. The PC gave individuals computation power and the ability to challenge and question assumptions made by the financial services companies. Again, much to their annoyance, the insurance and investment companies had to go on the defensive, providing rationales for long-held, often archaic, investment strategies.

The third event was the spread of the Internet in the 1990s, first by telephone modem and then by broadband. The speed of Internet delivery continues to accelerate today. This took the product and company transparency issue and the PC onto a whole new playing field. Anyone who now has access to the Internet has a method of challenging the status quo and finding others in cyberspace with similar concerns and questions. Financial services companies and ancillary Web sites these days default to providing more than enough financial information, sliced and diced in seemingly infinite ways.

The result of these three factors together is simply that deep, detailed financial services knowledge is available to everyone who wants to know. This evolution in communication has created a shift of power in education. The advisor once was the sole face-to-face educator on financial products and services for most Americans. Now, with a little Internet searching, second and third opinions, services, and products are readily available for the clients to compare. Within the past decade has evolved the danger of too much information! It's like the serfs of the Middle Ages having access to the castle blueprints, detailed listings of all the king's treasure, organizational charts, court visitors, treaties, trial results, battle updates, dungeon residents, tax systems, number and deployment of knights, jousting schedules, and the princess's Facebook pages. The king's authority would have been undermined through the power of the serfs' knowledge. Banks, insurance and investment companies, Wall Street, and the advisors were once kings monopolizing knowledge. Now, in a very real sense, they are servants to the clients. The good news is that this flood of information opens up opportunities for the advisor, as we'll see.

This brings us to the third of the four infrastructure systems: the Education system in this flat, decentralized information age. We'll look at three aspects of the Education system: (1) the education of the advisor, (2) the education of the advisor's assistants and team, and (3) the education of the advisor's clients.

Advisors

Core Competencies

As a financial advisor, what is your platform? Chapter 7 covered in detail all of an advisor's platform options. In whatever platform an advisor selects, the advisor must have certain core competencies. Core competencies represent the essential knowledge the advisor should have to begin a practice. This goes beyond the license classroom and testing material, which, while necessary, tends to be abstract and general in nature. The next section will discuss licensing. Here, we are answering the question, "What should a person know before he offers his services as an advisor?"

Three years ago, Danielle was just finishing the recruiting process. She had been selling airtime for a local cable company in the Denver area while finishing up her MBA. She had always been interested in investments and insurances since her father had passed away when Danielle was just 18. He had the foresight to have purchased a significant amount of life insurance, and Danielle—being the oldest of three children—had to learn how to invest it for the family's everyday needs and college funding.

She was part of a new advisor class in her firm where I was working with the sales manager, Art, to create the initial training program.

"My goal is to be a full financial planner," Danielle said. "First, get to know all the products, situations, and strategies that a normal family would face. Then, with experience, begin charging a fee for my planning services. I'll be studying for the CFP, and I'd like to sit for that in a year and a half."

Art and I reviewed the existing training materials and created a list of a dozen core competencies that a class of would-be financial planners should have down pat. As with all good communication, we clearly outlined our expectations. Danielle and her three classmates would spend the next two months getting all their licenses and doing classroom work. Once licensing was complete, they would begin contacting prospects. One month after that, they would be assessed on their ability to perform the 12 core competencies. If they successfully completed the licensing and performed well on the core competencies assessment, they could continue on the financing program.

Those 12 competencies are these:

1. Develop and maintain a minimum of five prospecting sources. Demonstrate prospecting skills (phone, objection handling) that turn a lead into an initial interview.
2. Have and demonstrate a simple, polished iconic presentation that describes what you do and why you do it and that stimulates the prospect's curiosity.
3. Show how to manage your prospect inventory in the CRM database.
4. Have at least two COIs, and demonstrate consistent referral-gathering language.
5. Demonstrate strong discovery skills: facts, feelings, client's network, and documentation.
6. Demonstrate a working knowledge of the planning software and presentation of the output.
7. Show a consistent, compliant series of steps in your sales process.
8. Have a memorized life insurance/risk management presentation.
9. Have a memorized fixed/variable annuity presentation.
10. Have a memorized mutual fund/brokerage account/managed assets presentation.
11. Have a memorized asset allocation presentation.
12. Have a memorized disability/long-term-care presentation.

The assessment of skills in these 12 areas would be through a combination of joint work, observation, and video role-play. This list is applicable to Danielle and Art's three other new advisors. The first 7 competencies are consistent through most of the platforms, as they focus on the four advisor geniuses: Relationship Building, Relationship Maintenance and Growth, Inspiring People to Action, and Solving Problems Creatively and Interpreting Information. The final 5 competencies are specific to the path leading to a full, fee-based financial planner practice. They relate to product knowledge, which will vary by chosen platform and financial discipline. A property and casualty–oriented practice would want competencies around personal auto, home, flood, and liability insurances, as well as understanding business owners' casualty needs. From these core competencies, a training program can be built.

While it's beyond the scope of this book to go into developing curriculum, keeping the basics in mind is critical, layering more advanced concepts, products, and situational knowledge as time and experience dictate.

Ultimately, Art developed a curriculum that emphasized the basics and eventually paralleled the CFP materials. In this way, the CFP designation coursework would be consistent with what Danielle was experiencing in "real life."

Three years later, one of that class of four had resigned due to an inability to pass the Series 7 exam. One had survived but had gone in a back-office direction, becoming a paraplanner to a senior advisor. Two, including Danielle, are CFPs and have prospering practices.

Licenses, Appointments, and Registrations

One of the more confusing aspects of becoming an advisor is trying to make sense of all the regulatory language imposed by the company, state, and federal overseers. In order to hold one's self out as a financial planner or as a practitioner in any of the various platforms, certain licenses, appointments, and registrations might be necessary. First, some terminology:

- A *license* authorizes an advisor to sell insurance in a specific state. One must pass a state test to obtain a license. Commonly, these include a life license, a health license (often combined into life/health), and a property and casualty license.
- An *appointment* authorizes an advisor to sell a particular company's products in a specific state. Normally, there are no tests for an appointment, just fees.
- A *registration* authorizes an advisor, who is a registered member of a Financial Industry Regulatory Authority (FINRA), a Broker/Dealer, and/or a Registered Investment Advisor (RIA) to solicit securities, such as mutual funds, stocks, and bonds. Eligibility is based on FINRA exams passed by the advisor. FINRA was established in 2007 from a consolidation of the National Association of Securities Dealers (NASD) and the member regulation, enforcement, and arbitration functions of the New York Stock Exchange. For anyone selling securities, it's the financial services' Big Brother.

To sell term, universal, and whole life insurance, all that is needed is a license and an appointment in the states you wish to operate. The same is true for health, fixed annuities, and property and casualty insurance. These are all products that at their core do not rely on the market returns and fluctuations for their performance, so they do not need to be registered.

A financial services practice can profitably be built around non-regulatory products. The overseers of those insurance-based practices will be the individual states where the advisor is licensed. The state insurance commissioners have formed the National Association of Insurance Commissioners (NAIC). This provides for some continuity among states in enforcement of regulations. Some states, notably New York and California, have the toughest regulations. These are the bellwether state regulations used by others to guide their policies.

Once the advisor steps into the variable insurances, variable and indexed annuities, mutual funds, and stocks and bonds arena, FINRA becomes another overseer in addition to the state regulators. Advisors who take the platform that involves registered products will have four sets of rules and regulations to keep in mind: the company, the state, FINRA, and the Securities and Exchange Commission (SEC). The SEC is the ultimate authority and weighs in with the über-rules and regulations.

What products you may solicit and sell as an advisor depends on the level of FINRA and SEC registration you have as well as the state licensing and appointments you hold. Here are the most common:

Full Registration

> *Series 7 General Securities.* This allows the holder to sell the full spectrum of investment products including the following: corporate stocks and bonds, rights, warrants, real estate investment trusts (REITs), collateralized mortgage obligations (CMOs), municipal securities, options (equity, debt, index, and foreign currency), investment company products and/or variable contracts, direct participation programs, unit investment trusts (UITs) and closed-end funds on the secondary market, and exchange-traded funds (ETFs).

Limited Registration

> *Series 6 Investment Company and Variable Contract Products.* This allows the holder to sell open-end and initial offerings of closed-end mutual funds, initial offerings of unit investment trusts, variable annuities, and variable life insurance. This is usually the minimum level of registration allowed to maintain a broker/dealer contract. Keep in mind that with variable products you must also hold the appropriate insurance licenses and appointments as well.

State Registration

> *Series 63 Uniform Securities Agent State Law Exam (Blue Sky).* Most states require this for registration with their state securities

department. Once you have taken this exam, it will be applied to all states in which you request registration.

Series 65 Uniform Investment Advisor Law Exam. This qualifies an investment professional to operate as an Investment Advisor Representative in certain states.

Series 66 Uniform Combined State Law Exam. This examination is a combination of the Series 63 and the Series 65, and it is preferred by many states and broker/dealers.

Registering with FINRA and the SEC is an exhaustive exercise. You'll endure background checks, fingerprints (three cards' worth), and the 28-page online U-4 form that requires full, detailed disclosure of the advisor's past professional activity. Other disclosure forms are often applicable (that is, Outside Business Activity Disclosure form, Private Securities Transaction form, and the Personal Brokerage Account Disclosure). All of this information is to be updated at regular intervals and will follow the advisor wherever he or she goes in the financial services world.

Running afoul of any FINRA or SEC regulations is serious business and can result in sanctions and heavy fines. It's no wonder some advisors choose to stay away from variable products altogether!

Licenses, appointments, and registrations must be renewed annually (with attendant fees), and there are also continuing-education requirements to be completed. Keeping track of all this can be daunting, especially if the advisor does business in multiple states.

Designations

The issue of having letters after one's name has been debated for years. One school of thought is that designations are nice but not necessary. Years of real-life, hands-on, practical experience can give the advisor the equivalent of a designation. This knowledge can easily be demonstrated to a prospect, and usually it is accompanied by a strong referral. Conrad, a 25-year veteran advisor in Georgia, is in this camp:

"I can remember only a handful of times when a client or prospect asked about the designations," he argued. "I've got years and years of practical experience in estate planning issues, and I can explain a grantor retained income trust better than any young whippersnapper. Besides," he added, "our company has a whole team of eggheads at the home office who have designations out the wazoo. I can point to them as my backup if a client doesn't trust me."

Conrad has utilized these home office folks and his network of estate planning attorneys (JDs), accountants (CPAs), and product specialists to form a formidable team.

The trust he has built within his top-tier clientele is unquestionable. In such situations the ultimate practice management question is this: If Conrad were to die, become disabled, or simply wish to sell his practice, would his top-tier clients stay with the successor? Will they be looking to the successor for some credibility in the form of a designation? Would Conrad's clients be at risk from competition that might bring the leverage of designations to bear?

"I see your point," Conrad admitted. "Without a specific successor named, there might be some poaching since I do have some high-profile clients and the vultures would be circling. Maybe it's a good idea to have a successor with some credentials."

If the mainstream media are to be believed, a reader, listener, or viewer looking for an advisor should examine designations first. Almost unanimously, business and popular finance columnists will guide the reader to find a Certified Financial Planner (CFP) in the area and to interview the CFP to see if your values mesh. It's a safe recommendation. The road to attaining the CFP designation from the CFP Board of Standards is a tough one. An advisor must show evidence of proficiency in such areas as the following:

- General principles of finance and financial planning
- Insurance planning
- Employee benefits planning
- Investment and securities planning
- State and federal income tax planning
- Estate tax, gift tax, and transfer tax planning
- Asset protection planning
- Retirement planning
- Estate planning

This is the bulk of the CFP "education requirement." Students are required to have at least a bachelor's degree from an accredited U.S. college or university plus documented course training in the above listed topic areas in order to qualify to sit for the exam. The exam is no picnic: the advisor must pass a grueling, two-day, 10-hour multiple-choice examination over a Friday and Saturday. If successful, the CFP designation is earned.

The Chartered Financial Consultant (ChFC) from the American College is also a recognized financial planning designation with parallel requirements. However, the media default to the CFP as the preferred standard.

In general, designations indicate that an advisor has sought out, studied, and acquired a deeper level of knowledge in a particular area. Normally, to achieve the designation, a test must be passed. That said, I recently went looking for a list of all the possible designations an advisor might achieve. There are over 60. Many of them are not permitted to be used by advisors until after due diligence by company compliance review boards. The content of the training and/or the required testing for a designation can be determined to be lightweight and simply a "cheap designation" as one compliance officer put it. "We're looking for integrity in the designations our advisors use within this broker/dealer," she commented. "There are plenty of designations an advisor can 'buy' that don't require much more than an online course and a true/false quiz at the end."

As a best practice, striving to achieve a designation is a good thing. Taking the course work as an educational exercise alone is valuable. Doug, an advisor in Minnesota, claims that his biggest clients came from a concept he learned in studying for his CLU designation. "At the time," he says, "in the late 1970s, there were some interesting estate tax ramifications that could be avoided by the use of a second-to-die policy. The concept of uniting the second-to-die policy with a third-party owner like a trust was very appealing to some of my wealthier prospects. Once I had the first one placed, the referrals were great."

Testing one's knowledge appeals to the competitive spirit most advisors possess, though many profess to be "bad test takers." There are plenty of ancillary companies that offer study guides, practice tests, chapter summaries, and outlines for the time-stressed advisor. It is possible, of course, that an advisor can pass a test without really getting to know the material. While this violates the spirit of achievement and specialized knowledge, it nonetheless is expedient.

Once attained, a designation looks good on a business card and lends credibility in marketing the advisor's services. Use of designations is affected by the advisor's licensing, affiliation, and registration. Every state, company, broker/dealer, RIA, and association group has its own approved designation list that is constantly updated as new designations pop up. Other than a select few, most people wouldn't know a serious designation from a fly-by-night one, which is why their use is tightly monitored. What follows is a list of the most commonly recognized designations in the financial services business:

AEP	Accredited Estate Planner
AIF	Accredited Investment Fiduciary

CAP	Chartered Advisor in Philanthropy
CASL	Chartered Advisor for Senior Living
CEA	Certified Estate Advisor
CEBS	Certified Employee Benefit Specialist
CFA	Chartered Financial Analyst
CFP	Certified Financial Planner
CFS	Certified Fund Specialist
ChFC	Chartered Financial Consultant
CLTC	Certified in Long-Term Care
CLU	Chartered Life Underwriter
CMFC	Charted Mutual Fund Counselor
CPA	Certified Public Accountant
CPC	Certified Pension Consultant
FSS	Financial Services Specialist
JD	Juris Doctor
LTCP	Long-Term Care Professional
LUTCF	Life Underwriters Training Council Fellow
MBA	Master in Business Administration
MSFS	Master of Science in Financial Services
PFS	Personal Financial Specialist
REBC	Registered Employee Benefits Consultant
RHU	Registered Health Underwriter
RPA	Retirement Plans Associate

Continuing-Education Meetings and Staying Current

Along with designations, licenses, appointments, and registrations come the continuing-education (CE) requirements. Keeping track of CE due dates can be challenging. Fortunately, most companies' compliance departments do a good job of this, alerting advisors and team members to upcoming deadlines. Many will provide the CE credit opportunities as well. Other advisors are on their own. For them, developing a CE tickler on the annual calendar is a best practice. A common trap advisors fall into is waiting until the last minute to get the necessary credits. These advisors end up snoozing through classes that have little application to their practice, creating wasted education opportunities. Selecting and scheduling CE courses that are useful and practical is possible when given enough notice. Mandatory annual compliance meetings are a necessary CE exercise. If done without any creativity, they can be positively onerous. When combined with other social and educational activities to promote camaraderie, these meetings can be a highlight of the year and something to look forward to.

The advisor has a duty to keep current on her chosen specialties and on general market conditions. The bull market of the 1990s made every investor look like a star. There was a wake-up call bear market exacerbated by the 9/11 terrorist attacks from 2000 through 2002. Traditional wisdom said to stay put—a recovery will be inevitable. For five years, it seemed to be true as plus-markets ensued and portfolio value was restored. And then came the mega-bear market beginning in late 2008 with the subprime collapse. Portfolio values fell back to 1997 levels. All investing wisdom seemed to be turned on its head, and huge infusions of government money into the markets promises to rewrite the free-market rules.

In this environment, meet Gary, an 18-year advisor in Illinois (and a CFP) and a self-styled student of the markets and economic trends. His educational intake includes his company's regular updates, research, and briefings, reading the *Wall Street Journal*, participating in conference calls, consulting selected online Web sites, and bouncing ideas off his mentor. Early in 2008, Gary began to get a sense of foreboding. "I didn't like the way the subprime markets were heading. The credit boom was coming to a head, as I saw it. Something had to give—there was lots of finger-pointing, but no one was taking responsibility for failing mortgages. California was the tipping point for me. They began to slip into red ink. So I put my top clients into 75 percent money markets and 25 percent balanced portfolios. Once Lehman Brothers put itself on the market and refused to sell below their too-high asking price, I knew I'd done the right thing."

How did your top clients fare from August through November 2008, when portfolios were losing up to 50 percent of their value?

"Their portfolios are down, but only by 5 percent. They are quite pleased. I don't get too many angst-ridden calls from that group."

Gary's not a psychic. Nor was he simply lucky. He has deliberately acquired a network of information providers and opinion makers that he feels provide him with enough evidence to challenge prevailing assumptions. He was willing to take action on behalf of his clients based on his reading of the situation and his accumulated experience. This is the hallmark of a best practices Education system: defining your own set of periodic (daily, weekly, monthly) resources that you feel are credible and reliable. Volume of information and opinions alone is not a formula for educational success, and it is to be avoided. Be selective.

Many advisor offices have a television on during business hours tuned to a financial network with ticker-tape-crawlers. While a nice diversion for clients in the waiting area, under normal circumstances, it can also be a mild distraction. During breaking events, it can completely sidetrack an office. The newspapers and magazines in the waiting area should also be current and reflective of your educational system. By the way, be ready to discuss any articles that might be in these periodicals—your clients will assume you read them.

Motivation, Inspiration, and Conferences

An important aspect of the advisor's education system is where he finds the doses of motivation and inspiration in the course of building a practice.

"It ain't easy," sighed Glen, a fourth-year advisor in the San Francisco Bay Area. "Today is one of those days. Three appointment cancellations, including one that was a sure sale, underwriting gave a table D rating to an applicant I thought was standard, my car's brakes have developed a loud squeak, and my new assistant showed up late." Glen and I have been working to establish his business systems, and it seems for every two steps forward we take one step back. This was one of those "step back" calls.

"You're feeling a little frustrated," I observed. My role with Glen, as with all my clients, is as a consultant. I'm not a coach who digs into psychological and behavioral issues and provides life guidance. My goal is to help construct a strong, systematized advisory practice. I learned long ago my role is behind the scenes.

"Yeah," Glen admitted. "But when events conspire against me and I feel like throwing in the towel, I go and close my door, put on some music and read."

I was intrigued. "What music? What do you read?"

"I hibernate for a half hour, and then I'm charged up again. The music is a CD of the harder-driving Beatles songs, like 'Lovely Rita,' 'Revolution,' 'Birthday,' 'Drive My Car,' and such. Sometimes the music is enough. Other times, I'll read *Life Is Tremendous* by Charlie T. Jones. Best little inspirational book ever. His SIB-KIS is the best: See It Big, Keep It Simple. That's the perspective I need to keep."

"And how does this practice management process we're working through fit into that perspective?"

Glen paused to consider. "It's definitely the big picture. Once we get it running, it will be more or less turnkey. IF I can keep an assistant!" he laughed. By just talking about his two safety valves, the Beatles and *Life Is Tremendous*, I could feel Glen's tension vanish.

The motivational and inspirational materials and resources are as varied as the advisors. Some regain their perspective by listening to classical music in the car, reading Bible passages, listening to audiobooks, or reaching out to a friend. There is an entire industry to support the advisor's motivational needs.

Tonya, an eight-year financial planner in Louisiana, has two events a year scheduled for this purpose.

"At this point in my practice," she related, "I look to the company-sponsored Gold Club meeting every summer as a big motivator. I meet other advisors, and there are workshops, good speakers, and sightseeing. I always come away with too many new ideas! The other event is something for my own development. This year I enrolled in a two-day seminar on maximizing the resources for retirees."

Where do you find inspiration on a daily or weekly basis?

"Ah, yes. I really am involved in our church, and that provides a great outlet for energy and inspiration. I also get a little invested in our kids' sports teams, though it is sometimes embarrassing to them!"

Well-designed conferences such as the one described by Tonya can align the company with the advisor's motivational aspirations, and that's a win-win. Other conferences are sponsored by financial service organizations such as the Million Dollar Round Table (MDRT), local CFP chapters, and the American College. Motivation and inspiration can be found in civic clubs, networking groups, public speaking organizations, volunteer and charitable activities, and a multitude of other offerings.

The best practice in this section would be to ensure that you have at least one inspirational and motivational event scheduled in a given year. Identify your reliable sources for dealing with the stresses and disappointments that are inevitable in our business. Depending on your place on the extroversion/introversion scale, these resources can run the gamut from intensely personal (as with Glen) to a social network (as with Tonya).

Mentoring and Joint Work

The term *mentor* has two meanings in the financial services world. First, a mentor is a wise, experienced, older advisor, member of management, or other sage person.

The second type of mentor is the person assigned to work with a new advisor who will "teach 'em the ropes." This type of mentor typically is a field sales manager for the first year and a more experienced advisor for years 2 and 3. It's this experienced advisor/rookie advisor relationship we'll explore here.

In the majority of financial services organizations I've encountered over the years, one consistent finding has been the lack of quantity and quality *second-line* sales managers. These are the people who bring new advisors into the business, supervise them in their first year or two, role-play, and go on appointments with them. A reason for this dearth of sales managers is a chronic tendency of firm and company management to convince young, successful advisors in their first few years to become sales managers. The skill set of a successful advisor and that of a successful manager are quite different. Usually, the hope is that the success of the experienced advisor will somehow rub off on the new person.

This form of osmosis has yet to be isolated in real life. What usually happens is that the experienced advisor's production falls off, she donates commissions to help the new advisor succeed, both incomes drop, the new advisor fails, and everyone is frustrated.

With this lack of sales managers so pervasive in our business, many companies and firms will instead assign a new advisor to a mentor. This mentor is an experienced, senior advisor without the field manager title but with similar osmotic expectations.

There are many variations in how these mentoring relationships are structured, but generally they fall into one of three categories: (1) consultative, (2) partner, or (3) assistant.

Consultative

A consultative mentoring relationship is the safest for the senior advisor. Here, the new advisor, Jan, is clearly building her own practice, apart from the senior advisor's practice. The senior advisor, Char, regularly meets with the new advisor, doing case reviews, reviewing activity, suggesting strategies, and doing some limited joint appointments. The joint case revenues are clearly split according to a specific formula. Jan can tap into Char's administrative and marketing team but only for educational purposes (not to have work done for her).

Partner

A partner mentoring relationship is more problematic. The senior advisor, Bill, agrees to allow the new advisor, Ethan, to use his established practice as a source of prospects, usually turning over his large book of C-level clients for Ethan to work. If Ethan finds new business from these C-level clients, he receives 75 percent of the revenue, with Bill retaining 25 percent. Ethan continues to bring his own prospects to the table, getting Bill's input and the support of his team. For these cases, Ethan gets 75 percent and Bill gets 25 percent. In short, Bill is allowing Ethan the use of his resources to get Ethan's own practice off the ground. The ulterior motive is to gauge how Ethan interacts with Bill's team and clientele to see if he might be a successor for Bill in the future, an upside to these types of arrangements.

However, a common outcome is for the relationship not to gel. They politely part ways, and Ethan continues to pursue his dream in another direction. The downside in this scenario is that as long as Ethan is in the business, a portion of his client base will belong to Bill and vice versa. Even if Ethan resigns, Bill retains the clients, but does not get their full revenue as Ethan's percentage goes to back to the company via the orphan pool.

Senior advisors will have attempted at least one of these arrangements in the course of their careers. They are seductive at the beginning since Ethan can solve some of his own prospecting shortfalls by being able to tap into Bill's large group of C-level clients. Theoretically, Bill has a new source of prospects from Ethan's networks. Seems like a win-win until the C-level clients (who are C-level clients for a reason) aren't being productive and Ethan's limited networks are not producing new prospects. Bill begins to hand off lower-quality referrals to Ethan, and his team members grumble about having to support a second producer. Without intervention, this situation will fester and result in hard feelings all around.

The partnering mentorship should have a limited trial period with specified expectations to be reviewed by both parties after about a month. If it's working, create a second, longer time period and establish the next set of expectations to be reviewed. Continue these reviews until the day the partnership becomes formalized and the two practices agree to merge or go their separate ways.

Assistant

An assistant relationship is the third type of mentoring used by experienced advisors to help bring on new advisors. The senior advisor, Rex, agrees to work with Jared, the new advisor. Rex's expectation is that Jared will act as his marketing assistant to learn the paperwork, track the underwriting, follow the investments, set up seminars, make prospecting calls, and run the database. Meanwhile, Jared is ostensibly developing his own practice.

Whether or not the mentorship is successful, Jared leaves Rex after a year or two to resign or to branch out on his own. This forces Rex to once again do his own marketing assistant work or to get another new advisor to train and develop. This revolving door of training, developing, and leaving becomes a formula for stagnation and frustration in the senior advisor's practice.

In all three of these field mentorships, a common element is education in the form of joint work during the different appointments in the Sales Process system. *Joint work* is defined as two or more advisors' working on a single case or client together. The five-part "MDRT split" described in an earlier chapter and repeated here provides a logical method of dividing up the caseload:

20 percent goes to the advisor who brought in the lead
20 percent goes to the advisor who does the discovery fact-and-feeling-finding
20 percent goes to the advisor who does the case preparation
20 percent goes to the advisor who presents and closes the case
20 percent goes to the advisor who will provide ongoing service to the new client

An advisor can find joint work an excellent venue for growing into new markets, learning advanced sales concepts, and observing other advisors' techniques. Ideally, working jointly with another advisor should have two elements: learning and earning.

In our partner mentoring relationship above, if Ethan simply brought Bill in to close cases, he'd be earning but not learning. Bill might retain his closing secrets and never teach them to Ethan. On the other hand, if Bill brought Ethan in on a case to observe and not participate, he'd be learning but not earning. A little of this can go a long way, especially if there is a well-defined Sale Process system to study. Eventually, a healthy balance of earning and learning should be maintained.

Study Groups

A *study group* can be defined as a group of people an advisor meets with regularly for the purpose of solving problems, brainstorming ideas, sharing perspectives, holding each member accountable, and growing personally and professionally.

A study group is not a referral-gathering process. While referrals might eventually be by-products of some study groups, they are not the primary reason for getting together. Growth, sharing, and accountability are the primary drivers of any study group.

Looking for a good study group can be a frustrating process. There are five distinct types of study groups that serve five different advisor needs: (1) the natural study group, (2) the specific-goal study group, (3) the interdisciplinary study group, (4) the open exchange study group, and (5) the common beliefs and passions study group.

I'll describe each type and then offer considerations for forming or joining a study group.

The Natural Study Group

The natural study group is one fostered exclusively in a particular financial services organization. All the participants are from the same company, broker/dealer, and/or office. These advisors share the same issues, products, compensation, incentives, and technology. They "speak a common language." Examples of these groups include these:

- In-office advisors who are roughly at the same experience level
- A group of advisors who have different areas of expertise
- Regional groups of advisors of all experience levels who meet after qualifying at a specific production level
- National groups of advisors of all experience levels who meet after qualifying at a specific production level

The Specific-Goal Study Group

The specific-goal study group is assembled by advisors who are striving for a common accomplishment. These groups generally follow a curriculum and usually target a test date as the end point for the group's life. Common examples include the CFP, Series 7, Series 63, CLU, CLTC, and numerous other licenses and designations.

The Interdisciplinary Study Group

The interdisciplinary study group is one in which the financial services advisor has assembled a group of fellow professionals from nonfinancial services disciplines. Generally, these other participants are at the same experience level in their own professions as the advisor is in hers. Examples of these groups include these:

- The advisor and other professionals in financially related occupations, such as a CPAs, trust or estate attorneys, bankers, mortgage lenders, property and casualty agents, and/or stock brokers.

- The advisor and other professionals in marketing-related occupations. If the advisor has the construction industry as his target market, a study group might consist of a general contractor, subcontractor, real estate agent, architect, supplier, and/or a financing expert.

The Open Exchange Study Group

The fourth type of study group is the open exchange group. With the availability of virtually unlimited communication opportunities via the Internet, all sorts of online collaborations are possible. Web sites, blogs, and publications offer forums for exchanges among their members on a wide variety of topics. These forums are not usually driven by a structured agenda, but by advisor's questions and the biases of the sponsor. Frequent participation in an open exchange group can lead to online relationships that can fulfill the purpose of a study group.

The Common Beliefs and Passions Study Group

This group format links the advisor with others who share a particular belief system or personal motivation. Examples would be these:

- Faith-based groups of advisors and other professionals such as Christian business associations or Bible-based investing
- Cause-based groups of advisors and other professionals such as financial literacy, cancer research, "green" investing, or chambers of commerce
- Coach-facilitated groups, sharing a common coach or coaching program and philosophy
- Avocation-related groups, sharing common interests such as golf or travel

The structure for each of these study group types will vary. The open exchange groups might not even have a true structure, and the specific-goal groups may have a very structured, preset agenda. What follows are questions to ask when considering joining or starting a study group:

Why are you together? Keep the purpose of the study group clear. Agree on a mission or vision statement, or common goals for the group.

How will you communicate as a group, and where will you meet?
What are the expectations of each group member? What are the
rules for the group?
What is our standard agenda? A structure for the group makes it
easier to get the meeting going and stay on track.

Reaching out to other advisors is the best method of finding a study
group that is open to new members. Organizations such as the Financial
Planning Association, Million Dollar Round Table, and the American
College try to foster study groups among their members as do many firms,
companies, and broker/dealers. Local chapters of the National Association
of Insurance and Financial Advisors (NAIFA) may also sponsor study
groups.

Assistants

Initial Education

In the Communication system, we developed a clear set of job duties and
expectations for the assistant. I suggested that this document would be crucial
in the training, supervision, and performance review of the assistant. Here is
where having this detailed summary pays off—the initial and ongoing training and development of the assistant. There were two specific sets of job
duties reviewed in Chapter 9: those of a marketing assistant and those of an
administrative assistant. From those two documents, the advisor can create a
specific set of duties for an assistant on either side or a hybrid of both. It's this
set of duties that should drive the training program, much as the core competencies drive the advisor curriculum. Figure 10.1 uses the marketing assistant
(MA) duties as the job description.

Figure 10.2 is a sample first week training schedule. Initially, the primary duties for the MA are to fill and coordinate the advisor's calendar and
to maintain the CRM and post information in it.

Consequently, those are the key activities in week 1: learning the programs, learning the call types and call scripts, and observing the advisor in
sales, review, and networking situations. There is time for telephone role-
play and coaching while the MA makes initial calls. Using the best practices operations manual and checklists makes the training job easier and
focused.

The following weeks of the training schedule will continue to layer on
the other job description duties. Once the CRM is understood and the MA

Figure 10.1

Marketing Assistant Job Duties

Time Management/Calendar

1. Fills advisor's calendar with the following:

   - Client annual reviews

   - Sales Process appointments: initial, discovery, presentation, and delivery appointments

   - COI and networking meetings

2. Coordinates and updates advisor's calendar:

   - To-do lists

   - Appointments

   - Forward planning

Client Relationship Management (CRM) Software

3. Maintains database for the following:

   - Client hard product information

   - Client soft information

   - Prospect tracking

   - Client segmentation

4. Postappointment:

   - Transcribes client notes and discovery materials into CRM database

   - Fulfills any follow-up

   - Creates unique client correspondence

5. Cultivates top clients by way of proactive interaction and client appreciation events.

(continued)

Figure 10.1

(Continued)

Client Management

6. Executes contact protocols for each client segment (newsletters, cards, and so on)

7. Maintains physical client files to be compliance ready

8. Culls through C-level clients to determine if they can grow to be A- or B-level clients

9. Prepares annual review materials and manages client opportunity inventory

Client Acquisition

10. Researches and provides advisor with prospect names and names to feed during referral-gathering appointments

11. Plans and executes seminars and other marketing efforts (campaigns) and manages the follow-up

Sales Process

12. Creates the discovery letters

13. Tracks activity and sales statistics

14. Executes and tracks trades

15. Packages appointment materials

16. Prefills application information

17. Reviews applications for submission

Case Development

18. Data input

19. Creates routine illustrations, hypotheticals, asset allocations, quotes, and other case prep work

20. Assembles presentation materials

Figure 10.2

Sample First Week Training Schedule for a Marketing Assistant (A = advisor, O = office manager or equivalent, T = trainer or equivalent)

Week 1	Assignment	Instructor	Time	Resources
Monday	Welcome. Introduction to personnel. Tour. Receive computer IDs and passwords. Identify workstation components. Organize desk.	O	0.5 hr	
	Benefits overview. Performance reviews. Compensation structure.	O	0.5 hr	Benefits booklet, supervision and review forms, compensation overview
	Review mission statement, policies, and procedures. Get copies of manuals.	O	0.5 hr	Office manual, best practices operations manual
	Review the job duties and expectations from the hiring process. Discuss advisor's marketing plan as it pertains to the MA.	A	2 hr	Business plan documents, job description
	Learn to access proprietary software, programs, and Web sites, with a brief description of how each is used.	O	1 hr	Passwords, IDs
	Time blocked to learn programs.	Self/T	2 hr	Program tutorials
	Observe advisor's first appointment.	A	1 hr	Sales Process checklist
	Learn do-not-call procedures.	Self	0.5 hr	Do-not-call section of Client Acquisition
Tuesday	Understand Client Acquisition system.	A/Self	1 hr	Client Acquisition system resources
	Review types of calls MA will be making. Identify scripts.	A	0.5 hr	Client Acquisition and Client Management system resources
	Telephone and calendar training.	T	2 hr	Video, audio role-play, calendar

Day	Task		Time	Resources
	Begin calling prospects, setting up reviews, and sales appointments.	T/Self	1 hr	Calendar
	Observe advisor on a discovery interview.	A	2 hr	Sales Process checklist
	Review initial interview and discovery with advisor. Show MA follow-up tasks in CRM.	A	1 hr	Sales Process checklist, CRM
Wednesday	Continue learning software and programs.	Self/T	2 hr	Tutorials
	Review day's calls to be made and expectations.	A	0.25 hr	Call lists, CRM, calendar
	Make calls.	Self/T if needed	2 hr	Calendar, CRM
	Observe advisor annual review appointment, with debrief on follow-up tasks in CRM.	A	2 hr	Client Management checklist
	Learn ethics and compliance basics.	Self/O	1 hr	Company tutorials, manuals, documentation
Thursday	Review day's calls to be made and expectations.	A	0.25 hr	Call lists, CRM, calendar
	Make calls.	Self	3 hr	Calendar, CRM
	Continue learning software and programs.	Self	2 hr	Tutorials
	Observe advisor in a networking situation with debrief on follow-up tasks in CRM.	A	2 hr	Client Acquisition checklist, CRM
Friday	Review day's calls to be made and expectations.	A	0.25 hr	Call lists, CRM, calendar
	Make calls.	Self	3 hr	Calendar, CRM
	Continue learning software and programs.	Self/T	2 hr	Tutorials
	Participate in team weekly meeting.	A	1 hr	Communication system meeting agenda
	Plan next week's training expectations. Review first week's progress.	A/O/T	1 hr	Marketing assistant job description

can navigate it, client service and contact protocols can be introduced. Mail policies, letters, and techniques are a natural for week 2, as is beginning to work on developing prospecting lists for the advisor. As we discussed in the Communication system, the advisor is in a supervisory role with the new MA and should avoid the extremes of micromanagement and abdication in favor of the monitoring style.

Cross Training

One of the benefits of having the Eight Business Systems detailed in a best practices operations manual is that cross training can be expedited. When an advisor has brought in a second assistant to support her practice, cross training becomes an important issue. If one assistant is gone for an extended period of time for illness, vacation, wedding, pregnancy, education, paternity leave, and the like, the other should be able to pick up the essential job duties.

Using the two assistant checklists from Chapter 9, the advisor should take some time at a team meeting to identify what the key job duties are for each assistant and what steps can be taken to ensure that no balls get dropped during an absence or emergency. Matt, an advisor in Cincinnati, Ohio, faced this challenge recently:

Matt: "We have three of us on the team. Greta does more of the administrative work, and Tyler helps me with the marketing side. Both were hired within six months of each other a year ago, so they've got their roles down pretty well."

Tyler: "All was progressing nicely until my emergency appendectomy."

Greta: "And I was pressed into dual service. Fortunately, Tyler was preparing his marketing operations manual, so I had something to guide me. But I did lose a couple of days' productivity trying to re-create some of the tasks he was doing at the time."

Matt: "What were the key items you had to quickly pick up?"

Greta: "The follow-up calls that were scheduled on the calendar and to-do list were the immediate concern. These included top clients and prospects. Then there was continuing to prepare for our January seminar. Finally, the job of entering client case notes."

Matt: "I did my own case preparation and paperwork for appointments, which is another Tyler responsibility. We made out okay and didn't lose much momentum. We did realize, however, that Tyler knows very little about what Greta does in the service and new business submission areas."

Greta: "So I started my own operations manual, with checklists. I'll be getting married in June of this year, and I plan to be off for at least 10 days."

Matt: "At least we can plan ahead for that one. And we can be sure of no more Tyler appendix attacks! Anyway, having the cross training in place has given me peace of mind just knowing Greta and Tyler know where to jump to in the event of an emergency."

Licensing, Appointments, and Registrations

The section earlier in this chapter concerning licenses, appointments, and registrations for advisors is mirrored on the assistant level. The advisor who does not deal with registered products needs only to be state licensed and appointed. The assistant to this advisor should be state licensed and appointed as well. This allows the assistant to help clients with policy advice, applications, material changes in coverages, and prospecting. An assistant who is not licensed and appointed can perform routine administrative tasks but cannot venture too far into the marketing duties. Getting licensed can also provide a bonus opportunity for the assistant.

Once an advisor is a Registered Representative (RR) and works with registered, market-driven variable products, the rules change for the assistant. If the assistant deals with a RR's clients on a regular basis, the assistant must be both FINRA registered and state registered. If the assistant deals with clients only occasionally, such as during vacation back-up, only FINRA registration is necessary. If the assistant deals only with the RR advisor and not the clients, no state or FINRA registration is necessary. The following duties do not require registration and can be done "on behalf of" the RR advisor:

- Set up and confirm the RR's appointments.
- Extend and confirm invitations and appointments to firm- or RR-sponsored events and seminars.
- Direct potential and/or current clients to the RR.

- Describe in general terms the types of investments that are available from the RR and/or firm.
- Distribute promotional material.
- Send out forms and requested documents to clients and/or prospects.
- Enter trade orders to be executed at the direction of the RR. The assistant cannot receive the order directly from the client; it must be received from the RR.
- Assist the RR in completing and processing client applications and service requests.
- Create and maintain client files.
- Make the following service requests on behalf of the clients:
  o Change addresses.
  o Cancel or suspend bank drafts, systematic exchanges, or withdrawals.
  o Order money market checks.

The following duties require the assistant to have both FINRA and state registrations:

- Meeting independently with clients to complete applications or client account information forms
- Discussing registered insurance or investment products with the clients or prospects
- Dispensing prospectuses and discussing content information
- Commenting in any way on the market or specific mutual funds or strategies
- Discussing the implications of moving funds among subaccounts in variable products or mutual fund families
- Soliciting or accepting new accounts or orders on behalf of the RR
- Prequalifying prospective customers as to financial status, investment history, or investment objectives
- Communicating with clients about the following:
  o Redemptions, loans, withdrawals, or liquidations of accounts
  o Tax implications of a policy loan
  o Reallocating client holdings
  o Changing the registration or RR on the account
  o Changing the dividend options
  o Establishing or reactivating a bank draft, or changing bank instructions or dollar amounts

During the annual compliance audit, a questionnaire must be completed by the assistant to attest to his or her understanding of these dos and don'ts. Any assistant who handles checks or securities must also be fingerprinted.

Advocacy: Designations, Continuing Education, Study Groups, Motivation, and Conferences

Once a good assistant has been hired, trained, and retained, the goal is to develop an advocate. I discussed the difference between a staff person and an advocate in the last chapter. Briefly, a staff person is one who clocks in, does his or her job, and clocks out. The advocate assistant will go above and beyond the simple duties and seek out marketing opportunities and proactively build client relationships on behalf of the advisor.

Once an assistant is in place, the advisor is tempted to leave well enough alone. This is *in*dependent thinking. The *inter*dependent advisor seeks to build the team, initially through cross training, regular team meetings, and strong supervision. Over and above this, offering assistants growth opportunities is imperative to their long-term retention and satisfaction. The equation is simple:

Advocates = profitable practice growth

Lisa, in St. Louis, Missouri, is 20 years into her career as a financial planner. She is perpetually in her company's top 10 percent with an annual revenue growth rate of 12 percent. She has two assistants, Dolores and Anthony.

Lisa: "I could never have gotten to where I am without those two. Dolores has been with me for five years, after she didn't make her advisor contract requirements in our office. She was fully licensed and seemed to have a good phone presence, so I brought her on as my marketing assistant. Anthony has a real knack for detail work and has worked with me for eight years now."

Anthony: "Lisa's great to work for. As she said, I do a lot of the detail work, like following up on paperwork, underwriting, trades, transfers, rollovers, service work. I finally got my Series 66 so I can do a lot more customer contact."

Dolores: "Lisa has her CLU and ChFC designations and is helping me get my CFP."

Lisa: "It will be a good fit for the team. Dolores can then do more of the discovery meetings with me and take a stronger role in case preparation."

Dolores: "Lisa's cofunding my CFP classes and is willing to review some of the tougher concepts, like options."

How else has Lisa promoted the creation of a team and advocates?

Anthony: "We get to go on the company conference trips. She qualifies every year and pays our way."

Dolores: "Yes, Orlando last year was great for my kids. I have two grade-schoolers, and we took them to Disney World. She paid for them, and my husband paid his own way. But going to the breakout sessions and hearing the platform speakers was very inspiring."

Anthony: "At the conferences we meet other assistants and have even started a telephone study group with two other offices. Five of us, every month. It's been instructive hearing how other assistants are handling similar issues."

Lisa: "We try to do continuing-education credits and compliance meetings together. With a little foresight, it can be done."

Dolores: "Plus the everyday things. We get to choose the music in the office, the beverages in the fridge, and give opinions about the décor."

Anthony: "And birthdays. She always remembers our birthday and anniversary date. I was just mentioning that to a friend of mine, and he was duly impressed. So I said he should meet Lisa, and we just set up the initial appointment."

Lisa: "There's the advocacy."

Designations for assistants run the gamut of those available to advisors. In addition, there are three others that commonly are obtained. Administrative assistants can work toward two designations rooted in serving an insurance practice but have expanded over the years to include investment knowledge:

AIAA   Associate Insurance Agency Administration
FLMI   Fellow, Life Management Institute
RP   Registered Paraplanner

Clients

The third component of the Education system is client education. Components of client education can be found in both the Client Management and the Case Development systems. As stated earlier in this chapter, clients have access to unprecedented amounts of financial information. Where once the client was forced to contact the advisor for account balances, she can now log onto the company Web sites and gather real-time values. With that information, she can go to a number of online blogs to discuss her investment performance versus that of other advisors and products. She can reallocate her portfolio online, and with some studying available from a reputable company Web site, she can jump in and do her own money management and market research and then buy and sell stocks at bargain transaction costs. This is certainly empowering for the client, but to what end?

Dr. Fred, my physician for the past 15 years, has a private practice in town. We get together for our quarterly blood work review in one of his examination rooms, and once the results have been analyzed, medications checked, and any appropriate chastising is done, we go off topic. Invariably, one of his pet peeves concerns patients who have overdosed on Internet medical information.

"This one guy today," he related, "comes in convinced he's got encephalitis." Dr. Fred pulled out five folded sheets of paper from his pocket and smoothed them out on the desk. "Here is his Internet research, from five different Web sites. This one says that the symptoms of encephalitis are fever, fatigue, sore throat, stiff neck and back, vomiting, headache, confusion, irritability, unsteady gait, drowsiness, and visual sensitivity to light." He looked up. "He has a cold. He's worn out from the cold and all the over-the-counter meds he's been taking. But he's convinced these indicate encephalitis. These other Web pages are pretty much the same."

"At least he came in to see you," I said.

"Yes, maybe I got through to him. But he was looking for validation of an opinion he had already formed and a treatment protocol for encephalitis. I basically told him to let the cold run its course, but he hinted at getting a referral to St. Mary's hospital to explore it further."

"More and more of this is happening," I stated.

"Ah, yes. A good percentage of patients no longer take my advice at face value. They go and dig up all sorts of data about medications, conditions, and therapies. Most of them mean well and just want to be better informed. But there's that hypochondriac fringe group, like this guy. Drives me nuts."

As with the medical profession, the explosion of available information impacts the financial advisor's clientele. In this environment, the advisor is no longer the ultimate authority but an additional resource—albeit a trusted resource—for the client. Making it more difficult is that today's consumer is jaded to "spin" and automatically tends to question information coming from only one source.

I recently presented a one-page graphic chart to my church adult education class. It was produced by BlackRock investments and demonstrated the recoveries that historically follow bear markets. As I explained the chart, two people stopped me and wanted to know, "Who are these BlackRock people?" I read their official blurb from the Web site: "BlackRock is a premier provider of global investment management, risk management, and advisory services to institutional and retail clients around the world." There were grunts and scoffs (it's a convivial group), but they gave me the benefit of the doubt. After I was finished with the review, the questions started.

"Are there other charts like that?" Fortunately, I had brought a similar document from Waddell & Reed. It showed a different angle (the posttax versus the pretax angle in the BlackRock piece), but it conveyed the same message.

"Which one is more accurate?" one asked.

"Do those charts show the impact of dividends?" asked another.

Sound like some of your clients? In subsequent conversation, the class was quoting what they remembered from five different Web sites, six business-cable shows, four different newspapers, and eight commentators and columnists. As their collective "financial advisor" for the day, I was overwhelmed and almost fell into a defensive posture.

Then I remembered Dr. Fred. He knew a cold when he saw one, despite the hysteria of a patient's Internet research. Dr. Fred's been in practice 35 years. That's why I see him—the collective experience he brings to the table. He's been through scares, epidemics, mutating viruses, and life and death issues with countless patients. I value his core medical knowledge, his philosophy, and his willingness to evolve as new discoveries, technologies, and medications develop. So toward the end of the class, I quieted everyone down.

"This is why we have financial advisors," I started. "I've met plenty of them over the years, and the best of them are students of the financial markets. They have opinions and rationales that feed the advice they give. I've lived through 25 professional years of market fluctuation. I know something about the history of the Great Depression and postwar recovery. I've endured the Cold War, gas crises, and price freezes, not to mention double-digit inflation, interest rate ups and downs, and terrorist attacks. You have lived through all this as well. In all those years, here are the historical trends." I gestured to the two presentation pieces. "If you and your financial advisor see something critically different in today's situation, please act on it. Meanwhile, here's how my advisor, my wife, and I are handling my portfolio." I shared the general trends of my own retirement fund and the reallocation strategy we were implementing.

Let's not forget that one of the advisor's geniuses is an ability to help clients interpret information. There is so much of it out in cyberspace and the media that the trusted advisor *should* be the one clients turn to for perspective and insight. If not you, then who?

From Dr. Fred and the Sunday adult ed class, we can extrapolate some best practices in the area of client education:

- Have a strong, flexible point of view. Most of the Prime and Mature practice advisors I've worked with possess a working philosophy about managing money, financial security, tax planning, retirement preparation, or some other specialty. An anchoring set of beliefs with which to endure and interpret the swirling winds of information will be well received by your clients.

- Engage in dialogue with top-tier clients. During periodic reviews (at least annually), give your best overview of the current financial environment and how it affects the planning you and the client have done so far. You have the knowledge and wisdom of experience. Don't be afraid to assert it.

- Provide learning opportunities for top clients. It's up to them to choose to take advantage of the opportunity. These can include seminars on current topics, wholesaler presentations, fund managers' conference calls, Webinars, and other "exclusive" events, and they give clients a feeling of being insiders at your invitation. Cito, an advisor in New Jersey, spent 22 years on Wall Street dealing in derivatives before joining a firm. His managing partner asked him to do a series of presentations on the evolution of the derivatives market for the firm's A-level clientele. Cito's unique insights proved a popular draw and gave the other advisors in the firm a credibility boost.

- Teach classes whenever the chance arises. Advisors are involved in community education programs, work site presentations, school business clubs, places of worship, civic organizations, and professional meetings.
- Build a library of books, articles, publications, and other media that support your philosophy and inspirational approach. Todd, in Wisconsin, has written a series of books about "real-life financial planning" for physicians, dentists, specialists, and other young professionals. Each is a slim volume that systematically describes Todd's reasoned approach to getting control of a busy practitioner's finances. These books are part of his initial package to referrals and interested prospects. Other advisors send favorite books to top clients. One of Todd's picks is *Golf Is Not a Game of Perfect* by Bob Rotella. Todd explained, "It has nothing to do with financial planning. But . . . since I'm addicted to the great sport of golf and am always trying to improve and see others improve, whenever I get a chance I send this book out to clients who play golf. It provides some great ideas on the mental side of the game." Another favorite is Mitch Anthony's *The New Retirementality*. It's a "great book for identifying the issues facing everyone as they prepare for their retirement years." Having this library of material to share is an excellent way to personalize their educational experience as clients of yours.
- Finally, be self-disclosing. I had no problem sharing with my class how Mike is advising us about our portfolio. The brilliance of the golden rule shines especially bright here. If you are dispensing advice you would not give to yourself in a similar situation, it smells of hypocrisy. There is no need to reveal your dollar amounts, but be able to show that there is consistency in practicing what you preach. Orrin, an advisor in Lexington, Kentucky, carries his portfolio and insurance statements with him on appointments and when appropriate, shares them with prospects and clients. "It's a snapshot of some—not all—of my financial holdings," he explained. "It's very powerful to show the performance over the years of my own portfolio versus that of a theoretical index. Most clients will tell me it's something they've never seen before and are highly complimentary."

Education System Best Practices Checklist

The Education System Best Practices Checklist is shown in Figure 10.3. There are 39 specific steps in this checklist. It's the blueprint for the seventh section of your best practices operations manual.

Each practice is unique, of course, and the checklist can be modified for each advisor. The resources referred to on the checklist are suggestions based on various best practices observed in the field. Any resource in italics refers to a piece reviewed or illustrated earlier in this chapter.

Figure 10.3

Education System Best Practices Checklist

Education Activities	Advisor	Marketing Assistant	Administrative Assistant	Firm	Resources
Advisor Education: Core Competencies					
7.1 Define the core competencies for your chosen practice platform: • Core Four business system skills • Product knowledge • Product features and benefits	X			S	*Sample above* Core Four best practices operations manual
7.2 Find or build a training and education curriculum that adequately addresses these core competencies.	X			S	Wide variety of broker/ dealer, company, firm, and third-party materials
7.3 Implement assessments to ensure mastery of core competencies: • Role-play (video/live) partners and feedback delivery process • Joint field work partners and feedback delivery process • Classroom demonstrations and feedback delivery process	X			S	

Note: X denotes primary accountability person, and S denotes shared accountability person.

	Advisor Education: Licenses, Appointments, and Registrations				
7.4	State license requirements: • Application • Completion • Submission • Continuing education needed to keep license • Renewal dates noted	X		S	
7.5	State and company appointment requirements: • Application • Completion • Submission • Continuing education needed to keep appointment • Renewal dates noted	X		S	
7.6	FINRA, state, and company registration requirements: • Application • Completion • Submission • Continuing education needed to keep registration • Renewal dates noted	X		S	
	Advisor Education: Designations				
7.7	Select an appropriate designation to pursue.	X			

(continued)

Figure 10.3

(Continued)

Education Activities		Advisor	Marketing Assistant	Administrative Assistant	Firm	Resources
7.8	Apply to the sponsoring organization.	X				
7.9	Receive materials and study guides.	X				
7.10	Schedule a timeline for completion.	X				
7.11	Take the appropriate tests.	X				
Advisor Education: Media Input						
7.12	Choose venues for staying current: • Internet • Print • Audio • Firm resources • Company resources • Broker/dealer resources • Maintain a library for tax, legal, financial, and product research	X			S	
Advisor Education: Motivation and Inspiration						
7.13	Establish sources for positive reinforcement: • People • Places • Media	X				

Advisor Education: Mentoring and Joint Work			
7.14	Clarify mentoring expectations.	X	S
7.15	Review and revise mentoring expectations at regular intervals.	X	S
7.16	Clarify joint work expectations: Learn and earn.	X	S
7.17	Agree on compensation splits.	X	S *MDRT split*
Advisor Education: Study Groups			
7.18	Determine study group preference: • Natural • Specific goal • Interdisciplinary • Open exchange • Common beliefs and passions	X	S
			S
7.19	Find sources for joining or starting a study group.	X	S
7.20	Clarify expectations of the study group: • Purpose • Communication methods • Member contributions • Agenda • Meeting place	X	
Advisor Education: Professional Organizations			
7.21	Evaluate the merits of joining different professional organizations.	X	S

(continued)

Figure 10.3

(Continued)

Education Activities		Advisor	Marketing Assistant	Administrative Assistant	Firm	Resources
7.22	Application completed/submitted with dues for professional organizations.	X				
7.23	Attend meetings and participate.	X				
7.24	Take a leadership role.	X				
Advisor Education: Due Diligence						
7.25	Evaluate the universe of products and services available for the platform chosen; select the most appropriate for your clients.	X			X	
7.26	Monitor the ongoing performance of the products and services to ensure their integrity.	X			X	
Assistant Education: Basic Training						
7.27	Clarify job duties, expectations, and core competencies for assistant.	X	S	S	S	
7.28	Find or build a training and education curriculum that adequately addresses these duties, expectations, and core competencies.	X	S	S	S	*Figure 10.1*, Wide variety of broker/dealer, company, firm, and third-party materials

#					
7.29	Implement assessments to ensure mastery of core competencies. Role-play (video/live) partners and feedback delivery process.	X	S	S	S
7.30	Identify key job duties on which to cross train assistants.	X	S	S	
Assistant Education: Licenses, Appointments and Registrations					
7.31	State license requirements: • Application • Completion • Submission • Continuing education needed to keep license • Renewal dates noted	X	S	S	S
7.32	State and company appointment requirements: • Application • Completion • Submission • Continuing education needed to keep appointment • Renewal dates noted	X	S	S	S
7.33	FINRA, state, and company registration requirements if dealing with RR clients: • Dos and don'ts clear • Application • Completion • Submission • Continuing education needed to keep registration • Renewal dates noted	X	S	S	S

(continued)

Figure 10.3

(Continued)

Education Activities	Advisor	Marketing Assistant	Administrative Assistant	Firm	Resources
Assistant Education: Ongoing					
7.34	Identify possible: • Designations to achieve • Study groups to join • Meetings to attend • Motivational opportunities • Other growth opportunities	X	S	S	S	
Client Education					
7.35	Know and be able to articulate your professional philosophy.	X				
7.36	Encourage educational dialogue with top-tier clients.	X				
7.37	Provide learning opportunities for top-tier clients.	X				
7.38	Keep a library of resource materials to share with clients.	X				
7.39	Consider what degree of self-disclosure might be appropriate in your Client Acquisition and Client Management systems.	X				

11

Infrastructure Business System 8: Financial Management

The last of the Eight Business Systems is a comprehensive look at how you structure the financial aspects of your practice. We'll start with the 10 elements to consider when creating a business model. This will take us in a number of directions, but all roads will lead to the Financial Management System Best Practices Checklist. Along the way we'll encounter how to compensate assistants, understanding and protecting your paycheck, and additional tools for a practice's financial management.

Let's visit Peggy.

The 10 Elements of the Advisor's Business Model

Peggy is an advisor operating out of Torrance, California. She has an associate advisor, Eva, and an assistant, Patricia. Peggy's 20-year professional résumé includes stints with Charles Schwab and Waddell & Reed, after which she settled on her current configuration as a hybrid money manager and financial planner. She is now affiliated with a large, national broker/dealer (BD) in San Diego.

From our previous chapter on the Education system, you will recognize her designations—Certified Financial Planner (CFP) practitioner, Certified

Estate Advisor (CEA), and Certified in Long-Term Care (CLTC)—as well as her licensure—Series 7, Series 65, Series 63, and Life/Health. Peggy also has her Series 24, making her officially a Registered Principal. The Series 24 exam, administered by FINRA (as is the Series 7), entitles the holder to supervise and manage branch activities in a registered, securities-based product environment.

Peggy volunteers her time in the community, and she serves as a professional on the board of the South Bay Estate Planning Council. She is active in the Financial Planning Association (FPA). The FPA is a national organization for advisors who practice financial planning as their primary vocation.

Let's examine Peggy's business model in light of 10 elements that should be addressed as an advisor develops his practice over time. These 10 decisions will be made by the advisor, or they will be made for the advisor by the companies, BDs, or partners the advisor is connected to, and in some cases they will be made by circumstances beyond the advisor's control:

- Type of platform from which the advisor wants to operate
- Level of compliance accountability the advisor wishes to assume
- Size of the practice
- Resources available
- Compensation arrangements
- Types of clients the advisor wishes to attract
- Location and setup of office
- Tax status of the advisor
- Tax structure of the practice
- Benefits package available to the advisor

How one element is positioned affects most of the others, as you will see. Smart, progressive financial services organizations wisely package many of these elements to attract and retain productive advisors. Let's pick them apart.

Elements 1 and 2: The Chosen Platforms and the Level of Compliance Accountability the Advisor Wishes to Assume

The nature of your advisory practice is the first element contributing to the business structure of your practice. Recall that there are many possibilities, and an advisor can use one or several of the following platforms, as discussed in the Case Development system:

- Full financial planner
- Comprehensive planner

- Modular planner
- Investment planner
- Wealth manager
- Financial instrument specialist
- Market specialist
- Insurance planner
- Benefits planner
- Executive business planner

Peggy's practice mix results in her primary platform's being that of a full financial planner and an investment planner, with a long-term-care product specialization, and an expertise in 1031 exchanges. In the past, Peggy has worked from other platforms. With Waddell & Reed, it was a two-part position, half management and half financial advisor. In her early days with Schwab it was product-oriented advising, offering a defined pool of mutual funds to sell. She's come to love working on true, comprehensive financial planning over the ensuing years, and this will be the direction in which her practice will continue to evolve. Peggy's two core platforms from which she operates are the investment side, consisting of assets under management (AUM), and the fee-based financial planning side.

For the investment management side of her business, Peggy has chosen to affiliate with a broker/dealer. One reason she has chosen to work with her particular BD is that it doesn't offer any proprietary products. The BD will do the due diligence on the products in the financial services universe, make recommendations, and approve vendors. It will also provide compliance guidance and regulatory backup for her. Peggy prefers not to be beholden to a particular company's product line. The BD also provides technology and education, and it is her connection to Wall Street. The broker/dealer assumes the burden of placing trades, confirmations, paperwork, and follow-up. Peggy is willing to pay for this affiliation (10 percent of the fees she collects on her assets under management).

Another advisor might be willing to take these burdens on himself or outsource them to a company that will do the detail work behind buying, selling, and trading investments. Lots of variations exit, but most advisors will choose to be part of a BD for many of the same reasons Peggy has.

This particular BD relationship works well for Peggy. She can utilize the company's expertise and efficiencies of scale on the investment side of her business. Her BD is the Registered Investment Advisor (RIA) in this arrangement. An RIA sponsor is required to transact securities business and is generally defined as an individual or entity that (1) provides advice or analysis by making direct or indirect recommendations regarding securities or securities markets; (2) does this for compensation in any form; and (3) engages in the regular business of providing advice regarding securities. For her BD, which acts as the RIA for the investment side of her business, Peggy is an Investment Advisor Representative (IAR). She also manages a branch office of the broker/dealer RIA (known as the *office of supervisory jurisdiction*, or OSJ), and she has a Registered Representative (Eva) working with her. Consequently, she needs to have the Series 24 license and to act as the branch's Registered Principal.

In the financial planning side of her practice, Peggy has chosen to be on her own and not affiliated with a BD. This creates a situation for which she needs to be her own RIA. "I'm very confident in my financial planning abilities, and I don't need the BD's help designing and preparing plans. I'm willing to do all the necessary compliance things. The buck stops with me on the planning side. The BD helps cover me on the AUM side."

So Peggy needed to register as an RIA. If she were to manage more than $25 million in assets, she would need to register as an RIA with the Securities and Exchange Commission as well as the state of California. Since she's under that amount, she is just RIA registered with the state.

(Have you had enough acronyms yet? I'm doing my best to try and use only the key acronyms and in the process am jettisoning plenty of others that haunt every advisor on a daily basis.)

So in answer to element 2, the level of compliance accountability the advisor wishes to assume, Peggy has decided to take on the challenges of being both a Registered Principal and an RIA. Many advisors prefer not to get involved this deeply and are content to allow BD and firm compliance departments to take care of the daily requirements of staying in bounds. As with all 10 elements, there are trade-offs for an advisor's choices. The larger the compliance department is, the more conservative the advisor needs to be. Some advisors have found this to be too restrictive an environment and they go in a more boutique direction. Others, like Peggy, take a two-tier approach: using a BD for one part of her business (AUM) and taking sole compliance accountability for the other (planning).

Elements 3 and 4: The Size of the Practice and the Available Resources

Two considerations in setting up a practice are how big the advisor wants the business to become and what the advisor is willing to pay for resources.

Peggy's path is an example of a common progression. Early in her career, she surrounded herself with large organizations for support, protection, and education. After 15 years and having attained a Mature practice status, she had gained the confidence to strike out on her own in some aspects and retain the resources of a larger BD in others.

"I'm happy being a boutique shop," she said. "I have all of the BD's research to fall back on, especially in the 1031 exchange world, and all the BD demands is its cut of my AUM business. Fair enough. The rest of the time, I like being queen of my own domain. For my planning business, I have assembled a library of materials and a network of specialists that I use for support and resources. It's fun to go out for coffee and pick each other's brain and share information and experiences."

Do you enjoy having a busy office environment with lots of activity and interaction? Or, like Peggy, do you prefer a more intimate practice? What are you willing to pay for support? The attraction of large BDs is their breadth and depth of knowledge and marketing assistance. Yet the Internet has opened up the knowledge base to be cherry-picked for affordable subscriptions to marketing and research sources.

The broker/dealer, insurance, and investment companies often struggle to retain good, producing senior advisors in this environment. It's easy enough to satisfy the needs of a newer associate getting a practice off the ground, but once an experienced advisor finds a niche that she wants to pursue, will the company or BD have what she needs? In Peggy's case, the BD did. However, for the financial planning side of her business, she outgrew the need of external support, and she chose not to utilize that service of the BD.

Element 5: The Compensation Arrangements

The holy grail of financial services compensation is to find a way to reward advisors for building, maintaining, and deepening relationships with clients—not just any clients but those who are willing to be honorable stewards of their money. This entails moving from a product-based compensation model to a client-based model. In a sense, Peggy has achieved this compensation arrangement.

"My bills get paid by the assets under management part of my practice," she related. "Those are based on a fee structure, and after the 10 percent goes to my BD, the rest goes to cover the expenses. For their fee, clients receive investment advice, trading, asset allocation, portfolio analysis, quarterly performance reports, and educational workshops."

A sample fee structure for assets under management looks like this:

A Client's Aggregate Assets	Advisor's Fee, %
Over $5,000,000	Negotiable
$3,000,000–$4,999,999	0.70
$2,000,000–$2,999,999	0.80
$1,000,000–$1,999,999	0.90
$500,000–$999,999	1.0
$250,000–$499,999	1.25
$100,000–$249,999	1.5
$25,000–$99,999	1.75

Let's take an advisor who has a $20 million portfolio. That $20M is spread among 40 different clients, all paying different fees based on their particular asset aggregation. For simplicity's sake, let's say the mix of all aggregate levels might yield an advisor an average of 1 percent in fees, or $200,000. If 10 percent goes to a BD, the advisor nets $180,000. This can provide a nice cushion for a practice. The advantages of an AUM fee-based account compensation model include an ongoing income stream, along with fewer expenses required to maintain the practice over the long run because the advisor doesn't have to constantly market new products. If the market rises, so does the advisor's income. Disadvantages include clients' leaving before the breakeven point is achieved. This is the amount an advisor would have earned if the client had instead purchased commission-based products. If the market falls, so does the advisor's income. And eventually, the clients will begin to withdraw money for retirement income or other purposes, and the asset base will shrink accordingly.

Peggy also has the financial planning side of her business, which has a different compensation structure. She focuses on an hourly fee as the basis. "$200 an hour is what my time is worth," Peggy stated. "If someone wants a comprehensive, no-holds-barred financial plan, I'll charge a minimum of 16 hours, or $3,200. Plus additional hours after that if necessary. There is also an annual retainer fee to regularly review and update the plan and to handle problems and questions that arise during the year. For consultations, it's a flat $200 an hour to deal with specific questions and needs, like retirement, long-term care, or helping with accountant and attorney clients on financial issues."

If Peggy does 10 financial plans a year, she'll realize a minimum of $32,000 in new fees as well as add to her ongoing retainer fee total. If she bills five hours a week for 40 full workweeks, that results in $40,000.

Hourly and planning fee advantages include compensating the advisor for the time spent working on a case and in the subsequent retainer fees that provide an ongoing stream of income. One disadvantage is the number of years it takes to build the practice and gain experience and credibility to offer real, comprehensive financial planning. Another disadvantage is the constant need to gauge the value clients receive for the fees being charged. The decisions on how much and when to raise the fees is often a touchy subject.

Fees for assets under management and set hourly planning fees are both consumer friendly in that they don't involve a product sale. The sale is instead about the expertise of the advisor and the money management tool she uses. There are advisors who are 100 percent planning and hourly fees, and advisors who are 100 percent AUM fee compensated. Both of these avoid, for the most part, the sticky world of product selling and commissions. The investment-only advisor compensation is normally driven by a grid. The grid relates the volume of assets to how much the advisor makes. Peggy's flat 10 percent to the BD is simple and is in place due to her Registered Principal status; otherwise, her investment activity would be subject to a grid.

Gross Dealer Concessions

One term that is necessary to understand going forward is *gross dealer concession* (GDC). When a product is developed ("manufactured") by a company or broker/dealer, the pricing of the product incorporates the costs of the product's development, ongoing support, a profit margin, and a percentage to be dedicated to the sales and marketing of the product. This last-named percentage is known as the "gross dealer concession."

The *gross* is the base percentage set aside for selling and marketing the product. The *dealer* is the entity producing and/or sponsoring the product. The word *concession* makes it sound like the developing company is being forced to give the product away, but the term actually refers to the act of "conceding" some of the profit to the seller. At any rate, GDC is another name for the amount of money set aside in the sale of a product or transaction to go to the seller of that product or transaction. For insurance products, it's known as the "commission." In the mutual fund world, it's known as the "load." In the securities business, it's known variously as "fees," "charges," or "commissions."

Here's how it works: The advisor agrees to sell products, trade securities, collect fees, and otherwise generate income and funnel it all through a broker/dealer. All of the GDCs generated from these activities are "put on the grid." As the GDC accumulates through the year, each time it exceeds one of the breakpoints, all year-to-date GDC is credited with the new rate.

XYZ Broker/Dealer Gross Dealer Concessions	Retroactive Advisor Payout Rate, %
Under $25,000	25
$25,001–$35,000	30
$35,001–$55,000	35
$55,001–$75,000	40
$75,001–$100,000	45
$100,001–$125,000	50
$125,001–$150,000	53
Over $150,000	57

Let's say an advisor sells a variety of products exclusively through his BD. These produce a mix of commissions, loads, fees, and charges that on March 31 total $70,000. The advisor's quarterly payout will be 40 percent of this GDC, or $28,000. He continues to be productive, and by June 30, his GDC has grown to $110,000. His quarterly payout will be the entire $110,000 times the new breakpoint percentage of 50 percent, or $55,000 minus the $28,000 already paid in quarter 1. His check: $27,000. By the end of the year, if he crosses the $150,000 GDC point, he'll be getting 57 percent of the total, retroactively adjusted.

What "hits the grid" varies by BD. If the BD develops and sponsors a full range of proprietary products, its grid might include the GDC generated by these:

- Proprietary mutual funds
- Proprietary variable, universal, and term life
- Proprietary variable and fixed indexed annuities
- Proprietary trust fees
- Financial planning fees
- General securities trades
- Select nonproprietary variable annuities
- Select nonproprietary variable life
- Brokerage

Careful examination of a BD's grid is highly recommended in making compensation arrangement decisions. The sample grid above is just the starting point in negotiations. Grids are quite flexible for all sorts of competitive reasons. A valuable advisor being wooed from another firm might be offered 100 percent payouts on certain product's GDC, or even off-the-grid deals. There are bonus percentages offered for stellar levels of production and other product sale incentives.

As we have seen in our examination of Peggy's practice, she is off the grid. As such, a third compensation source for Peggy is product sales. Generally, a financial plan will include the suggestion to purchase an insurance product. It could be term or permanent life, disability, long-term care, health, liability, auto, home insurance, or an annuity. Some of these products will be variable in nature (having their performance based on underlying securities), such as variable life and variable annuities. The advice Peggy gives to a planning client is part of the fee; the products that she recommends that the client purchase are not. The client may go anywhere he chooses to buy the product. If sufficient trust has been established in the relationship, Peggy can go find the appropriate insurance or annuity from a broad spectrum of companies. Since her BD does not have proprietary products, Peggy is free to search for the right product that fits the situation. She would then need to be appointed by the carrier of the selected policy to sell it in California. For this, she receives a commission from the company. If the insurance product is one for which she is not licensed, such as home, auto, and liability, she can recommend an agent who's a specialist in property and casualty.

If her BD did offer a product line, there would be pressure to sell those policies, usually sweetened with additional bonuses or credits of some kind. Peggy's happy not to have that lurking in the background while researching the best product for her clients.

In trying to keep it simple, I must issue a caveat: advisor compensation can become a very bizarre business. Full disclosure on compensation issues is often hard to obtain. It is often easier to explain derivatives than it is to explain how an advisor is paid.

Commissions

So far, we've looked at AUM fees, planning fees, hourly fees, and compensation through a grid. Another compensation choice is that of going strictly on a commission (also known as a load or charge) basis. Advisors who are paid on this basis work on commission or other compensation tied directly to the sale of a product.

In this world, there are generally two kinds of advisors: captive or independent. *Captive advisors* work exclusively for one company and are obliged to give business only to them. Some captive advisors can access products from affiliated carriers with their parent company's permission.

The captive advisor's income is based primarily on generating business for the parent company. In exchange for this loyalty, the company provides its advisors with a solid benefits package, office support allowance, and production bonuses. This is the model of the old-line insurers, and it is relatively simple but expensive to maintain. Consequently, the population of captive advisors is shrinking as the public increasingly prefers doing business with advisors who can offer many options or simply shopping for products online.

Advantages of Being a Captive Advisor

Starting resources are often provided by the parent company. This remains the single biggest positive: it allows a person new to the financial services business a relatively safe nest of support. However, fewer and fewer companies are dedicating resources to the on-boarding of the next generation of advisors.

The company offers financial support for two or three years, allowing a new person to survive while learning the craft of building a practice.

A benefits package is part of the deal, which is a powerful incentive in today's marketplace.

Disadvantages of Being a Captive Advisor

There is a limited number of products to market, and most of the products are proprietary.

The parent company can discontinue selling certain products it views as unprofitable and introduce new ones to replace them. This is known as an *internal replacement*, and it is usually not very advantageous for either clients or advisors.

Parent companies often push certain products or product families over others, and they require advisors to meet established quotas.

Independent advisors, on the other hand, represent multiple investment and insurance companies and ostensibly work on behalf of the clients rather than the captive, who works primarily for the parent company. With this company and product independence comes the advisor's responsibility for providing his own resources to start his practice, grow it, and maintain it. Many companies will offer incentives to sell their products, and keeping track of all the due diligence involved can be difficult.

Advantages of Being an Independent Advisor

The advisor is free of the strict regulations of a parent company.

The advisor is free to offer a larger portfolio of products and services.

Most commission income is front-end loaded (paid up front).

The advisor can compare prices, products, and services and can select the best solutions for the clients.

Disadvantages of Being an Independent Advisor

Advisors must use personal resources to start and continue the business, and early profits are reinvested to keep the practice afloat.

There is no help for staying compliant and abreast of regulatory changes.

Advisors must devise their own benefits packages.

The products sold might not have much of a residual or trail commission with which to build a long-range income stream.

Most insurance products still provide the advisor with a large commission paid at the time of the sale and a dwindling amount over the life of the policy. A typical payout is 70 percent of premium for term life. For example, I sell you a term policy for a $500,000 death benefit that costs you a yearly premium of $1,000. I make $700 dollars at the time of the sale. As long as the policy stays on the books for a year, I get to keep my $700. When you pay your second premium of $1,000, I receive a renewal commission of 2 percent, or $20. This renewal continues for a number of years and eventually drops to 1 percent in the tenth year.

Client Term Insurance Premium	Advisor Commission		
	Year 1	Years 2–9	Years 10+
$1,000	$700	$20 per year	$10 per year

Permanent life insurance, disability insurance, and long-term-care insurance are similarly front-end loaded. These products are designed for long stretches of time and consequently cost more. I sell you a permanent life policy with a premium of the same $1,000; I'll normally get 50 percent of the premium in the first year, 5 percent for years 2 through 10, and 1 percent forever more, until death do us part (or the policy is replaced by another product).

Client Permanent Insurance Premium	Advisor Commission		
	Year 1	Years 2–9	Years 10+
$1,000	$500	$50 per year	$10 per year

Our brethren in the property and casualty business have a sensible commission structure designed to provide an ever-growing income stream. A $1,000 premium for a homeowner's policy might result in a 20 percent first-year commission and an ongoing 15 percent for the life of the policy. This encourages building relationships with clients for the long run, as opposed to the front-loaded insurances. There's a lesson here that has long been ignored.

There are countless variables in the structuring of commission tables, so please study them carefully before committing to a contract with a particular company. As with the grid, my examples above are designed to give you a sense of the type of compensation arrangement commissions entail. When switching companies, firms, or broker/dealers, it's appropriate to have your attorney review the compensation language prior to signing on the dotted line.

Overrides

The last compensation type that I'd like to present is the *override*. Peggy has an associate advisor, Eva. Since Peggy is responsible for Eva's compliance, well-being, and aspects of her development and growth, she receives an override on all of the business Eva places through the broker/dealer. Overrides generally fall between 10 and 30 percent, depending on how much supervision is required. If Eva earns $1,000 on a particular transaction, the BD takes its percentage, and then it credits Peggy's account with the decided-upon override percentage. As with all other aspects of advisor compensation, the concept of overrides can be construed and paid out in many, often confusing, ways. In some cases, they are used to give an experienced advisor some additional income as incentive to stay with the firm.

In summary, the choices available to an advisor in choosing a compensation arrangement include a mix of the following:

- Fees, hourly and for financial planning
- Assets under management fees
- Funneling production through a grid
- Being a captive advisor on commission
- Being an independent advisor on commission
- Receiving overrides

It's important to fully understand the compensation agreement you are entering into, so consult an attorney or other advisor as needed.

Elements 6 and 7: The Types of Clients the Advisor Wishes to Attract and the Office Location and Setup

These two elements of setting up a practice need to be complementary. As an advisor cycles through his life cycle stages, the first three, Developing,

Emerging, and Formative, are *dependent* stages. As such, the advisor will be located in a "bullpen" or some other shared space, and he is less selective when prospecting for clients.

As the practice grows into Maturity, both of these choices begin to exert themselves. The advisor begins to target specific groups of people to approach and often wants to move into an independent location. This decision is another tough one as the more independent the advisor grows, the more business costs she needs to pick up. Companies can exert some pull by offering to offset private office expenses if the advisor will continue to stay in the main firm location. Peggy settled on her primary target market after years of exploring different venues and niches.

"It's the Torrance, California, area and the so-called middle-class millionaires," she says. "These are couples with combined incomes in the $250,000 range and net worth of between $2 million and $10 million dollars. With this market came the location and office decisions. I found a good location in an executive plaza in Torrance. We have 770 square feet that I must say we have designed really well. I'm proud of that. It's appropriate for the clientele I want to work with—warm and friendly. People constantly tell me that they like to come here; that it's comfortable."

Tell me more about your office décor.

"Sure. When clients arrive, they sit in a waiting area that has a water fountain and a selection of chocolates, and Patricia brings them their favorite beverage, which we find out ahead of time. The office has a green theme, and there are crystals in strategic locations. I take them back to my office to meet Fred the fish and peek at the recognition awards and diplomas on the wall. I have a small fountain bubbling away in there, and, yes, some crystals exerting their influence! All very impressive and professional and very much tailored to the kinds of people I enjoy being with."

Peggy has reached a consistency in her practice between clientele, location, and office setup. How consistent are these three elements in your practice?

Element 8: The Tax Status of the Advisor

Taxability is a key element in making decisions about structuring your practice. As with the other elements, there are early career defaults in place as part of being sponsored by a parent organization. In the financial services world, there are three distinct classifications of advisor: (1) independent contractor, (2) common-law employee, and (3) statutory employee.

It is critical that you know if the services you are providing are correctly determined to be that of an employee or an independent contractor.

Generally, an employer must withhold income taxes, withhold and pay Social Security and Medicare taxes, and pay unemployment taxes on wages paid to an employee. Employers generally do not have to withhold any taxes on payments to independent contractors.

In determining whether the advisor is an employee or an independent contractor, we must consider evidence of the employer's degree of control over the advisor and how independent she really is. The IRS Common Law Rules spell out three areas to examine in this control determination:

> *Behavioral.* Does the company control or have the right to control what the worker does and how the worker does his or her job?
>
> *Financial.* Are the business aspects of the worker's job controlled by the payer? (These include things like how worker is paid, whether expenses are reimbursed, and who provides sales materials.)
>
> *Type of relationship.* Are there written contracts or employee types of benefits (pension plan, insurance, or vacation pay)? Will the relationship continue, and is the work performed a key aspect of the business?

Companies must weigh all these factors when determining whether an advisor is an employee or independent contractor. Some factors may indicate that the advisor is an employee, while other factors indicate that the advisor is an independent contractor. There is no magic or set number of factors that makes the advisor an employee or an independent contractor, and no one factor stands alone in making this determination. Also, factors that are relevant in one situation may not be relevant in another.

The key is to look at the entire relationship, as well as the degree or extent of the right to direct and control, and to document each of the factors used in coming up with the determination.

> *Independent contractor.* An individual is an independent contractor if the company for whom the services are performed has the right to control or direct only the result of the work and not the means and methods of accomplishing the result.
>
> *Common-law employee.* Under common-law rules, an advisor who performs services is an employee if the company can control what will be done and how it will be done. The company has the right to control the details of how the services are performed.
>
> *Statutory employee.* Even if an advisor is not an employee under the usual common-law rules, his or her pay may still be subject

to Social Security, Medicare, and FUTA taxes. This advisor is a *statutory employee*. To be considered a statutory employee, an advisor needs to meet all eight elements of the statutory employee test:

1. Works full time for one person or company except, possibly, for sideline sales activities on behalf of some other person
2. Sells on behalf of, and turns his or her orders over to, the person or company for which he or she works
3. Sells to wholesalers, retailers, contractors, or operators of hotels, restaurants, or similar establishments
4. Sells merchandise for resale, or supplies for use in the customer's business
5. Agrees to do substantially all of this work personally
6. Has no substantial investment in the facilities used to do the work, other than in facilities for transportation
7. Maintains a continuing relationship with the person or company for which he or she works
8. Is an employee under common-law rules

All advisors fall into one of the three categories, and sometimes fall into two categories simultaneously. I am not a CPA, but there are ramifications for falling into each of the three categories. You certainly do not want to fall into the IRS's naughty audit club. The compliance department or Registered Principal should be able to explain why you are being treated the way you are for tax purposes. Generally, the following is true:

Employees. When an advisor is paid on the form W-2, the employer will automatically withhold and pay all of the necessary employee income taxes that are required by the IRS. The applicable taxes include federal income tax, state income tax, and FICA (Social Security and Medicare). In addition, the employer will pay all of the necessary employer taxes. These taxes include FICA (Social Security and Medicare), FUTA (Federal Unemployment Tax), and SUI (State Unemployment Tax). In most cases, the employer will provide the equipment and office space you will need. You may be eligible for some or all of the benefits your employer may offer to permanent employees such as medical, life, and disability insurances, pension plans, sick days, and paid holidays.

Independent contractor. Working on a 1099 basis actually means that you are working as a true independent contractor under the

IRS rules. You work on a 1099 basis when you are self-employed as either a sole proprietor or a corporation. Your clients will report the monies they pay you to the IRS on a 1099 form. Your clients will typically contract with you to work on a specific project. You should have a written contract with each client that will outline the work you will perform, the fees and/or cost the client will pay, and how the client will pay you. You will forward invoices to the client according to the contract terms. Independent contractors are responsible for maintaining all business expenses and income and for making quarterly federal and state income tax payments.

Element 9: The Tax Structure of the Practice

Understanding how you are treated for tax purposes often leads to questions about setting yourself up tax efficiently as an independent entity. There are five major types to choose from: four are pass-through entities and one is a taxable entity. You should always consult with your attorney and accountant to ensure that your business is set up properly.

Pass-Through Entities

Advisors can choose to set themselves up as *pass-through entities*. This is where the entity itself does not pay taxes. Profits and losses pass through to the advisor's personal tax returns. There are four commonly used pass-through entities.

1. *Sole Proprietorships.* Being a sole proprietor is the simplest and least expensive model to put in practice. It is a pass-through entity using the advisor's personal Form 1040 tax return. Business income and expenses are reported on Schedule C. Legally, there is no differentiation between the business entity and the individual. If you get sued over a business transaction, your personal assets are at risk. Peggy is a sole proprietor.

2. *Partnerships.* A partnership is co-ownership in a business with two or more advisors. It is a pass-through entity. Partnerships are required to file a Form 1065 tax return. The pass-through profit or loss is recorded on a K-1 form that each partner reports on Schedule E of their Form 1040 tax return. Liability for the partnership is determined by who is a general partner (liable for the percentage of ownership in the business) and who is a limited

partner (liable for only the amount invested in the business). A balance sheet and income statement are usually required.

3. *Limited Liability Companies (LLCs).* An LLC is relatively easy to set up, like a partnership. Rules for creating an LLC are state sensitive. It is a pass-through entity that files the Form 1065 (like a partnership) or a Schedule C (like a sole proprietor) depending on which form of organization the advisor chooses. Liability is limited as with corporations.

4. *S Corporations.* An S corporation is a complex hybrid of a C corporation and a partnership. It is a pass-through entity like a partnership: the stockholders receive a K-1 form. The limited liability protection remains the same as for the C corporation. The S corporation files a Form 1120-S to report tax information.

Taxable Entities: C Corporations

The one taxable entity is the C corporation. This is a business entity created under state law, and it stands as an independent legal "person" apart from its shareholders and directors. A corporation's owners or shareholders receive the benefit of limited liability for the obligations of the corporation, and they are thus ordinarily shielded from the corporation's creditors even in the event that the corporation cannot pay its obligations.

A C corporation pays its own taxes based on taxable income, filing a Form 1120. Most people hire an attorney to initiate the process of obtaining the articles of incorporation, establishing the bylaws, issuing stock certificates, writing a stockholders' agreement, and chairing the first stockholders' meeting where the new officers are voted in. Annual stockholders' meetings are required. A balance sheet and income statement are also required. If there are profits distributed to stockholders in the form of dividends, there is the danger of "double taxation" to the advisor/stockholder: taxes on the corporation and taxes on the dividends at the personal level. Creating a C corporation might be advantageous if there is no profit!

Element 10: The Benefits Packages Available to the Advisor

In the world of employee benefits, more and more of us are having to cope on our own. Like Peggy, I am a sole proprietor and independent contractor. Unlike Peggy, I have to assemble my own makeshift benefits package for our family. There are times when I take a hard look at going back to becoming an employee for the benefits. Having a C corporation (profitable or not) might allow an advisor to get group benefit rates.

Indeed, many advisors I work with have chosen to be more "captive" in their compensation arrangements in order to secure a benefits package, including matching retirement funds and sharing the Social Security burden with their employer.

Oh, and Peggy's secret?
"Meet Dan," she smiles. "I married a benefits package."
She's one smart cookie, that Peggy.

Now that we've navigated the 10 key elements of putting together a business model, there are a number of other best practices that are worth examining. Most of these topics intersect with the business model elements. I'll highlight each one and provide insights I've found to be helpful to the advisors I've consulted with over the years.

Tracking the Advisor's New Business Compensation

It is good to have faith. In fact, it's one of the legendary trio of faith, hope, and charity. Advisors as a whole are quite charitable in their volunteer and pro bono work. Many new advisors are so charitable, in fact, that they never sell much and leave to join a nonprofit organization. Most advisors I have encountered are hopeful for the future.

This is the hallmark of a positive mindset, seeing the opportunities in every prospect encounter, turning lemons into lemonade. Faith is a strong characteristic of a successful advisor. It doesn't take long to get into a religious discussion with many advisors, and a surprising percentage of them have a strong, faith-based background that provides the core to their financial advising.

I find that advisors tend to also have faith in how their paychecks are calculated. But sometimes when looking at paychecks, a different kind of faith would be helpful, the kind of faith framed by President Reagan's Cold War philosophy of "trust, but verify."

As we've seen, with all the permutations of fees, grids, and commissions feeding into a paycheck, things can get as complicated as a credit default swap.

Tommy, an experienced advisor out of Philadelphia, Pennsylvania, once gave me a copy of his quarterly pay statement. It was a 25-page document with dreary graphics, small print, and lots and lots of acronyms. With the copy, Tommy sent along a note: "If the devil is in the details, this is an evil statement!"

I understand the complexity of trail commissions, renewals, and products sold long ago that are producing a few cents of income every quarter. While all that adds up, it's not practical to follow that money. My preference is to have a system of auditing the major components of your compensation.

Every practice should have four spreadsheet inventories for ongoing tracking that measure your practice's health: (1) prospects, (2) open cases, (3) submitted cases, and (4) opportunities.

We covered the prospects and opportunities inventories in Chapters 4 and 5. The other two are important for auditing compensation purposes.

The open-cases spreadsheet, as shown in Figure 11.1, is a listing of prospects and clients whom you have asked to purchase a product or service but who have yet to say yes or no but who you expect will do so in the next 30 days. While the prospects and opportunities inventories reflect the longer-term health of your practice, the open-cases list addresses the next cycle of new business to be written. In Figure 11.1 we see the advisor has asked for a potential of $7,300 in revenue that has yet to close. Monitoring these open cases gives the advisor a sense of future new business production.

Figure 11.1

Open-Cases Spreadsheet

Open Cases				
Name	Date Asked	Product and Amount	Potential Revenue	Notes
Roberts	11/24	$250,000 variable life	$2,500	Did medical for preliminary underwriting quote
Cassman	11/18	$120,000 rollover from 401(k) into wrap account	$1,200	Waiting to see final statement from employer
Billings	11/16	Long-term-care joint policy	$3,000	
Levon	11/12	$500,000 term	$600	
Total			**$7,300**	

Once a piece of business is agreed upon and the advisor has collected the check or set the transfer of funds in motion, it goes on the submitted-cases spreadsheet, as shown in Figure 11.2. Here, the business is tracked until it is issued or completed. This is an important auditing tool for your compensation. With this tool, you project what you think your payout ought to be and compare it to the actual number that hits the pay statement. Once verified, it drops off the submitted-cases spreadsheet.

Notice that the information contained on the open-cases spreadsheet is separate from any underwriting or investment process flowchart, which tracks the individual steps as they are completed. That process is covered in the Sales Process system. All we want from the submitted-cases spreadsheet is an at-a-glance amount that is being processed and an audit when it's completed.

As a rule of thumb, a healthy number in submitted cases is to have at least a month's new business income pending at any point in time. If an advisor would like to achieve $100,000 in new business from all sources this year, then the number is $8,333. Open cases should similarly provide a minimum of a month's income, or $8,333. Looking at our two earlier examples, the advisor has $7,300 in open cases and $8,862 in pending income. These would be very healthy practice indicators for that $100,000 aspirant.

These are the major components in new business auditing of your paycheck. Once every six months, study the flow of ongoing payouts from current clients to see if they feel right. Ask the company to provide you with a payout profile for your top clients. Verify accuracy. I have yet to encounter an organization who purposely defrauds advisors. Many compensation systems are so overwrought, however, that mistakes are made on a regular basis.

Tracking the Advisor's Bonuses and Incentives

And let's not forget to track an advisor's bonuses and incentives. These vary by company and broker/dealer. The important point here is to keep abreast of bonus breakpoints. Mac was an advisor in his fifth year when we took a look at his marketing game plan for the upcoming year. In that process, we looked back at his previous year's production, tallied up his life sales, and projected them to grow 10 percent.

"This is great," I noticed. "You sold 16 of these Variable Max policies last year. They upped the bonus point to 18 from last year's 15. The new bonus is the same, $5,000."

"Hold on," Mac jumped. "I sold 16 and the bonus was 15?"

"That's what this says." I rechecked the bonus charts.

"I didn't see that. I forgot. No one told me!" he yelped.

Figure 11.2

Submitted-Cases Spreadsheet

Submitted Cases

Name	Case Number and Date Submitted	Product Type and Amount	Premium or Deposit	Mode	Percent of Case	Projected Revenue and Company Credits	Actual Revenue and Credits	Date Completed
Miles	V4567 11/18	$200,000 variable life	$3,500	Qtr	100	$1,750 1,750 cr		
LeVay	Q9809v 11/21	$75,000 QAnnuity	$75,000	1×	100	$3250 3,000 cr		
Cross	BR5568 11/01	Wrap rollover	$150,000	1×	100	$1,500 500 cr		
Billings	TR3456 11/13	$250,000 term	$560	Annual	50	$112 90 cr		
Brill	DB677909	$12,000 per month DI	$5,500	Annual	100	$2,250 2,250 cr		
Total						**$8,862 7,590 cr**		

"You mean you didn't get the bonus?" I arched my eyebrows.

"I never got a bonus." Mac shook his head.

"I'm sure you can get it retroactively," I assured him.

"You don't know the challenge process they'll put me through," he sighed. "I'll give it a go."

Mac eventually got his bonus after three executives reviewed the case, but it took three months.

Some advisors share their bonuses with their assistants and have empowered the assistants to keep track of progress toward these additional dollars. That leads us to the ever-popular topic of compensating assistants.

Staff Compensation, Bonuses, and Incentives

In the Communication system, I outlined the best practices in supervising and reviewing the performance of assistants. In this Financial Management system we address their compensation.

First, there's the base pay; then we'll tackle incentives.

Base Pay

Assistants with Experience

To calculate the base compensation ranges, I'll use actual historical pay rates for assistants that I've worked with over the years.

There are overriding factors that come into play in implementing any pay scale:

> *Job duties and expectations.* For this exercise, I'll use the two job descriptions for full-time positions seen in Chapter 9: Figure 9.2, "Sample Job Description Checklist for a Marketing Assistant," and Figure 9.3, "Sample Job Description Checklist for an Administrative Assistant."
>
> *Local economic conditions.* This is perhaps the heaviest hand in establishing a pay range. In a depressed economic environment, a highly competent assistant can be hired on the low end of the scale. A booming economy makes the competition tighter, and the high end of the scale would be appropriate. For this calculation, the best numbers to use are the national unemployment rate versus the local unemployment rate. That ratio gives us an indicator of where your location sits in the boom/bust cycle.
>
> *Regional pay scale.* This goes hand-in-hand with the local economic conditions. While not being specific to a particular

locality, it does provide a detached look at what others are paying for similar services.

Advisor's budget. What's realistically affordable? What fits within the parameters of the advisor's budget?

Cooperation. Will there be cost sharing on the assistant's compensation? Will the firm or company pick up part of the salary? Can an assistant be hired to work with two or three advisors to help spread out the expense?

Hourly or salaried. Hourly employees (nonexempt) are governed by wage, hour, and overtime laws. Salaried (exempt) employees generally are not. Salaried assistants can work overtime as part of a salary, while hourly earners have to be paid for any hours they work beyond their designated workweek.

Licensed or not. An assistant who has invested in education and applicable licensing brings more to the practice and should be compensated accordingly.

Payroll outsourced or in-house. Who has the job of withholding appropriate taxes in producing a regular paycheck? Who produces the tax information for the assistant's IRS filing?

Benefits. Will benefits be part of the base compensation? Typically, a base salary includes major medical coverage but not dental or disability.

Space. Where will the assistant sit? What will this cost the advisor?

Enough variables for you? This is why it's so difficult to answer the perpetual questions "How much do I pay an assistant if I get one?" and "Am I paying my assistant too much (or not enough)?"

From my research, a national average for an assistant with the following qualifications was approximately $40,000 in 2009. Thereafter, it will need to be adjusted annually for the cost of living index:

- Performs either all 20 marketing duties or all 20 administrative duties, *or* is a hybrid (a total of 20 duties drawn from both lists)
- Has at least five years' administrative and/or marketing experience
- Is insurance licensed with Series 6 and 63
- Has received satisfactory annual performance reviews (as discussed in the Communication system)

Jean had her practice in Cherry Hill, New Jersey, across the Delaware River from Philadelphia, Pennsylvania. As such, she was part of the Philadelphia Metropolitan Area for the Bureau of Labor Statistics (BLS) purposes. In her sixth year, Jean had gotten as far as she could on her own. She had successfully used the help of interns from the local business college, but she had decided it was time to take the plunge and hire a full-time assistant. She interviewed and decided to hire Bill. Bill had six years' experience with a large real estate sales broker, and he wanted out of the big office environment. Jean's reference calls to the real estate office were all positive and verified that his performance had been stellar and that they were sorry to see him go. During the period between Jean's decision to bring him aboard and his giving his two weeks' notice, Bill obtained his Life/Health license. He also agreed to sit for his Series 6 and 63 within his first six months.

To determine an appropriate salary for Bill, Jean went through the following calculations based on the variables above. Using the $40,000 figure, she applied the four factors that *would* adjust the base:

> *Job duties and expectations variable.* Jean wanted Bill to be a hybrid assistant, combining marketing and administrative work. There are a total of 40 job duties listed for both the marketing and administrative assistants. When she posted the position, Jean had selected 22 of the 40 as the job description: 8 marketing and 14 administrative. Since the $40,000 was based on 20 job duties, she added $1,000 to the base salary for each additional duty. She would have subtracted $1,000 for each job duty under 20:
>
> + $2,000 for two additional duties

> *Local economy variable.* On the Bureau of Labor Statistics Web site (www.bls.gov), you can find the national unemployment rate and the unemployment rates for a variety of metropolitan areas and states. Accepting the national unemployment percentage as a baseline, Jean could adjust the base salary figure accordingly. She found that the national unemployment rate was 6 percent and Cherry Hill's was only 5 percent. That indicated that jobs were tighter locally than nationally by a factor of 17 percent (taking the 1 percent difference and dividing it by 6 percent). This added $6,800 to Bill's base salary ($40,000 times 1.17 percent). The reverse would be true as well. I like this unemployment calculation because your chamber of commerce should have a precise local figure to apply against the national rate. Using the unemployment rate, Jean made this change:
>
> + $6,800 for local economic conditions

> *Regional pay scale variable.* This calculation uses the Occupational Pay Comparisons among Metropolitan Areas, also on the Bureau of Labor Statistics Web site. Here, the BLS does a calculation of

pay—wages, salaries, commissions, and production bonuses—for a given metropolitan area relative to the nation as a whole. The calculation controls for differences among areas in occupational composition, establishment and occupational characteristics, and the fact that data are collected for areas at different times during the year. The national pay scale is set at 100. Jean finds that the Office Administration and Support pay category for the Philadelphia Metropolitan Area is 106, or 6 percentage points above the national average. The category of Sales and Related Occupations has a factor of 98, or 2 percent below the national average. These are the two most relevant to Bill's job description in the BLS report, so Jean decides to split the difference and give this variable a 102, or +2 percent. Since 2 percent of $40,000 equals $800, Jane made this change:

> \+ $800 for the regional pay differential

Registered status variable. An assistant who becomes registered, obtaining a Series 7, increases the base by $5,000. Jean had this in mind in another year or two, but Bill didn't have a Series 7 at the current time. So this was not a factor in her base salary calculations:

> $40,000 base
> \+ 2,000 for additional duties
> \+ 6,800 for a highly competitive location
> \+ 800 for the regional pay differential
> = $49,600 base for Bill

The following six factors *would not* affect the base amount, but they needed to be taken into account:

1. *Advisor's budget.* Jean understood that this was an investment in her practice. She knew that when Bill was up and running, he would provide her with 8 productive hours a week in genius time. Her rationale was simple: 8 hours a week multiplied by 42 full workweeks a year would result in 336 freed-up hours. Jean knew her time was valuable and was charging $200 an hour for financial planning. Assuming she utilized those freed-up genius hours productively, 336 hours times $200 would result in $67,200 in new revenue. This would more than offset Bill's first-year salary. Jean was also anxious to pursue the dental insurance market, having established COIs and credibility in that market

over the past couple of years. Jean's freed-up time generated by Bill's work would will allow her to establish more contacts and prepare materials for approaching dentists and oral surgeons.

2. *Cooperation.* Jean had experience in sharing the interns with another advisor in the office. She was convinced that a dedicated assistant was the way to go. The shared intern often had conflicting priorities that delayed the implementation of some of Jean's client service mailings. Her firm, a branch of a large broker/dealer, provided a group health plan in which Bill, as a full-time assistant, could participate. In reviewing the decision to hire an assistant, Jean's sales manager pointed out that if her production increased by 20 percent (well within the anticipated $67,200 increase), she would be eligible for a plan in which her BD would help offset Bill's salary.

3. *Hourly or salaried.* There were seminar marketing plans that Jean wanted to execute that would be time intensive and involve some evenings and weekends. She had no desire to track these hours and preferred a salary so that Bill's schedule could be flexible.

4. *Payroll outsourced or in-house.* Jean's branch had a payroll service that managed its 12 support people. Branch management agreed to add Bill to the list at no additional cost.

5. *Benefits.* Jean decided to wait a year before offering Bill a retirement plan with a matching amount. She also decided to provide a bonus opportunity, which is discussed below.

6. *Space.* Initially, Bill would sit at the work station used by the interns as they rotated through. Jean understood that this was one of the value propositions offered by being part of a firm. If she had owned a detached office, the decision of where to put Bill would possibly have involved finding additional space, purchasing new equipment, setting up a network, and other considerations she didn't want to deal with.

The end result for Jean was an experienced assistant who had a market value of $49,600. She reviewed her calculations with Bill, and that became the initial offer. Factors in Bill's personal situation were discussed. He would be getting married in eight months, his father was undergoing chemotherapy but sadly was losing the battle with cancer, and Bill was buying a townhouse after renting an apartment for the past seven years. All of these events would somewhat affect Bill's availability in the coming year. After some give-and-take on both Jean's and Bill's parts, they agreed on

$45,000 as base pay with bonus potential (covered below) and three weeks paid time off. A one-week vacation is the office standard for a first-year employee. Jean was fine with two weeks for Bill's wedding preparations and honeymoon and another five days to be used at Bill's discretion as his dad's condition worsened.

Assistants without Experience

Jean's example is useful in gauging the pay of an experienced assistant. For an advisor in an early career stage who wants to stick his toe in the water before jumping in, we can take a similar approach. My research has determined that the minimum salary for a full-time inexperienced assistant is $25,000. This assumes that the advisor would like the assistant to learn 20 of the job duties pulled from the marketing and administrative checklists.

Using $40,000 as a target for a good fifth-year assistant, an entry-level position begins at $25,000. If we break the $25,000 into an hourly wage, it becomes $12.00 an hour:

$$52 \text{ weeks} \times 40 \text{ hours per week} = 2,080 \text{ hours a year}$$
$$\$25,000/2,080 = \$12.02, \text{ rounded down to}$$
$$\$12.00 \text{ an hour}$$

The same exercise Jean took us through above can be used to localize the base pay of $12.00 an hour up or down.

The $12.00 hourly figure ($25,000 a year) works nicely as the assistant grows in knowledge and experience. If you increase her pay 12 percent a year, the fifth year's pay will be at the $40,000 level:

$25,000 × 1.12 = $28,000 in year 2	($13.46/hour)
$28,000 × 1.12 = $31,360 in year 3	($15.08/hour)
$31,360 × 1.12 = $35,123 in year 4	($16.89/hour)
$35,123 × 1.12 = $39,338 in year 5	($18.91/hour)

An increase of 12 percent a year does *not* include the cost of living. If an assistant is truly meeting expectations, a 12 percent raise on the base is suggested. If the cost of living index is up 3 percent, that percentage should be added, resulting in a total raise of 15 percent.

Virtual Assistants

Using a virtual assistant (VA) is an option for a cost-saving means of getting work done. Virtual assistants are independent contractors anywhere in the world who have access to a state-of-the-art computer and communication system. They can be found through virtual staffing agencies or through posting by individuals on a variety of online job sites. Most are paid only for the time spent working in the advisor's service, making their use very efficient.

My experience with advisors who have used a VA suggests that compliance departments are not particularly fond of them for both company and client security reasons. Also, without a Web-based CRM database, the VA has limited value in building relationships with your clients. A relationship-based practice might find hiring a VA useful in managing the C-level clients, doing such things as routine contacts, mail, e-mail, or telephone campaigns. Still, the bigger question is whether or not they can even talk to clients with registered products. For transactional practices, such as those who sell property and casualty and unregistered insurance products, the VA can perform more effectively, not having to worry about licensing.

Financial services organizations would be wise to explore the use of VAs. Putting together a VA network for producers could help everyone hold down costs, especially in the human resources budget. Consider all the communication methods available to us in our wired world:

> *E-mail.* E-mail allows you to quickly attach a file and send it to your VA so that she may make changes, print a letter and mail it, or keep it as a reference. Compliance rules around e-mail have been well established over the past decade.
>
> *Telephone.* By setting up your VA on speed dial with both office and cell phones, accessibility is not an issue during business hours.
>
> *Instant messaging (IM).* IM is underutilized when it comes to communicating with virtual assistants. There are several excellent instant messaging programs, and most are easy to use. IM should be used for quick questions rather than lengthy communications.
>
> *Texting.* Texting has replaced IM in my teenagers' world, and it is a new language to learn. But once you are fluent with the T9 feature (auto word completion) on your cell phone, texting can be a useful and convenient tool.
>
> *Snail mail.* While not as popular as other forms of communication, it is sometimes necessary. Much of the work in financial services still requires a paper trail.
>
> *Faxing.* Faxing your VA is a popular means of communicating tasks and lists. With the rise of inexpensive scanning programs, faxes have gone electronic and soon there will be little need for hard copy fax machines.

Voice over instant messaging (VOIM). VOIM is another
communication option. VOIM allows you to pull up your instant
messaging program, click your VA's name, click the call button, and
ring through the computer to your VA. Once the connection is
established (which only takes a second or two), you can talk with
your VA through the computer—no phone line involved. You can
then quickly delegate tasks, give instructions, or ask questions
without typing out a lengthy e-mail or IM.

All of these communication tools are, naturally, not limited to VAs.
The use of the VA in a relationship-based practice is still evolving. As compliance departments and technology units become more comfortable with
the privacy and security issues, VAs will become more common. As costs rise
and budgets shrink, the use of VAs will be economically necessary.

Bonuses and Incentives for Assistants

We have established the base pay element of an assistant's compensation.
The second element is determining an assistant's incentives.

Advisors are notorious for giving ad hoc or discretionary bonuses.
These are payments made to assistants for good performance at a feel-good
moment. There have been no qualifications established for these bonuses,
and the assistants aren't always sure what they did right. Discretionary
bonuses are fine for what they are—instant gratification—but they should
not be expected to motivate behavior. Without a clear reason for creating a
bonus, advisors may be rewarding assistants for simply doing what the assistants were hired to do. This creates an air of entitlement, and it might as
well be built into the base salary. If Jean, our advisor hiring Bill, expected to
give him a Christmas bonus of $100 if he did a competent job, she might as
well have added it to the $45,000 they settled on. Holding the payment until
December would simply be a delayed payment of an entitlement.

Performance-based incentives are the best practice. These are
additional income opportunities based on the assistants' actual performance
above and beyond the salary expectations. A critical element in performance-
based incentives is for the advisor to have a functioning performance review
process. This can be found in the Communication system chapter. Advisors
who have poor or nonexistent performance review processes are often guilted
into providing discretionary bonuses as a way of saying, "Sorry I ignored
giving you feedback all year, so here's some money to make up for it."

Jean and Bill worked out an incentive program that highlighted two
areas: professional growth and practice growth. She did not want Bill to suffer

because of circumstances beyond his control, such as a market reversal or her having personal issues. He should participate in the practice's growth but not be penalized for its failure to grow. If Bill was performing all the duties she hired him to do as part of his salary, and doing them well, that was his job. If the practice failed to grow, it would be due to external factors or her strategies' backfiring. This is why Jean put in a professional growth incentive piece. Even if the practice did not grow, Bill could still earn a bonus.

Incentives for the Practice's Growth

There are a number of ways to measure the practice's growth from year to year:

- Gross dealer concessions (GDC) earned
- Net profit from a profit and loss statement
- New assets under management (AUM)
- Total AUM in force
- New clients obtained
- Referrals obtained
- Client retention
- Client satisfaction (via survey)

All can each be measured against the previous year's numbers. Jean's goal was to acquire 24 new clients (households, businesses) in the coming year and to increase her AUM by $8 million. She and Bill discussed the fairness of these goals, and then they committed to these goals. If exceeded, Bill would receive a bonus at the end of the year.

They structured it this way: Bill would receive a percent of his income for each percent above 24 clients and $8 million in new AUM, up to 6 percent in each category.

If the practice grew by $9 million in assets, the additional $1 million would represent a growth of 12.5 percent ($1 million divided by the goal of $8 million). So Bill would earn the capped 6 percent bonus of $2,700 ($45,000 base times 6 percent).

If the practice grew by 25 clients, 1 more than the goal, the percentage would be 4.17 (1 client divided by the goal of 24). The bonus on this portion would be $1,877 ($45,000 times 4.17 percent). Bill's yearly income in this scenario would be as follows:

$45,000 base salary
\+ 2,700 AUM bonus
\+ 1,877 new client bonus
= $49,577 salary and bonus

This was economical for Jean due to the extra income from the $1 million in AUM (worth about $10,000 to Jean) and the 1 extra new client (worth $2,500 to Jean based on her previous year's average). The two practice bonuses would total $4,577, or 37 percent of the additional profit ($4,577 divided by $12,500 expected increase). If all this came to fruition, Bill would have proven himself to be an advocate of the practice, and it would be well worth sharing the additional income with him.

Incentives for Professional Growth

Jean and Bill also agreed that if he successfully passed his Series 6 and 63, she would reimburse his costs and give him $2,500 on top of that. Again, this would strongly indicate that Bill was committed to the practice and was an advocate for his own growth and development. Other ideas for professional growth include these:

- Achieving licenses
- Achieving designations
- Educational achievements toward a college or postgraduate degree
- Educational achievement for product and services
- Learning new technology
- Implementation of new programs
- Client experience (via survey)

Even if the practice bonuses did not work out, Bill could still be reimbursed for his work in passing the Series 6 and 63. Bill's total potential income would become the following:

$45,000 base salary
+ 2,700 AUM practice growth bonus
+ 1,877 new client practice growth bonus
+ 2,500 professional growth bonus
+ 500 professional reimbursement
= $52,577 salary and bonus

This $7,577 in possible additional compensation would be 16.8 percent over and above Bill's base salary.

To sum up, the assistant's compensation should be based on a base salary, plus incentives reflecting practice and professional growth. These should exist in a strong supervision and performance review environment lest the advisor risk watering down their effectiveness.

My research has revealed some additional factors to keep in mind when bringing on an assistant. All could be considered best practices:

One broker/dealer suggests that there should be one assistant for every $400,000 to $500,000 of GDC.

For an independent advisory practice, the total overhead (including payroll) should be 40 to 45 percent of the total practice gross compensation.

A housed advisor's total overhead can be as low as 15 to 25 percent through group cost sharing.

The salary, wages, bonuses, and payroll taxes portions of the independent advisor's practice's budget should be about 15 percent of total gross compensation. In our example above, if Jean did $350,000 in GDC, Bill's total possible compensation of $52,577 would be almost exactly 15 percent.

Commission Sharing

There is one other rule of thumb for compensating assistants. It is that assistants, even if licensed, should *not* share in commissions. In order to shave down the total compensation for an assistant, advisors are often tempted to invite assistants to get licensed and share in the sales. However, it's usually a bad idea for the following reasons:

> The advisor is the one building a practice. Giving part ownership of a new or existing client to an assistant by way of a commission split dilutes the value of the entire practice. If the assistant leaves, the client may not know the difference, but the advisor's paycheck will.
>
> An advisor can't share commissions with someone who isn't appointed with the company. The cost to appoint someone is offset by production for the company. If the assistant isn't really producing, it's a cost deficit for the company to keep the assistant on the books as a producer.
>
> If an assistant is involved in sharing commissions for variable sales, then the broker/dealer has to supervise the assistant. Again, the cost benefit isn't there.
>
> Many companies have minimum requirements for producers, even those on part-time contracts. Will the assistant generate enough business via the splits to validate a minimal contract?
>
> Reducing the base salary with the intention to share commissions usually ends up in resentment and broken promises. After a time, the assistant might think the advisor shares whenever the advisor feels like it, not based on clear expectations for the assistant. There is no consistent flow or amount of dollars to replace base pay, so the assistant ends up realizing he or she can

make a better salary elsewhere. A steady, predictable income is important to assistants. The ups and downs of the advisor's pay usually holds little attraction for them. That's why we strongly recommend that incentives be *in addition to* a salary for assistants, not a *replacement for* a base salary.

Incentives should be based on the assistant's efforts, not the advisor's. In a joint case with another advisor, the two share commissions with certain criteria in mind, such as the MDRT split. Applying this to an assistant is a very different animal and difficult to manage. Throwing the assistant a commission on an irregular basis doesn't tie the incentive to the assistant's performance, nor does it allow him or her to be in control of reaching the incentive goal.

Other Financial Management Considerations

The Financial Management system encompasses six other best-practice items in addition to the 10 elements for setting up a practice and compensating assistants: (1) business profitability assessment tools, (2) budgets, (3) accountants, attorneys, and coaches, (4) product selection, (5) key person coverage, and (6) exit strategies.

Business Profitability Assessment Tools

Are you making a profit? This is a starting point in a practice financial assessment. Understanding the flow of revenue in and out is a vital statistical exercise. While many advisors help their business clients analyze their financial statements, they never get around to examining their own books. Not being an accountant, I'm going to keep it pretty simple:

If Jean is generating $350,000 of GDC and is getting a 55 percent payout, her net operating revenue is $192,500. If her total overhead, including Bill, is $84,700, that leaves her with an income of $107,800:

$350,000 GDC × 55 percent payout = $192,500 operating revenue
− $84,700 total overhead = $107,800 profit

In managing all this money, it is wise to have separate accounts for business and personal funds. It's tempting, especially for sole proprietors, to put it all in one checking account. But in determining profitability and income taxes, having the business expenses broken out is handy, especially in the case of an IRS audit. I recommend a business checking account, credit card, and line of credit for an advisor's practice. This allows for financial matters to be delegated to assistants once the practice is large enough and to an accountant when it grows even larger. Other reasons for not commingling personal and business funds include these:

> Having separate accounts is helpful in clarifying monetary issues in the event of a divorce, partnership dissolution, lawsuit, and/or compliance audit.
>
> Maintaining separate accounts allows you to produce financial analysis statements such as revenue per client, revenue per staff member, cash flow, profit and loss, and budget analyses.
>
> Financial statements based on business-only accounts give advisors a solid grounding for annual planning and goal setting.

Business Budgets

All good business practices have budgets. I find that the more captive an advisor is, the less likely he is to have a budget on paper. Conversely, the more autonomous an advisor is, the more acute is his awareness of income and expenses. I encounter online budgeting software being used quite a bit in these practices. More expansive practices, with more team members, often have a financial person in place who is dedicated to monitoring the budget.

Doing a budget analysis is always an eye-opening experience, whether it's for the family or the business. My best practices recommendation is to create a realistic monthly budget, monitor it, adjust it as needed, and examine the annual totals with an accountability partner.

Figure 11.3 is a template for the budgeting exercise that includes the most common expenses for a financial services practice.

Accountants, Attorneys, and Coaches

For the financial security of your own practice, reviewing the structural and taxation issues by fellow professionals is a best practice. Once in a Mature life cycle stage, your practice should have legal and tax guidance from an attorney and an accountant (preferably a CPA). I have discussed quite an array of possibilities in setting up your business model as you progress from independence to interdependence. These two professionals speak to the interdependence you are trying to achieve.

A coach can come in many forms. After a certain point, having this dispassionate point of view is valuable on issues outside of the legal and tax worlds.

One other professional to consider for your practice is a financial planner. Most advisors employ themselves as their financial professional, advisor,

Figure 11.3

Business Budget Analysis

Category	Expense	Annual Budgeted	Monthly Budgeted	Annual Actual Total
Office	Space rental (office)			
	Furniture and fixtures			
	Supplies			
	Copier, supplies and service			
	Stationery and business cards			
	Brochures			
	Mail, postage, delivery			
	Utilities (includes garbage)			
Insurances	Fire, theft			
	Errors and omissions			
	Unemployment			
	Business overhead			
	Buy/sell			
Telephone and fax	Local			
	Long distance			
	Cellular			
	Headset and other equipment			
Computer	Broadband			
	Hardware and services			
	Software and services			

(continued)

Figure 11.3

(Continued)

Category	Expense	Annual Budgeted	Monthly Budgeted	Annual Actual Total
Sales tools	Newsletters, premiums			
	Marketing campaigns			
	Prospecting leads, lists			
	Advertising and publicity			
	Sales presentation materials			
	Community involvement			
	Information resources			
Business expense	Business entertainment			
	Business auto use			
	Business travel			
Dues and subscriptions	Professional associations			
	Continuing education			
	State licenses			
	FINRA/SEC costs			
	Periodicals			
Salary and benefits	Staff salary/ hourly pay			
	Staff benefits			

(continued)

Figure 11.3

(Continued)

Category	Expense	Annual Budgeted	Monthly Budgeted	Annual Actual Total
	Self/family salary			
	Self/family insurances			
	Self/family retirement			
Taxes	Federal			
	State			
	Social Security/ Medicare			
Other	1099 expenses			
	Payroll services			
	Tax preparation			
	Legal fees			

and planner. Chuck and Linda, two experienced advisors in Connecticut, have a working partnership. One of their informal bylaws is to examine each other's financial plan annually.

"We have somewhat different philosophies in how we approach the mix and allocation of variable products," said Linda. "So it's a good exercise to bounce ideas off each other. It's our families who benefit the most."

"Her conservative approach," Chuck rejoined, "has paid off in the recent bear markets. My gung-ho strategies after the 9/11 down market were good for about five years. Linda suggested that college money be used in 2010 for my oldest twins be put into conservative funds and money markets. It was," he smiled, "a wise move."

Product Selection

The balancing act between the right product and the right compensation for placing that product can be frustrating. Part of the advisor's genius is the ability to do the due diligence, study the universe of products and services available, and select the right one for the client. Most advisors are compensated by a product manufacturer either directly or indirectly. In many cases, product accessibility is a primary reason for selecting a firm or BD.

At one end of the spectrum is the fee-only advisor. She might place only no-load mutual funds and forego any ties to products that have any kind of load or commission structure. Fees alone support her practice. It's a tough road to create a viable business model on the strength of fees alone.

At the other end is a captive advisor to a particular company. He's able to sell only one family of products and doesn't have any control over the pricing and compensation from those products.

Either extreme is relatively rare these days. Most advisors have multiple product choices and make compensation trade-offs with the clients' best interest in mind. However, I've seen firsthand the carnage wrought by high front-end commissions. Let me tell you of a recent experience I had.

A Cautionary Product Abuse Tale

Recently, I've interviewed plaintiffs who were part of a large class action lawsuit. The company and the states involved, while recognizable, aren't important. I was part of a team of independent financial services consultants who were brought on to help these plaintiffs understand their options as part of the settlement. Each one, whose average age was over 75, had purchased an indexed annuity product. The crux of the lawsuit involved the improper sale of these annuities, particularly in how bonuses were offered to plaintiffs as a purchase incentive.

The sad fact is that there have been far too many of these lawsuits over the past 20 years. That's why the names don't really matter. The underlying issue remains that product pushers and their boilerroom tactics represent the past while today's clients want a relationship-based sale. Companies who continue to set commission and bonus structures that favor the product pushers will be caught in regulatory cross-hairs and become more vulnerable to individual and class action lawsuits.

In all 40 of my interviews, I learned that the plaintiffs had signed all the necessary compliance paperwork, but they didn't really understand what they had purchased. The commissions generated on the products in question were typically front loaded with minimal trails, which provided more incentive to sell it now and less incentive to keep it on the books over the long haul. Rose's story is typical of what I heard.

"The guy that sold me that annuity was nice enough," she explained. "He came out to the house and told me he was working with people retired from the electric co-op. My husband worked for them for many years and passed away two years ago. So I have his pension and Social Security for income, plus a little bit set aside for emergencies."

This "little bit" was $76,000, nonqualified, in a large-cap mutual fund. Rose, who was 76, had taken the money out of that mutual fund and rolled it into the indexed annuity four years earlier.

"The agent showed me that my mutual fund was not doing so well. Then he showed me his annuity that paid a 10 percent bonus and that would never lose money no matter what the markets did. That sounded like a really good deal, so I signed up." It was a one-interview sale and took all of 90 minutes.

"I got the annuity in the mail and never heard from him again. When this settlement letter showed up, I tried calling him, but I never got a response. I felt kind of foolish. But he seemed like a nice young man."

The most frequently misunderstood elements of the annuity that got the state attorney general's attention were the engendering of new back-end sales charges, not disclosing where the bonus money actually went, the tax status of the funds, and how the whole indexing process worked.

When I questioned Rose on these four items, she recalled talking about them and "sort of understanding them at the time. But I couldn't tell you about them now." Nearly every plaintiff I've interviewed echoed Rose's postsale confusion.

But each case had its unique elements. Rose's son, Jim, who lives in Texas, eventually joined us on one of our conference calls to "make sure mom's making the right decision." He was the beneficiary, and the three of us spent a good deal of time discussing her current situation.

She was still living in the family home in a small town, where neighbors looked out for each other. If she were to need ongoing care, the $76,000 was earmarked for the costs associated with nursing homes or in-home assistance. Her income was fixed and didn't allow for much self-funded traveling or entertainment. She still drove, but she tried to keep it to a minimum and only during daylight. She played bridge, was involved in community and church activities, and had a network of friends and relatives. Was the indexed annuity the right product for all of her remaining nest egg? I would certainly question the appropriateness in Rose's case.

Since I was acting as a one-time, impartial consultant to Rose, we reached a general understanding of all these issues for the time being, and the annuity seemed like something worth keeping after weighing all the pros and cons. However, the complexity of the product could not be ignored. It required that Rose and Jim have a go-to person to refresh their understanding of how the annuity worked at least once per year. In other words, having a *relationship* with an advisor would be critical. When they need to make significant decisions, who would they turn to for their options? Since Rose and Jim did not have a financial advisor they could trust, and my role was temporary, should they keep the policy or accept the proposed buyout? With the buyout, approximately $80,000, they could put it into something safe, like laddered CDs, to keep things simple and have the funds accessible.

Rose kept returning to a simple question, one that was important to her. She had a friend whose husband had recently suffered a stroke. As a result, he needed in-home care and their house needed to be made wheelchair friendly. It has put a severe strain on their finances and relationship. So Rose asked, at regular intervals, "What if I have a stroke?" My advice to Rose and Jim was to take the buyout and put the money somewhere safe and accessible. What would you have suggested?

The majority of you reading this are relationship-oriented advisors. In that sense, I'm preaching to the choir, at least where your top clients are concerned. Yet, take a look at your book of business. Do you have B- or C-level senior-aged clients with just a product or two who might be seduced by a product pusher like the one who rolled Rose's funds? If so, reach out to them by mail or phone. Let them know you or someone on your team can be available to review their product or portfolio at least annually.

Do your part to disable the product pushers. I've seen plenty of the frustration, confusion, anger, and lawsuits created in their wake. Your clients, even those with smaller assets, deserve better.

If you have the clout, consider lobbying product providers to take the emphasis off up-front commissions and to spread them out over time. The recurring nature of this compensation will help reward relationship building over transactions. It's your playing field. Consider helping level it.

Key Person Coverage

What if you were hit by a truck and didn't survive?

What if you were hit by a truck and did survive but suffered permanent brain damage?

What if either happened to a key assistant?

As may be true for your business clients, are the key people in your practice covered in the event of death or disability? Life and disability insurance indemnify these losses, providing funds to keep the business running and buying the time to bring a successor up to speed. For partnerships, buy-sell life and disability policies are *de rigueur*.

Exit Strategies

No chapter about a Financial Management system would be complete without mentioning the end game. We covered this ground in early chapters, making an argument that systems enhance the value of a practice at its ultimate disposition. Without going into detail, there are essentially five ways to exit your practice:

1. Die with your boots on. Remember that from Chapter 2? You die and the clientele go into the orphan pool of the company or firm for whom you work.
2. Transfer your practice to a family member.
3. Sell the practice to a familiar entity: another advisor, key employees, or back to the firm or company.
4. Sell the practice to an unfamiliar outside third party.
5. Dismantle the practice by giving top clients away to select advisors and by passing on the rest to the orphan pool to be worked by new associates.

Whichever you choose, there's a strategy to go with it. The Eight Business Systems are designed to provide assistance in these transitions.

Financial Management System Best Practices Checklist

The Financial Management System Best Practices Checklist is shown in Figure 11.4. There are 40 specific steps in this checklist. It's the blueprint for the eighth section of your best practices operations manual.

In Figure 11.4, we have assumed that the advisor is with a broker/dealer in a detached location, with a full-time administrative assistant and a full-time paraplanner/marketing assistant. The advisor is in a Mature life cycle stage. Each practice is unique, of course, and the checklist can be modified for each advisor.

The resources referred to on the checklist are suggestions based on various best practices observed in the field. Any resource in italics refers to a piece reviewed or illustrated earlier in this chapter.

Figure 11.4

Financial Management System Best Practices Checklist

Financial Management Activities	Advisor	Marketing Assistant	Administrative Assistant	Firm	Resources
10 Elements of Setting up a Practice					
8.1 The platforms from which the advisor wants to operate—check all that apply: • Full financial planner • Comprehensive planner • Modular planner • Investment planner • Wealth manager • Financial instrument specialist • Market specialist • Insurance planner • Benefits planner • Executive business planner	X			X	Case Development system discussion; Company/BD/firm
8.2 The level of compliance accountability the advisor wishes to assume: • High • Medium • Low	X			X	Company/BD/firm

Note: X denotes primary accountability person, and S denotes shared accountability person.

8.3	Size of the practice: • Small (1–3 people) • Medium (3–7 people) • Large (8+ people)	X			Company/BD/firm
8.4	Resources available: • Broker/dealer • Firm • Company • Online • Other media • Personal library	X		X	Company/BD/firm
8.5	Compensation arrangements: • Fees, hourly and for financial planning • Assets under management fees • Funneling production through a grid • Being a captive advisor • Being an independent advisor • Receiving overrides	X		X	Company/BD/firm; *Element 5 in this chapter*
8.6	Type of clients the advisor wishes to attract: system • Ideal client profile	X			Client Acquisition
8.7	Location and setup of office: • Home office • Stand-alone office	X		X	Company/BD/firm

(*continued*)

Figure 11.4

(Continued)

Financial Management Activities	Advisor	Marketing Assistant	Administrative Assistant	Firm	Resources
• Suburban office park • Downtown high-rise					
8.8 Tax status of the advisor: • Independent contractor • Common law employee • Statutory employee	X			X	Company/BD/firm, CPA
8.9 Tax structure of the practice: • Sole proprietor • Partnership • LLC • S corporation • C corporation	X			X	Company/BD/firm, CPA, attorney
8.10 Benefits package available to the advisor: • Matching funds • Major medical • Dental • Disability • Long-term care • Vision • Other perks	X			X	Company/BD/firm

Understanding and Securing Your Paycheck

8.11	Understand the elements of advisor compensation.	X		Company/BD/firm
8.12	Monitor the compensation flow: • Prospect inventory • Open cases • Submitted business • Opportunities inventory	X		*Figures 11.1 & 11.2*
8.13	Audit the compensation flow for accuracy.	X		Company/BD/firm
8.14	Establish tracking to ensure that advisor bonus and incentive points are not missed.	X	X	
8.15	Audit bonuses and incentives for accuracy.	X	X	

Assistant Compensation

8.16	Establish base salary range for marketing, administrative, and hybrid assistants.	X	X	Company/BD/firm
8.17	Establish an assistant bonus and/or incentive based on the practice's performance.	X	X	Company/BD/firm
8.18	Establish an assistant bonus and/or incentive based on professional development.	X	X	Company/BD/firm
8.19	Establish staff benefits package.	X	X	Company/BD/firm
8.20	Integrate the total compensation package elements into the hiring, selection, supervision, and performance review systems in the Communication business system.	X		Communication system

(continued)

Figure 11.4

(Continued)

	Financial Management Activities	Advisor	Marketing Assistant	Administrative Assistant	Firm	Resources
8.21	Administer the staff pay.	X				Company/BD/firm, third party
8.22	Administer the staff benefits.	X				Company/BD/firm, third party
8.23	Administer the staff bonus and/or incentives.	X				Company/BD/firm, third party
8.24	Audit total staff compensation.	X				Company/BD/firm, third party
	Financial Management Tools					
8.25	Establish measures of profitability.	X			X	
8.26	Open business checking/debit account.	X				Professional referrals
8.27	Open a business credit card.	X				"
8.28	Open a business line of credit.	X				"
8.29	Contract with a bill-paying service for the practice.			X		"

Business Budget

#	Task						Reference
8.30	Create an annual budget.	X	S				*Sample budget, Figure 11.3*
8.31	Monitor and adjust budget.	X	S				

Other Business Professionals

#	Task						Reference
8.32	Legal work and advice for advisor and the practice.	X	X				Professional referrals
8.33	Tax preparation and advice for advisor and the practice.	X	X				"
8.34	Performance coach for advisor and the practice.	X	X				"
8.35	Financial planning for advisor and the practice.				X		"

Product Selection

#	Task						Reference
8.36	Establish an array of products for use in the practice.	X				X	Company/BD/firm, third party
8.37	Due diligence: Monitor product performance as compared to expectations.	X				X	Company/BD/firm, third party

Transfer Issues

#	Task						Reference
8.38	Develop a disability or premature death strategy (key person, buyout, business overhead) for advisor.	X				X	Company/BD/firm, third party
8.39	Develop a disability or premature death strategy (key person, buyout, business overhead) for key associates.	X				X	Company/BD/firm, third party

(continued)

Figure 11.4

(Continued)

Financial Management Activities		Advisor	Marketing Assistant	Administrative Assistant	Firm	Resources
8.40	Develop an exit strategy (successor planning): • Die with your boots on. • Transfer your practice to a family member. • Sell the practice to a familiar entity: another advisor, key employees, or back to the firm or company. • Sell the practice to an unfamiliar outside third party. • Dismantle the practice by giving top clients away to select advisors and passing on the rest to the orphan pool to be worked by new associates.	X			X	Company/BD/firm, third party

1 2

Epilogue: On Balance and Blending

We began the Introduction to this book with a visit to the Survivors' Club and its membership of seasoned Prudential producers. It was working with them that inspired me onto the practice management path. One of the most powerful characteristics of these men was how difficult it was to separate their personal and professional lives.

Up to that point, I had always worked from a "balanced" point of view: a person had only so many hours in the day and only so much energy to give. It made sense to allocate time and energy to all the various aspects of one's life. There were personal things: family, spouse, faith, entertainment, friends, hobbies, and sports. There were work things: prospecting, selling, preparing cases, paperwork, attending meetings, holding training sessions, and studying for licenses and designations. They were mutually exclusive. Of the 168 hours in a week, 55 were being devoted to work. If any additional work hours were needed, permission had to be granted from the personal side and vice versa. This was always an uneasy give-and-take. It felt like I was keeping a series of plates spinning on sticks, tending to each before the momentum died and it crashed. There was guilt if I brought work home. Personal calls at work were frowned upon. This is the world of balance.

Yet here was a bunch of very experienced advisors who seemed unconcerned about balance. They spoke of playing golf with clients/best friends after a policy review; going out to dinner regularly with clients/best friends and spouses; stopping by a client/best friend's office to shoot the breeze; bringing his family to a client/best friend's children's birthday party; attending holiday parties thrown by clients/best friends; or going to brunch after church with clients/best friends.

It was always "client/best friend." They were sharing their lives with their clients! The concept of client management merged into friendship maintenance. Top clients equals top friends was an equation alien to me at that point. I observed the Survivors' Club members easily and selflessly interacting: eating, drinking, playing cards and cribbage, taking walks, and discussing mutual clients and friends. I was welcomed in any of these activities. My balancing act was working OK, but I was witnessing the potential of a different mindset. A blended mindset.

I began noticing how futile it was to train and develop advisors who were having relationship troubles at home such as marital discord or carrying too much debt. The personal issues inevitably affected their on-the-job performance. Some advisors were quiet, distracted, and preoccupied in class. Others would throw themselves hyperactively and completely into their work. Management would surreptitiously ignore the former behavior and reward the latter. In either case, the long-range effect on advisor productivity was inevitably chaotic and detrimental.

Conversely, trouble meeting sales quotas or contract requirements at work affected the mood at home. In individual conversations with advisors, home front stories began to emerge: silence in place of discussions about "how work went." Tension that grew out of a critical piece of business submitted and stalled while the clock ticked on a compensation deadline resulting in arguments or keeping the advisor up at night. In not addressing those pressures, an advisor's physical and mental health was becoming compromised and his or her relationships strained.

The evidence was slowly accumulating and becoming quite clear: we lead one *interdependent* life, not a set of *independent* lives. Who we are spiritually, professionally, privately, at home, in the community, and participating in sports or hobbies are inevitably interconnected. They draw on one source of power: a strong sense of self-worth. It's this sense of self-worth that allows your gift—your genius—to flow and magnify.

The financial services advisory business is one of relationships, and as such is uniquely suited to the concept of blending. Yet even within this industry, in the regional and home offices that support the advisors, many employees' jobs are routine, and they perform them with minimal human interaction. In these work environments, blending is stifled and balance is promoted. A 9 to 5 job exemplifies this balanced thinking. In the early stages of the advisor's career, the search for balance is appropriate (and even necessary) to get a career off on the right foot. But as time goes on, many of the advisors who do not eventually blend the parts of their lives and become truly *inter*dependent leave the business or, if they stay, become increasingly frustrated.

In Chapter 8, we dissected the 168 hours in a week with the objective of identifying "genius" time. This is a balanced approach to time management because it calls for segregating tasks and activities. Most of all, an advisor is learning what her potential roles are in life and how much energy and time need to be devoted to performing well in each. It's a time of trial and error, and it is a terrain that must be traversed before one can enter into a blended way of thinking. The advisors who survive those early years have a choice to build transactional- or relationship-based practices. The interpersonal relationships developed over time will provide the bridge necessary to answer the question, "How do I go from balancing to blending?"

You will notice that there is no "Balance and Blending Best Practices Checklist" at the end of this chapter. The reason is simple enough. Balance can be taught, worked on, put into modules, and supervised. We did that back in Chapter 8. Blending can be learned only gradually by experience and having a role model to emulate. No checklists to becoming blended exist because it's tough to put a "done" checkmark next to "philosophical framework of life reformed" or "paradigm shift completed."

Instead, let me tell you about Charles, my teacher.

Charles was my favorite in the Survivors' Club. It was always Charles. Never "Chuck," unless you were beating him at cribbage and wanted to further annoy him. Charles was the co-chef and wine steward of the club. He was as erudite in life as he was in life insurance. He invited me to visit his home a number of times, and I spent a couple of days tagging along as he went about his business.

A typical day with Charles would begin with a stop at his office, which was in a downtown building that he owned. "Downtown" was modest as befits a small Minnesota town an hour outside of St. Cloud with 13,000 residents. In the office, he prepared the day's presentations and met with his assistant to check her to-dos, service work, and his calendar. He fielded phone calls and left messages. It was an interesting mix of calls—community event planning, dinner preparations, prospects, client reviews, and some I never did figure out. After a couple of hours, we hopped in his Buick and dropped by people's homes and offices to deliver policies, collect premiums, visit, get signatures, collect documents, and visit some more. We stopped by the liquor store to examine the new wines that had recently arrived. The owner was a client and we talked oenology. They dickered over price, vintage, and corking. Charles finally bought two bottles. Lunch at the downtown café was a blizzard of networking, visiting tables and booths, introducing me as Tonto to his Lone Ranger. In the afternoon, we stopped at the office before going on a presentation appointment.

At a furniture store, we met with the partners and reviewed their buy/sell arrangement. Both men signed up for additional life insurance coverage—it seemed business was prospering. Charles had all the paperwork ready, and we collected the check. We lingered, looking for the "right corner desk for the Missus," as he referred to his wife, Ellie.

We dropped the application and check off at his office. After getting messages, returning calls, and reviewing the next day's calendar, we headed out to the Little League fields. It was late afternoon, a lovely day in June. Charles was sponsoring a boy's seventh grade baseball team. The players wore powder blue team shirts with the Prudential logo and Charles's office address and phone number. "Charles!" the kids yelled. They seemed genuinely happy to see him. He had their names and numbers memorized. As we watched them play, he called out their names and cheered them on. After the game, having lost 12 to 8, the team and coach gathered in the mesh-protected bench area. Charles approached.

"Good effort, my men," he said in his soft, modulated voice. "We didn't win. However," he paused dramatically and reached into his pocket, "our play of the day goes to young Martin, who heaved a mighty toss from right field in an effort to throw out an opposing player trying to score. It was accurate, if late. No matter—Martin, for an excellent effort." Everyone clapped as Charles gave Martin two Susan B. Anthony dollar coins.

It turned out that Charles carried a supply of odd dollar and half-dollar coins as well as a supply of $2 bills. He distributed them at will, catching people doing nice things and giving monetary acknowledgment. For the team, Charles was methodically awarding two Susan B.'s for a "play of the game." There were 13 players and 16 scheduled games. He figured on a few rainouts and would find a good play by a different player in each game, thereby awarding everyone once. And if there were no rainouts? "Oh, we can award the coach, assistant coach, and the bat boy," he replied without hesitation.

After the game, we headed to his home. Charles and Ellie prepared dinner—pot roast, which was a favorite—while I chatted with them in the kitchen, sipping a well-researched and smooth Chardonnay. The neighbors dropped by for a glass of wine and ended up staying for dinner. The conversation ranged from investments to children to insurance and neighborhood concerns. They were life insurance and mutual fund clients, and at one point, Charles took a prospectus from his briefcase and gave it to the couple. "Since we just spoke of this fund, I am legally bound to give you this prospectus," he announced, bowing. "Pleasant reading."

After dinner, he and I took a "constitutional" stroll around the block.

"Charles, how many hours a week do you work?" I asked.

He looked at me as if I were speaking Greek. I wouldn't have been surprised if he knew Greek and answered me with it. "Young man," he intoned. "That's trouble with your generation. Looking to work and then play, turning it on and off like a faucet. The question is absurd."

"Absurd?" I thought, then said, "Enlighten me, please."

Charles sighed. "Maybe you will be one who will understand. You've seen my day, Tonto. What did you witness?"

"A mix of business and personal things," I answered.

"Very good," he replied. "Did you see a theme?"

"A theme," I restated. "You made some money, spent some money, met a lot of people. The theme is, ..." I stammered, "... is that you built your business. Through people. Relationships. Is that the theme? Relationships?"

"Hmmm," Charles murmured, straightening his jacket collar. "I'm 64 years old. You learn a lot in 64 years." His eyes took on a faraway look for a moment. "Lots of things, many by trial and error, like marriage. Many by practice and more practice, like life insurance selling.

"But we have one life to live. We are born with a gift. That gift is what we need to nurture and grow. I understand that I have a gift. My past is the slow revelation of the nature of my gift. The present is for sharing my gift. The future is leaving a legacy through my gift."

"Your gift, what is it?" I asked, intrigued.

"My gift is my ability to unlock the potential in others." He stopped. "I figured that out about 20 years ago, and life has been much more rewarding since."

"When did you first suspect it was your gift?" I pushed my glasses back up the bridge of my nose and looked up at Charles. He was six-feet-two to my five-feet-eight. More like Mutt and Jeff than the Lone Ranger and Tonto.

"I recognized it when my first spouse, the lovely Katrina, left me. I was getting started in this business, and we were both young, too young, it turned out. I was right out of college and returning home. She was right out of high school and wanted to work before going to college. After a couple of years, she found that she wasn't happy in this small-town world, and she wanted to move off to the big city of St. Cloud, perhaps even the Twin Cities. I, on the other hand, am a born and raised small-town boy and proud of it. So we compromised, and she took classes at St. Cloud State toward her bachelor's degree. I worked extra hard to afford that education. She commuted four days a week, and those days got longer and longer. By the end, she had gotten an education and a degree, and she had found a kindred soul in her English class who wooed her away. While I was sad that we parted, there was a part of me that was satisfied to see her grow and find someone who could—one would hope—bring out the best in her."

"Was that your gift starting to exert itself?" I asked.

"Yes, indeed. Ten years later, I met Ellie. With her and our three children, my role was and is always to be a provocateur for the instigation and rewarding of good acts and trying one's best. It's what I do. That's my gift. See?"

"I think so. It is why you are here on Earth, your purpose. Your gift drives all the different aspects of your life." I was starting to understand.

"You see why the question of how many hours I work is absurd?" he looked at me with satisfaction. I thought for a minute, walking in silence.

"So," I finally said, "you are always looking for good acts and finding people who are trying their best."

"Very good. You win a Susan B." He smiled and presented me with the dollar coin.

I took it and held it in the palm of my left hand. "So, Charles, everything you do serves your purpose, your gift. It's not about the work or the activities."

"Well, I've chosen the right business to be in. I can deal with people like the neighbors you met because they are curious and want to learn more. I can help them do that while I'm earning an income. Others who don't care or feel like life owes them a living—I have no time for them. My gift is wasted on them. It's very clarifying to just be myself wherever I am."

"The baseball players, the furniture store partners, your assistant, the liquor store owner—they shared the common theme of doing their best and wanting to do better. You bring that force to everything you do."

"Indeed." Charles smiled.

We rounded the corner, and he led me to my car. As I got in, he leaned over and asked, "How many hours are you working this week?"

I almost said "55" but caught myself. Instead, I laughed. "Don't be absurd!" I said and drove off.

Charles has since passed away. My career took me far afield, and I lost touch with him until an old associate forwarded me his obituary. With the sadness came the knowledge that Charles's gift continued. He had shared that when we last met.

"I'm leaving my gift legacy in three ways," he said one afternoon over a cup of coffee at his favorite café. "Genes—the kids have them whether or not they want them. I believe the gift is in there somewhere and will manifest itself in their lives. I'm also leaving a lot of good forward-thinking clients who will have heirs benefiting from the life insurance I have put in force. And Ellie is the third. She's getting all my coins and $2 bills, and she knows what to do with them. Maybe you'll get yourself a pocketful!" he winked.

Charles never did find a successor for his practice. He tried to send his best clients to specific advisors in the firm, with mixed success. This was the one aspect of his practice that was left unfulfilled: his best friends/best clients lost any continuity after Charles died. All they received was a call from a new advisor with a whole new agenda.

Yet in another sense—a life sense—Charles was very successful. He had achieved a blended life. He shared his gift with clients and friends who would accept it. My mission statement is the result of my conversations with Charles. It describes the gift I have found that provides my life's theme:

> *To challenge people to turn wishes and dreams into goals and into action.*

It's what I do best—challenge others to takes steps to grow. If you're not up for the challenge, I move on.

In the mapping exercise conducted with Paul in Chapter 4 (Figure 4.1), we identified well over 10 roles he played in his life. I'm no different. In my old balanced approach, I was looking for how much of my time and energy to spend in each role. Charles turned that inside out. His blended life simply asked, "What roles can I most effectively play with the gift I've been given?" His gift was replenished by what he did, not spent and exhausted. With that wisdom, I resigned from organizations in which I was giving the gift of challenge but receiving no response. I began an adult education class at church where we have developed a great, challenging rapport. My family relationships are spurred by our recognizing each member's achievements and our encouraging (challenging) the next level of growth. As a consultant, it's a nonstop challenge to get you to systematize your practice, to unleash your genius, and increase its value. Some respond, some don't. I work with those of you who do.

In this book, I challenge you to take some serious steps to manage your practice through the life cycle stages and into an interdependent mindset. With interdependence comes the opportunity to live the blended life. It's an end game to aspire to, one above the practice value, exit planning, and the amount of new business generated.

Charles got it.

I'm getting it.

Will you join in the journey?

I've got a pocketful of Susan B. Anthony dollars to share if you do!

Index

About the Author

Al Depman, CLU, ChFC, CMFC, BH, is a graduate of the University of Notre Dame. After graduation, Al combined his liberal arts studies with his 10 years of management experience in the McDonald's Corporation (including a BH degree from Hamburger University) to enter the financial services world 25 years ago. Since then, he has evolved from an award-winning sales rep into a full-time consultant specializing in helping advisors engineer their business practices to the proverbial "next level" through the use of transferable systems.

Al is the creator of the Practice Management Assessment diagnostic tool and best-practice resource materials. He has authored numerous articles in professional and mass-market publications, most recently *Horsesmouth*, *Wealth Manager*, and *GAMA International*. He also writes a popular monthly column for *Mitch Anthony's Intuitive Advisor* newsletter, in which he offers practice management insight to financial advisors. In addition, Al serves as the national practice management consultant for Securian (Minnesota Life). He has also worked with advisors from Waddell & Reed, Morgan Stanley, LPL

Financial, State Farm, Prudential, New York Life, Wachovia, and many independents across the country.

Al resides in Rochester, Minnesota, with his wife, Barb, and their three children. Al's areas of interest include studying classic comic strips, reading, battling the *New York Times* crossword puzzle, and conducting adult education classes at his church.